William Q. Judge
1851-1896

LETTERS
THAT
HAVE HELPED ME

WILLIAM Q. JUDGE
(1851-1896)

THE THEOSOPHY COMPANY
LOS ANGELES AND NEW YORK
1946

Semicentennial Edition
March 21, 1946

Printed in the United States of America

CONTENTS

Book I

Book II

Book III

BOOK I

To
Z. L. Z.
The Greatest of
the Exiles, and Friend
of all Creatures, from his
Younger Brother, the Compiler
JASPER NIEMAND
1891

Reprinted from
"THE PATH"

THE MASTER'S LOVE IS BOUNTIFUL: ITS LIGHT SHINES UPON THY FACE AND SHALL MAKE ALL THE CROOKED WAYS STRAIGHT FOR THEE.

Farewell Book

PREFACE

Seeking for freedom, I go to that God who is the light of his own thoughts. A man who knows him truly passes over death; there is no other path to go.

—UPANISHADS

IN the *Path* for May, 1886, we find these words: "We need a literature, not solely for highly intellectual persons, but of a more simple character, which attempts to appeal to ordinary common-sense minds who are really fainting for such moral and mental assistance as is not reached by the more pretentious works."

The experience of one student is, on the whole, the experience of all. Details differ, however. Some are made more instantly rich than others: they are those who put forth more vigorous and generous effort; or they have a Karmic store which brings aid. What Theosophists know as Karma, or the law of spiritual action and reaction, decides this, as it works on all the planes, physical, moral, mental, psychical, and spiritual alike. Our Karma may be worked out on any one of these planes when our life is chiefly concentrated upon it, no matter upon what other plane any special initiative impulse or branch of it originated.

The writer, when first he became a Theosophical student, had the aid of an advanced occultist in his studies. This friend sent him, among others, the letters which, in the hope that they may assist others as they have the original recipient, are here published. They are not exhaustive treatises; they are hints given by one who knew that the first need of a student is to learn *how to think*. The true direction is pointed out, and the student is left to clarify his own perceptions, to draw upon and enlarge his own intuitions, and to develop, as every created thing must at last develop, by his own inward exertions. Such students have passed the point where their external environment can affect their growth favorably. They may learn from it, but the time has also come to resist it and turn to the internal adjustment to higher relations only.

The brevity of these letters should not mislead the reader. Every statement in them is a statement of law. They point to causes of which life is an effect; that life arising from the action of Spirit in

Nature, and which we must understand as it is manifested within us before we can advance on the Path. There is a scientific meaning within all these devotional or ethical injunctions, for the Wisdom-Religion never relaxes her hold upon Science nor attempts to dissever an effect from its cause. Most of these admonitions have their base in the constitution of the Archæus, or World-Soul, and the correlation of its energies; others, still, adhere in the Eternal.

No less should the reader guard himself against a slight estimate arising from the exquisite modesty of Z. An occultist is never so truly a man of power as when he has wholly learned and exhibits this truth:

"And the power the disciple shall covet is that which shall make him appear as nothing *in the eyes of men.*"

The inner eye, the *power of seeing,* looks deeper into the source of a man's knowledge and takes it at its true value. Those men who are sharers in the Divine, whose first office is to give, are often protected from the demands and curiosity of the careless by a simple exterior which deceives the worldly sense. Some men are great because of the Power which stands behind them, the divine energies which flow through them; they are great through having learned how to receive this celestial influx from higher spheres of Being; they are the appointed ministrants, the true servitors of the Law and pupils of Masters whose office is humanitarian and universal.

Such aid is never volunteered; it follows the Karmic behest, and, when given, leaves the student free to follow it or not, as his intuitions may direct. There is not a shadow or vestige of *authority* in the matter, as the world understands the word *authority.* Those who travel the unknown way send messages back, and he who can receives them. Only a few of the first steps are here recorded and the first impediments surmounted. No hints of magic lore are to be found; no formulas of creed or occult powers; the questions of an awakening soul are answered, and the pilgrim is shown where lies the entrance to the Path. The world at large seeks the facts of occult science, but the student who has resolved to attain desires to find the true road. What may seem to others as mere ethics is to him practical instruction, for as he follows it he soon perceives its relation to facts and laws which he is enabled to verify, and what seemed to him the language of devotion merely, is found to be that of science; but the science is spiritual, for the Great Cause is pure Spirit.

Many students must at some time stand where the writer then stood, at the beginning of the way. For all these this correspondence is made public, and they are urged to look within the printed words for their imperishable meaning. They may be cheered to find the foot-prints of a comrade upon the rugged Path, above which the light of Truth ever shines. Yet even this light is not always a clear splendor. It may seem "in the day-time a cloud, and by night a pillar of fire." We must question every external aspect, even that of Faith itself, for the secret and germ of things lies at their core. Let us purify even our Faith; let us seek Truth herself, and not our preconceptions of Truth. In her mirror we shall never see our own familiar face: that which we see is still ourselves, because our real self is truth.

As the Theosophical movement gathers new momentum, fresh recruits may be aided by those letters which so greatly sustained me, or encouraged by some co-partnership of thought, and that, too, in the real issue confronting them. We first take this issue to be the acquirement of occult knowledge. Soon we find that the meaning of all really informed occult writers eludes us. We find that books only serve to remind us of what we knew in the long past, perhaps when "journeying with Deity," and the echoes awakened within us are so faint that they are rarely to be caught. Whether we study philosophies, metaphysics, physics, ethics, harmony, astrology, natural sciences, astralism, magnetism or what not, we meet with endless contradiction and differentation; we forever require to strike the balance of our own intuition. We discover that the final word has not yet been *written down* upon any of the higher subjects (unless it be on mathematics, and scarcely on that), and that all our learning is but a finger-post to that supreme knowledge of Truth which is only found and closely guarded within the human heart. Thrown back upon our inner perceptions for continual readjustment, on every side of experience this warning confronts us: *Stand ready to abandon all thou hast learned!* Not knowing the one center, we cannot thoroughly know any sub-center. The cause unknown, effects mislead us. Then we turn to that mysterious center whereby the One is manifest in man, and we begin the study of the heart, both in itself and in the life it has instituted about us.

To be put into more direct communication with the world of cause is now the student's most pressing need. One thing alone prevents this,—himself. He is of such gross fibre that he cannot be "porous to thought, bibulous of the sea of light." To the refinement and dispersal of this lower self—of the man he now takes himself to be—he then directs his will. Each man has a different mode of doing this, but each who advances at all finds that with every new period of his inner life a new self rises before him. Looking back over a group of weeks or months, he is amazed to see what manner of man he was then, and smiles that pitying smile which we bestow upon the faded letters of our youth.

Yet some there be who ossify there in their rut; let them struggle mightily to break up the mass which has resisted all environment, all change, all the conditions of progressive life. They have done for themselves what the enemy strives to do for others; they are the rock in their own path.

What our Eastern brothers call "the sheaths of the heart" fall away one by one; when the last bursts open there is a silence, the silence of the mystic death. But "the dead shall arise," and from that death springs up the first tender growth of eternal life.

Up to this point we shall not travel in the ensuing pages. Yet having realized the real issues so forcibly that his whole strength was at the start directed towards self-knowledge and the right use of Thought, the writer offers a part of his first instructions to those of his comrades who, single-hearted and of royal Faith, hold Truth to be dearer than all material life and seek it on the hidden way. There is no tie in the universe equal to that which binds such comrades together. It has been forged in the fires of unspeakable anguish; it has been rivetted by a dauntless purpose and a unique, because Divine, Love. The fierce hatred of seen and unseen worlds cannot tamper with it so long as a man remains true to himself, for this larger life is himself, and as he grows towards it his self-imposed fetters fall away and he stands, at last, a free soul, in the celestial Light which is Freedom itself, obedient only to the Law of its own divine Being. To reach it, let us obey the law of our own Being, for, truly, *Being is One.*

My comrades, wherever you are, I salute you.

JASPER NIEMAND, F. T. S.

LETTERS THAT HAVE HELPED ME

I

My Dear Jasper:

NOW let me elevate a signal. Do not think much of me, please. Think kindly of me; but oh, my friend, direct your thoughts to the Eternal Truth. I am, like you, struggling on the road. Perhaps a veil might in an instant fall down from your spirit, and you would be long ahead of us all. The reason you have had help is that in other lives you gave it to others. In every effort you made to lighten another mind and open it to Truth, you were helped yourself. Those pearls you found for another and gave to him, you really retained for yourself in the act of benevolence. For when one lives thus to help others, he is thereby putting in practice the rule to try and "kill out all sense of separateness," and thus gets little by little in possession of the true light.

Never lose, then, that attitude of mind. Hold fast in silence to all that is your own, for you will need it in the fight; but never, *never* desire to get knowledge or power for any other purpose than to give it on the altar, for thus alone can it be saved to you.

So many are there around me who are ardent desirers and seekers, devotees; but they are doing it because the possession seems valuable. Perhaps I see in you—I hope I mistake not—a pure desire to seek Knowledge for its own sake, and that all others may be benefited. So I would point out to you the only royal road, the one vehicle. Do all those acts, physical, mental, moral, for the reason that they must be done, instantly resigning all interest in them, offering them upon the altar. What altar? Why, the great spiritual altar, which is, if one desires it, in the heart. Yet still use earthly discrimination, prudence, and wisdom.

It is not that you must rush madly or boldly out *to do, to do*. Do what you find to do. Desire ardently to do, and even when you shall not have succeeded in carrying out anything but some small duties, some words of warning, your strong desire will strike like Vulcan upon other hearts in the world, and suddenly you will find that done which you had longed to be the doer of. Then rejoice that another had been so fortunate as to make such a meritorious Karma. Thus, like the rivers running into the unswelling, passive ocean, will your desires enter into your heart.

I find all your remarks just; and besides, there seems to be a real spirit behind them. Do not fear nor fail because you feel dark and heavy. The very rage you feel will break the shrine that covers the mystery after a while. No one can really help you. No one can open your doors. You locked them up, and only you can open them. When you open any door, beyond it you find others standing who had passed you long ago, but now, unable to proceed, they are there waiting; others are there *waiting for you.* Then you come, opening a door, and those waiting disciples perhaps may pass on; thus on and on. What a privilege this, to reflect that we may perhaps be able to help those who seemed greater than ourselves!

Oh, what a groan Nature gives to see the heavy Karma which man has piled upon himself and all the creatures of the three worlds! That deep sigh pierces through my heart. How can the load be lifted? Am I to stand for myself, while the few strong hands of Blessed Masters and Their friends hold back the awful cloud? Such a vow I registered ages ago to help them, and I must. Would to great Karma I could do more! And you—do what you can.

Place your only faith, reliance, and trust on Karma.

Z.

II

My Dear Brother:

Your last long letter came duly to hand and has been read with much pleasure. It is quite rare to find one willing to enter this movement on the basis you have laid down for yourself, and my previous letter was written in order to see what your attitude really was, and also because I then felt from your writing that you were really in earnest. And before yours of to-day, I fell to thinking about you and wondering whether a future of power, a brilliancy of knowledge, was not your aspiration, and what effect certain occurrences would have upon that.

Judge, then, my pleasure in reading your present words exactly answering my mental inquiries of yesterday and placing you in the right position.

It is true, we must aspire ardently, and blessed is the one who, after the first aspiration, is wise enough to see the Truth.

Three qualities forever encompass us: *Satwa* (truth and stability), *Rajas* (action, war, aspiration, ambition), *Tamas* (indifference, ignorance, darkness).

None may be ignored. So the path lies from Tamas, up through war, ambition, and aspiration, to Satwa, or truth and stability. We are now in Rajasika regions, sometimes lifting our fingers up to the hem of the garment of Satwa, ever aspiring, ever trying to purify our thoughts and free ourselves from the attachment to actions and objects. So, of course, the ardent student naturally aspires for power. This is wise. But he must soon begin to see what he must do for real progress. For continual aspiration for power, merely, is sure to sow for us the giant weed of self, which is the giant spoken of in *Light on the Path*.*

As to the Theosophical Society, all should be admitted, for we can refuse *no one*. If this is a Universal Brotherhood, we can make no distinctions; but we can put ourselves right in the beginning by seeing that people do not enter with mistaken notions of what we have. And yet with all our precautions, how often we find persons who, not really sincere themselves, judge us by their standard, unbelieving in our sincerity. They enter; they find that each must study for himself and that no guides are told off to each one; then they are disgusted. They forget that "the kingdom of heaven must be taken by violence." We have also had to suffer from our friends. People have joined us in secret like Nicodemus; they have stood idly by, waiting for the Cause to get strong or to get fashionable, leaving all the hard fighting to be done by a few earnest men who defied the hosts of Materialism and of Conventionality. Had they spoken for their Cause, more earnest people would long ago have heard of the Movement, instead of being kept away until now, like yourself, for want of knowledge that it existed.

You will find that other members care for nothing but Theosophy, and are yet forced by circumstances to work in other fields as well. What moments they have left are devoted to the Cause, and in consequence they have no unoccupied hours; each moment, day and evening, is filled up, and therefore they are happy. Yet they are unhappy that they cannot give their entire working time

---

* By Mabel Collins. (Orig. Pub., 1885.) Jasper states (*Path*, IV, 101, July, 1889): "Advanced occultists identify *Light on the Path* with an ancient, untranslated and unpublished M.S.S. called 'The Book of the * * * ,' to which M.C. could not have had access, and whose precepts must have been communicated to her through occult methods."—Eds. [Footnotes signed "Eds." have in all cases been added in the present edition.]

to the Cause in which some have been from the beginning. They feel, like Claude St. Martin, a burning desire within them to get these truths to the ears of all men. They are truths, and you are in the right path. In America it is as easy to find the Light of Lights as in India, but all around you are those who do not know these things, who never heard of them; and yet many of our fellow members are anxious to study only for their own benefit. Sometimes, if it were not for my reliance on those Great Beings who beckon me ever on, I would faint, and, leaving these people to themselves, rush off into the forest. So many people like Theosophy, and yet they at once wish to make it select and of high tone. It is for all men. It is for the common people, who are ever with us. Others, again, come in and wait like young birds for food to be put into them: they *will not think,* and ages must pass before they will progress.

You misunderstood a little the words "Do not think much of me." Underline *"much,"* but not "think." You will please think all the thoughts you will of me, but do not place me on any pinnacle: that's all I meant.

A constant endeavor towards perfecting the mere mortal machine is folly. Thereby we sometimes fail to live up to our own intuitions. This habit goes on for some time, but will get weaker as other senses (inner ones) begin to appear. Yet know the new fully before being off with the old.

Inasmuch as we learn almost solely from each other, as we are all here for each other, the effect of affinities upon our acts and thoughts is enormous and wide. It anon saves us, and anon damns. For we may meet in our lives a person who has a remarkable effect, either for good or ill, because of the affinities engendered in past lives. And now our eyes are open, we act to-day for the future.

That you may pass beyond the sea of darkness, I offer you my life and help.

Z.

III

Say, Brother Jasper, are you tired? I am. Not tired of fate nor of the great "Leaders of the World," but of all these people who gape and gape and are (excuse me) so Americanly "independent"—as if men were ever independent of each other.

You ask about the "moment of choice." It is made up of all moments. It is not in space or time, but is the aggregation of those moments flying by us each instant. It is referred to in *Esoteric Buddhism** as a period not yet arrived for the race, when it will as a whole be compelled to make the choice for good or evil. But any single individual can bring on the period for himself. When it will or has come, the uninstructed cannot tell. For the student of occultism it may come in the next instant, or it may come one hundred lives after. But it cannot come this instant unless all the previous lives have led up to it. Yet as regards the student, even if it be presented to him and he refuse, he will be brought to the choice in future existences, with the whole body of his race.

Race influences are insidious and powerful. For instance, my race has its peculiarities deeply seated and inherited from an extraordinary past. I must be under their influence in this body as a necessary part of my experience. In another life I might have been a prosaic Hottentot, or an Englishman, and in a succeeding one I might be under the influence of other race peculiarities. Those influences are, then, guiding me every moment, and each thought I have adds to them now, for either my own future use or for some other person who will come under the power of part of the force generated now by me.

As to the sub-conscious mind. It is difficult to explain. I find constantly I have ideas that internally I thoroughly understand, and yet can find no language for. Call it sub-conscious if you like. It is there and can be affected; indeed, it is affected every moment. It is a nearness to the universal mind. So if I desire to influence—say, your mind—I do not formulate your sub-conscious plane, but firmly and kindly think of you and the subject I wish you to think of. This must reach you. If I am selfish, then the thought has more difficulty to get there; but if it be brotherly, then it gets there more easily, being in harmony with the universal mind and the Law. The Psychical Society speaks of it, and says that the influence "emerges into the lower mind" by one or more of the channels. But they do not know what those "channels" are, nor even if they do exist. In fact, the whole subject of mind is only faintly understood in the West. They say "mind," meaning the vast range and departments of that which they call mind, whereas there must be a need for the names of those departments. When

* By A. P. Sinnett. (Orig. Pub., 1883.)—Eds.

the true ideas are grasped, the names will follow. Meanwhile we must be satisfied with "mind" as including the whole thing. But it does not. Certainly it is not ordinary mental motion—ratiocination—to grasp in an instant a whole subject, premises and conclusions, without stopping to reason. It cannot be called a *picture*, for with some it comes as an idea, and not as a picture. Memory. What is that? Is it brain-impression; or similarity of vibration, recognized upon being repeated and then producing a picture? If so, then the power to recognize the vibration as the same as before is separate from the matter which vibrates. And how is it possible for the power to inhere in the brain cells, when we know they are constantly being changed? Yet memory is perfect, no matter what happens. That it is above brain is clear, because a man may be killed by having his brain blown to atoms, and yet his "shell" can give all the incidents of his life; they are not taken from the brain, for that is dead. Where, then, is the sub-conscious mind? And where are the channels, and how are they connected? I think through the heart, and that the heart is the key to it all, and that the brain is only the servant of the heart,* for remember that there is in it the "small dwarf who sits at the centre." Think it out on that line now for yourself—or any other line that you may choose, but *think*.

As ever, Z.

IV

Dear Sir and Brother:

In cogitating lately I thought of you in respect to some of my own thoughts. I was reading a book and looking around within myself to see how I could enlarge my idea of brotherhood. Practice in benevolence will not give it its full growth. I had to find some means of reaching further, and struck on this, which is as old as old age.

I am not separate from anything. "I am that which is." That is, I am Brahma, and Brahma is everything. But being in an illusionary world, I am surrounded by certain appearances that seem to make me separate. So I will proceed to mentally state and accept that I am all these illusions. I am my friends,—and then I went to them in general and in particular. I am my enemies; then I felt them all. I am the poor and the wicked; I am the ignorant.

* Not the physical heart, but the real centre of life in man.—J. N.

Those moments of intellectual gloom are the moments when I am influenced by those ignorant ones who are myself. All this in my nation. But there are many nations, and to those I go in mind; I feel and I am them all, with what they hold of superstition or of wisdom or evil. All, all is myself. Unwisely, I was then about to stop, but the whole is Brahma, so I went to the Devas and Asuras;* the elemental world, that too is myself. After pursuing this course a while, I found it easier to return to a contemplation of all men as myself. It is a good method and ought to be pursued, for it is a step toward getting into contemplation of the All. I tried last night to reach up to Brahma, but darkness is about his pavilion.

Now what does all this insanity sound like? I'll tell you what: if it were not for this insanity I would go insane. But shall I not take heart, even when a dear friend deserts me and stabs me deep, when I know that he is myself?

NAMASTAE!

Z.

I found the above letter still more valuable when I remembered that Brahma is "the universal expansive force of Nature"—from *Brih,* to expand; and so stated in an article by H. P. Blavatsky in *Five Years of Theosophy* [1st ed., p. 184]. In the *Dhammapada* we are told to think ourselves to be the sun and stars, the wet and dry, heat and cold; in short, to feel all experience, for we can live all out in the mind. J. N.

V

Dear Jasper:

I wish I could answer your letter as you ought to have it done. But I feel my inability. However, our duty is to never consider our ability, but to do what comes to be done in whatever way we can, no matter how inadequate the work appears to others. When we stop to consider our weakness, we think, by comparison, of how another would do it. Our *only right is in the act itself.* The consequences are in the great Brahm. So I will just say what comes.

I feel the sadness in your letter, but know that you will rebound from that. Do not let the sadness of knowledge create despair;

* Gods and demons.—J. N.

that sadness is less than the joy of Truth. Abstract Truth, even, has necessarily in it all the mercy there is in the whole. Its sternness is only a reflection from our own imperfections, which make us recognize the stern aspect alone. We are not the only ones to suffer upon the Path. Like ourselves, Masters have wept, though They do not now weep. One of them wrote some years ago: "Do you suppose we have not passed through many times worse trials than you now think you are in?" The Master often seems to reject and to hide his (spiritual) face, in order that the disciple may try. On the doors and walls of the temple the word *"Try"* is written. ("The Brothers" is a better designation than Mahâtmas or Masters.)

Along the path of the true student is sadness, but also there is great joy and hope. Sadness comes from a more just appreciation of the difficulties in one's way, and of the great wickedness of the individual and collective heart of man. But look at the great fountain of hope and of joy in the consideration that the Brothers exist, that They were men too; They had to fight the fight; They triumphed, and They work for those left after Them. Then beyond Them are "the Fathers," that is, the spirits of "just men made perfect," those Who lived and worked for humanity ages ago and Who are now out of our sphere, but Who nevertheless still influence us in that Their spiritual forces flow down upon this earth for all pure souls. Their immediate influence is felt by Masters, and by us through the latter.

Now, as you say, it is all Faith; but what is Faith? It is the intuitional feeling—*"that is true."* So, formulate to yourself certain things as true that you feel to be true, and then increase your faith in them.

Don't be anxious. Don't get "maddened." Because in the fact that you are "maddened" (of course in the metaphorical sense) is found the proof that you are anxious. In a worldly sense it is perhaps well to be anxious about a highly important matter, but in occultism it is different, for the Law takes no account of our projects and objects, or our desire to be ahead or behind. So, if we are anxious, we raise a barrier against progress, by perturbation, and straining harshly. You wrote to B. that what is his, is his. Then the converse is true; what is not, is not. Why don't you take your own medicine?

Yours, Z.

VI

Dear Jasper:

It is a great advance that you hear the bells, which few hear, and evidence that you are where you can hear them; that is a great deal indeed. Do not look for the voice of the bells, but regard the *ideas* which thereupon come into the head, and apply to them the touchstone of your own Soul, just as you advised B. The fact that you feel "dead" is something you should not worry about. It is likely that you are under the operation of a law which prevails in nature, and which you will find referred to in an article in *Path* Magazine for April, '86, page 14.* It is that the soul goes to a new place or new surroundings and becomes silent awhile—what you call "dead"—and draws strength there, and begins to get accustomed to its new surroundings, after which it begins to move about. This is seen in ordinary life in the bashfulness of a boy. That is, the bashfulness is the shyness felt in new surroundings, and is just what happens when the soul goes to a new place or into new surroundings.

There can be no loss or detriment to our efforts. Every aspiration higher brightens up the road connecting the higher and lower self. No doubt of that. It is not *what* is done, but the spirit in which the least thing is done that is counted. Hear the word of the Master:

"He who does the best he knows how and that he can do, does enough for us."

The mere fact that a man appreciates these truths and feels these aspirations is proof that he is on the right road. It is well to tread it *now*. We will not always live. Death must come. How much better, then, to embrace death while thus at work than to swerve off only to be brought up with suddenness in after lives. Immediate rebirth is for those who are always working with their hearts on Master's work and free from self-interest.

The one Spirit is in all, is the property of each; therefore It is always there, always with us, and by reflecting on that, little room is left for sorrow or delusion. If we believe that the soul of all is measured by the whole of Time and not by a part, then we care not for these moments which relate alone to our body. If we

---

* See "Seership," reprinted in *Theosophy*, VI, 19.—Eds.

live in our hearts we soon prove that space and time exist not. Nothing foreign to Master enters there; our faults are not there. The heart reaches Him always, and no doubt He replies. He does, I know. He helps us while He leaves us to ourselves. He needs not stoop to see our devotion, for that is of a supernal quality and reaches anywhere.

No, I do not say nor have I said that you ought to do something other than you do. We each do what we can. None of us can be the judge of any creature existing; so I do not judge you in the least respect. Your life may in the great sum total be greater than any life I ever led or that anyone has led. Whether you are in America, Europe, or India makes no difference. That is seeking conditions. I have come to understand that Masters themselves must have worked up out of much worse conditions than we are in. No matter where we are, the same spirit pervades all and is accessible. What need, then, to change places? We do not change ourselves by moving the body to another *locus*. We only put it under a different influence. And in order to change we must have got to dislike the place we moved from. That is *attachment by opposites*, and that will produce detriment, as does all that disturbs the equilibrium of the soul. You know the same result is produced by two exact opposites, and thus extremes meet.

That hot flame you speak of is one of the experiences, as are also the sounds. There are so many, many of these things. Often they result from extreme tension or vibration in the aura of an aspirant of pure devotion. They are himself, and he should be on his guard against taking them for wonders. Often they are "apparitions in Brahm." They are like new lights and sights to a mariner on an unfamiliar coast. They will go on, or alter, or stop. You are only to carefully note them, and "do not exhibit wonder nor form association."

I cannot say more. All help you extend to any other soul is help to yourself. It is our duty to help all, and we must begin on those nearest to us, for to run abroad to souls we might possibly help we again forsake our present duty. It is better to die in our own duty, however mean, than to try another one. So lift your head and look around upon the hulks of past imagined faults. They were means and teachers. Cast all doubt, all fear, all regret aside, and freely take of truth what you may contain right on every step. It will thus be well. Eternal Truth is one and indivisible, and we may get from the Fathers (Pitris) flashes now and then of what is true.

Words are things. With me and in fact. Upon the lower plane of social intercourse they are things, but soulless and dead because that convention in which they have their birth has made abortions of them. But when we step away from that conventionality, words become alive in proportion to the reality and purity of the thought that is behind them. So in communication between two students they are things, and students must be careful that the ground of intercourse is fully understood. Let us use with care those living messengers called words.

Where I see you mistaken I will speak, to warn my Brother who temporarily knows not. For did I not call on the bugle, perhaps other things might switch him off to where for the time he would be pleased, but would again be sorry; and then when his mistake was plain, he would justly sigh to me across dark centuries of separation that I had been false to my duty of warning.

As ever, Z.

The new plane to which the soul may go, referred to in this letter, is the astral plane. It is the plane next above the material one, and consists of a subtile order of matter. When a student turns his attention to the higher life and desires intensely to find the way, his soul has begun to awaken and to speak. It has heard the voice of the spirit. Then the inner senses begin to unfold, at first ever so gently, so tenderly, we scarce hear their report. But the soul has then turned its attention to the astral plane, that being the next one to be learned on the way upward; its energy is transferred from the material plane to this one, and we have an influx of many confused dreams and strange experiences, awake and asleep. These may or may not continue; all depends upon the individual soul and upon Karma. It is a most confusing plane, and generally speaking, we may say that those students are more fortunate who make a marked degree of progress in spiritual things without having any conscious experience of the astral plane. For then they can later on learn it *from above*, instead of from below, and with far less danger to themselves. The whole must be known, but we may progress in various ways, even by discontinuous degrees, only then we must go back later on, to what we passed by. Such a going back does not imply detriment or loss of degree, for such cannot be lost when once gained in reality.

With regard to the astral plane being a more subtile order of matter, this truth is often denied by clairvoyants and untrained seers. They do not distinguish between the psychic senses and the spiritual. They can see through gross matter, such as a wall, the human body, and so forth, as if it were glass; but they cannot see through astral substance, and hence they believe its forms and all the pictures and shapes in the astral light to be real. Only the adept sees through these illusions, which are far more powerful because composed of a subtile order of matter: subtile energies, fine forces have a highly increased rate of power over grosser ones. The adept has at his command the rate of vibration which dispels them or drives them asunder. In speaking of the astral plane, I mean the lower soul plane, and not that higher and purified quality which the author of *Light on the Path* calls the "divine astral."

By anxiety we exert the constrictive power of egoism, which densifies and perturbs our magnetic sphere, rendering us less permeable to the efflux from above. J. N.

VII

Dear Jasper:

I have your letter, Comrade, in which you say how much you wish there were some Adepts sent to the United States to help all true students. Yet you know well They do not need to come here in person, in order to help. By going carefully over your letter there appears to me the possibility of the seed of doubt in your heart as to the wise ordering of all things, for all are under the Law, and Masters first of all. Mind, I only say the *"possibility of the seed of doubt."* For I judge from my own experience. Well do I remember when I thought, as you say—how much better 'twould be if some one were there.

If that is allowed to remain, it will metamorphose itself into a seed, and afterward a plant, of doubt. Cast it right out! It does not now show as seed of doubt, but in the case of metamorphosis, the change would be so great as to deceive you into thinking it were never from the same root. The best stand to take is—it is all right as it is now, and when the time comes for it to be better, it will be so. Meanwhile we have a duty to see that we do all we can *in our own place* as we see best, undisturbed and undismayed by aught.

How much I have in years gone away said and thought those very words of yours, and to no profit! Why do you care what becomes of a million human beings? Are not millions going to death daily with no one to tell them of all this? But did you suppose that all this was not provided for? "And heavenly death itself is also well provided for." Now, then, you and I must learn to look on the deaths or the famishing of millions of beings with unfaltering heart. Else we had better give it all up now. Consider that at this moment are so many persons in various far-distant places who cannot ever hear these truths. Do you grieve for them? Do you realize their state? No; you realize the same thing only partially among those with whom it was your present lot to be born—I mean the nation. Do you want to do more than your best? Do you covet the work of another? No; you do not. You will sit calmly where you are, then, and with an unaffected heart, picture to yourself the moral and physical deaths and famines which are now without the possibility of prevention or amelioration. Your faith will know that *all* is provided for.

I do not say that you must attain to that calm *now* or give up seeking the Way; but I do say that you must admit that such an attainment must be absolutely tried for. For of such is the trial, and why should we care? *We must some day be able to stand any shock,* and to get ready for that time we must be triumphant now over some smaller things. Among others is the very position you and I are now in; that is, standing our ground and feeling ourselves so much and so awfully alone. But we know that They have left us a commandment. That we keep, although now and then objects, senses, men, and time conspire to show us that Masters laugh at us. It is all a delusion. It is only one consequence of our past Karma now burning itself out before our eyes. The whole phantasmagoria is only a picture thrown up against the Screen of Time by the mighty magic of Prakriti (Nature). But you and I are superior to Nature. Why, then, mind these pictures? Part of that very screen, however, being our own mortal bodies, we cannot help the *sensation* derived therefrom through our connection with the body. It is only another form of cold or heat; and what are they? They are vibrations; they are *felt;* they do not really exist in themselves. So we can calmly look on the picture as it passes fragmentarily through those few square feet contained within the superficial boundaries of our elementary frame. We *must* do so, for it is a copy of the greater, of the universal form. For otherwise we will never be able to understand the greater picture. Now, then, is there not many a cubic inch of your own body which is entitled to know and to be the Truth in greater measure than now? And yet you grieve for the ignorance of so many other human beings! Grieve on; and I grieve, too. Do not imagine that I *am* what is there written. Not so. I am grieving just the same outwardly, but inwardly trying what I have just told you. And what a dream all this is. Here I am writing you so seriously, and now I see that you know it all quite well and much better than I do.

Yet, my dear Jasper, now and then I feel—not Doubt of Masters, who hear any heartbeat in the right direction, but—a terrible Despair of these people. Oh, my God! The age is black as hell, hard as iron. It is iron, it is Kali Yuga. Kali is always painted black. Yet Kali Yuga, by its very nature and terrible, swift momentum, permits one to do more with his energies in a shorter time than in any other Yuga. But heavens, what a combat! Demons from all the spheres; waving clouds of smoky Karma; dreadful shapes; stupefying exhalations from every side. Exposed at each turn to new dangers. Imagine a friend walking with you who you see is in the same road, but all at once he is permeated by these things of death and shows a disposition to obstruct your path, the path of himself. Yes; the gods are asleep for a while. But noble hearts still walk here, fighting over again the ancient fight. They seek each other, so as to be of mutual help. We will not fail them. To fail would be nothing, but to stop working for Humanity and Brotherhood would be awful. We cannot; we will not. Yet we have not a clear road. No, it is not clear. I am content if I can see the next step in advance, only. You seek *The Warrior*. He is here, somewhere. No one can find him for you. You must do that. Still He fights on. No doubt He sees you and tries to make you see Him. Still He fights on and on.

How plainly the lines are drawn, how easily the bands are seen. Some want a certificate, or an uttered pledge, or a secret meeting, or a declaration, but, without any of that, I see those who—up to this hour—I find are my "companions." They need no such folly. They are there; they hear and understand the battle-cry, they recognize the sign. Now where are the rest? Many have I halted, and spoken the exact words to them, have exposed to them my real heart, and they heard nothing; they thought that heart was something else. I sigh to think how many. Perhaps I overlooked some; perhaps some did not belong to me. There are some who partly understood the words and the sign, but they are not sure of themselves; they know that they partake of the nature, but are still held back.

Do you not see, Jasper, that your place in the ranks is well known? You need no assurances because they are *within* you.

Now what a dreadful letter; but it is all true.

A student of occultism after a while gets into what we may call a psychic whirl, or a vortex of occultism. At first he is affected by the feelings and influences of those about him. That begins to be pushed off and he passes into the whirl caused by the mighty effort of his Higher Self to make him remember his past lives. Then those past lives affect him. They become like clouds throwing shadows on his path. Now they seem tangible and then fade away, only a cloud. Then they begin to affect his impulse to action in many various ways. To-day he has vague calling longings to do something, and critically regarding himself, he cannot see in this life any cause. It is the bugle note of a past life blown almost in his face. It startles him; it may throw him down. Then it starts before him, a phantom, or, like a person behind you as you look at a mirror, it looks over his shoulder. Although dead and past they yet have a power. He gets, too, a power and a choice. If all his previous past lives were full of good, then irresistible is the force for his benefit. But all alike marshal up in front, and he hastens their coming by his effort. Into this vortex about him others are drawn, and their germs for good or ill ripen with activity. This is a phase of the operation of Karmic stamina. The choice is this: these events arrive one after the other and, as it were, offer themselves. If he chooses wrong, then hard is the fight. The one chosen attracts old ones like itself perhaps, for all have a life of their own. Do you wonder that in the case of those who rush unprepared into the "circle of ascetics" and before the ripe moment, insanity sometimes results? But then that insanity is their safety for the next life, or for their return to sanity.

Receive my brotherly assurances, my constant desire to help you.

In respect to Karmic action it is well to recall the statement of Patanjali that "works exist only in the shape of mental deposits." (Book 2, Aph. 12, A.) By "works" is here meant Karma, the stock of works, or Action. Its results remain as mental deposits or potential energies in the higher part of the fifth principle, and when it reincarnates those seeds are there to "ripen on the tablets of the mind" whenever they are exposed to favoring circumstances. Sometimes they remain dormant for want of something to arouse them, as in the case of children. "The mental deposits of works, collected from time without beginning in the ground of the mind, as they by degrees arrive at maturation, so do they, existing in lesser or greater measure (the sum of merit being less than that of demerit, or conversely), lead to their effects in the shape of rank, raised or lowered . . . or experience of good or ill." (Book 2, Aph. 13, B.).* The mind energizes and impels us to fresh action. The impulse lies within, in germ, and may be ripened by interior or exterior suggestion. Can we, then, be too careful to guard the ground of the mind, to keep close watch over our thoughts? Thoughts are dynamic. Each one as it leaves the mind has a *vis viva* of its own, proportionate to the intensity with which it was propelled. As the work done by a moving body is proportionate to the square of its velocity, we may say that the force of thoughts is to be measured by the square or quadrupled power of their spirituality, so greatly do these finer forces increase by activity. The spiritual force, being impersonal, fluidic, not bound to any constricting center, acts with unimaginable swiftness. A thought, on its departure from the mind, is said to associate itself with an elemental; it is attracted wherever there is a similar vibration, or, let us say, a suitable soil, just as the winged thistle-seed floats off and sows itself in this spot and not in that, in the soil of its natural selection. Thus the man of virtue, by admitting a material or sensual thought into his mind—even though he expel it—sends it forth to swell the evil impulses of the man of vice, from whom he imagines himself separated by a wide gulf, yet to whom he may have just given a fresh impulse to sin. Many men are like sponges, porous and bibulous, ready to suck up every element of the order preferred by their nature. We all have more or less of this quality; we attract what we love, and we may derive a greater strength from the vitality of thoughts infused from without than from those self-reproduced within us at a time when our nervous vitality is exhausted. It is a solemn thought, this, of our responsibility for the impulse of

* The foregoing passages are not cited from Mr. Judge's rendition of Patanjali, but from some other edition. For a parallel discussion, see the corresponding rendition by Mr. Judge; also, Book IV, Aphs. 7-11.—Eds.

another. We live in one another, and our widely different deeds have often a common source. The occultist cannot go far upon his way without realizing to what a great extent he is "his brother's keeper." Our affinities are ourselves, in whatever ground they may live and ripen. J. N.

VIII

Dear Jasper:

I seize a few moments to acknowledge your letter. This is a period of waiting, of silence. Nothing seems alive. All oracles are silent. But the great clock of the Universe still goes on, unheeding. On Sunday I engaged in Meditation and received some benefit. I wished I could see you to speak of it. Yet these things are too high for words, and when we approach the subjects we are not able to give expression to our thoughts. We do not live up to our highest soul possibilities. All that prevents our reaching up to the high thoughts of the far past is our own weakness, and not the work of any other. How petty seem the cares of this earth when we indulge in deep reflection; they are then seen for what they are, and later on they are obliterated. It is true that the road to the gods is dark and difficult, and as you say, we get nothing from them at first call; we have to call often. But we can on the way stop to look ahead, for no matter how sombre or howsoever weak ourselves, the Spectator sees it all and beckons to us, and whispers, "Be of good courage, for I have prepared a place for you where you will be with me forever." He is the Great Self; He is ourselves.

The Leaders of the world are always trying to help us. May we pass the clouds and see them ever. We must be patient. All our obstructions are of our own making. All our power is the storage of the past. That store we all must have; who in this life feels it near is he who has in this life directed his thoughts to the proper channel. That others do not feel it is because they have lived but blindly. That you do not feel it and see it more is because you have not yet directed all your mental energies to it. This great root of Karmic energy can be drawn upon by directing to it the fire of our minds. Towards Love of course is the right way—the Love of the Divine and of all beings. If we feel that after all we are not yet "Great Souls" who participate in the totality of those "Souls who wait upon the gods," it need not cast us down:

we are waiting our hour in hope. Let us wait patiently, in the silence which follows all effort, knowing that thus Nature works, for in her periods of obscuration she does naught where that obscuration lies, while doubtless she and we, too, are then at work on other spheres.

That described by you is not the soul; it is only a partial experience. Did you know the Soul, then could you yourself reply to all those questions, for all knowledge is there. In the soul is every creature and every thought alike. That sinking down of your thoughts to the center is practice. It can be done and we cannot explain it; we can only say "do it." Still, do not hunger to do these things. The first step in *becoming* is Resignation. Resignation is the sure, true, and royal road. Our subtle motives, ever changing, elude us when we seek it. You are near to it; it needs a great care. But while the body may be requiring time to feel its full results, we can instantly change the attitude of the mind. After Resignation, follow (in their own order) Satisfaction, Contentment, Knowledge. Anxiety to do these things is an obscurant and deterrent. So, try to acquire patient Resignation. The lesson intended by the Karma of your present life is *the higher patience.* I can tell you nothing on this head; it is a matter for self and practice. Throw away every wish to get the power, and seek only for understanding of thyself. Insist on carelessness. Assert to yourself that it is not of the slightest consequence what you were yesterday, but in every moment strive for that moment; the results will follow of themselves.

The Past! What is it? Nothing. Gone! Dismiss it. You are the past of yourself. Therefore it concerns you not as such. It only concerns you as you now are. In you, as you now exist, lies *all* the past. So follow the Hindu maxim: "Regret nothing; never be sorry; and cut all doubts with the sword of spiritual knowledge." Regret is productive only of error. I care not what I *was,* or what any one *was.* I only look for what I am each moment. For as each moment is and at once is not, it must follow that if we think of the past we forget the present, and while we forget, the moments fly by us, making more past. Then regret nothing, not even the greatest follies of your life, for they are gone, and you are to work in the present which is both past and future at once. So then, with the absolute knowledge that all your limitations are due to Karma, past or in this life, and with a firm reliance ever upon Karma as the only judge, which will be good or bad as you make it, yourself, you can stand anything that may happen and feel serene, despite the occasional despondencies which all feel, but which the light of Truth always dispels. This verse always settles everything:

"In him who knows that all spiritual beings are the same in kind with the Supreme Being, what room can there be for delusion and what room for sorrow when he reflects upon the unity of spirit?"

In all these inner experiences there are tides, as well as in the ocean. We rise and fall. Anon the gods descend, and then they return to heaven. Do not think of getting *them* to descend, but strive to raise *yourself* higher on the road down which they periodically return, and thus get nearer to them, so that you shall in fact receive their influences sooner than before.

Adios. May you ever feel the surge of the vast deeps that lie beyond the heart's small ebb. Perhaps our comrades are coming nearer. Who knows? But even if not, then we will wait; the sun must burst some day from the clouds. This will keep us strong, as, in the company of the Dweller of the Threshold, we have perforce to stare and sham awhile.

Z.

The "higher patience" alluded to also requires a care. It is the fine line between pride and humility. Both are extremes and mistakes; oscillations from one to the other are only a trifle better. How shall we be proud when we are so small? How dare we be humble when we are so great? In both we blaspheme. But there is that firm spot between the two which is the place "neither too high nor too low" on which Krishna told Arjuna to sit; a spot *of his own*. It is the firm place which our faith has won from the world. On it we are always to stand calmly, not overshadowed by any man however great, because each of us contains the potentialities of every other. "Not overshadowed" does not mean that we are not to show reverence to those through whom the soul speaks. It is the great soul we reverence, and not the mortal clay. We are to examine thoughtfully all that comes to us from such persons, and all that comes to us from any source wearing the aspect of truth, and try faithfully to see wherein it may be true, laying it aside, if we fail, as fruit not ripe for us yet. We are not to yield up our intuitions to any being, while we may largely doubt our judgment at all times. We are not to act without the inner asseveration, but we must not remain ignorant of the serious difficulties of separating this intuitive voice from the babble and prattle of fancy, desire, or pride. If we are just to ourselves we shall hold the balance evenly. How can we be just to any other, who are not just to ourselves? In the Law, a man suffers as much from injustice to himself as to another; it matters not in whose interests he has opposed the universal currents; the Law only knows that he has tried to deflect them by an injustice. It takes no account of persons nor even of ignorance of the Law. It is an impartial, impersonal force, only to be understood by the aid of the higher patience, which at once dares all and endures all.

"Never regret anything." Regret is a thought, hence an energy. If we turn its tide upon the past, it plays upon the seeds of that past and vivifies them; it causes them to sprout and grow in the ground of the mind: from thence to expression in action is but a step. A child once said to me when I used the word "Ghosts," "Hush! Don't think of them. What we think of always happens." There are no impartial observers like children when they think away from themselves. J. N.

IX

Dear Sir and Brother:

Tell your friend and inquirer this: No one was ever converted to Theosophy. Each one who *really* comes into it does so because it is only "an extension of previous beliefs." This will show you that Karma is a true thing. For no idea we get is any more than an extension of previous ones. That is, they are cause and effect in endless succession. Each one is the producer of the next and inheres in that successor. Thus we are all different, and some similar. My ideas of today, and yours, are tinged with those of youth, and we will thus forever proceed on the inevitable line we have marked out in the beginning. We of course alter a little always, but never until our old ideas are extended. Those *false* ideas now and then discarded are not to be counted; yet they give a shadow here and there. But through Brotherhood we receive the knowledge of others, which we consider until (if it fits us) it is ours. As far as your private conclusions are concerned, use your discrimination always. Do not adopt any conclusions merely because they are uttered by one in whom you have confidence, but adopt them when they coincide with your intuition. To be even unconsciously deluded by the influence of another is to have a counterfeit faith.

Spiritual knowledge includes every action. Inquirers ought to read the *Bhagavad-Gîtâ.** It will give them food for centuries if they read with spiritual eyes at all. Underneath its shell is the living spirit that will light us all. I read it ten times before I saw things that I did not see at first. In the night the ideas contained in it are digested and returned partly next day to the mind. It is the study of adepts.

Let no man be unaware that while there is a great joy in this belief there is also a great sorrow. Being true, being *the Law,* all the great forces are set in motion by the student. He now thinks he has given up ambition and comfort. The ambition and comfort he has given up are those of the lower plane, the mere reflections of the great ambitions and comforts of a larger life. The rays of truth burn up the covers time has placed upon those seeds, and then the seeds begin to sprout and cause new struggles. Do not leave any earnest inquirer in ignorance of this. It has cost others many years and tears of blood to self-learn it.

How difficult the path of action is! I see the future dimly, and unconsciously in such case one makes efforts either for or against it. Then Karma results. I could almost wish I did not hear these whispers. But he who conquers himself is greater than the conquerors of worlds.

Perhaps you see more clearly now how Karma operates. If one directs himself to eliminating all old Karma, the struggle very often becomes tremendous, for the whole load of ancient sin rushes to the front on a man and the events succeed each other rapidly; the strain is terrific, and the whole life fabric groans and rocks. As is said in the East, you may go through the appointed course in 700 births, in seven years, or in seven minutes.

The sentence in *Light on the Path* referred to by so many students is not so difficult as some others. One answer will do for all. The book is written on the basis of Reincarnation, and when it says the soiled garment will fall again on you, it means that this will happen in some other life, not necessarily in this, though that

* Mr. Judge's rendition, and his *Notes on the Bhagavad-Gita* are in print. —Eds.

may be, too. To "turn away in horror" is *not* detachment. Before we can hope to prevent any particular state of mind or events reaching us in this or in another life, *we* must in fact be detached from these things. Now, *we* are not our bodies nor mere minds, but the *real* part of us in which Karma inheres. Karma brings everything about. It attaches to our real inner selves by attachment and repulsion. That is, if we love vice or anything, it seizes on us by attachment; if we hate anything, it seizes on our inner selves by reason of the strong horror we feel for it. In order to prevent a thing we must understand it; we cannot understand while we fear or hate it. We are not to love vice, but are to recognize that it is a part of the whole, and, trying to understand it, we thus get above it. This is the "doctrine of opposites" spoken of in *Bhagavad-Gîtâ.* So if we turn in horror from the bad (we may feel sad and charitable, though), in a future life we will feel that horror and develop it by reaction into a reincarnation in a body and place where we must in material life go through the very thing we now hate. As we are striving to reach God, we must learn to be as near like Him as possible. He loves and hates not; so, we must strive to regard the greatest vice as being something we must not hate while we will not engage in it, and then we may approach that state where we will know the greater love that takes in good and evil men and things alike.

Good and Evil are only the two poles of the one thing. In the Absolute, Evil is the same thing as Good in this way. One with absolute knowledge can *see* both Good and Evil, but he does not *feel* Evil to be a thing to flee from, and thus he has to call it merely the other pole. We say Good or Evil as certain events seem pleasant or unpleasant to us or to our present civilization. And so we have coined those two words. They are bad words to use. For in the Absolute one is just as necessary as the other, and often what seem evil and "pain" are not absolutely so, but only necessary adjustments in the progress of the soul. Read *Bhagavad-Gîtâ* as to how the self seems to suffer pain. What is Evil now? Loss of friends? No; if you are self-centered. Slander? Not if you rely on Karma. There is only evil when you rebel against immutable decrees that must be worked out. You know that there must be these balancings which we call Good and Evil. Just imagine one man who really was a high soul, now living as a miser and enjoying it. You call it an evil; he a good. Who is right? You say "Evil" because you are speaking out of the True; but the True did know that he could never have passed some one certain point unless he had that experience, and so we see him now in an evil state. Experience we must have, and if we accept it at our own hands we are wise. That is, while striving to do our whole duty to the world and ourselves, we will not live the past over again by vain and hurtful regrets, nor condemn any man, whatever his deeds, since we cannot know their true cause. We are not Karma, we are not the Law, and it is a species of that hypocrisy so deeply condemned by It for us to condemn any man. That the Law lets a man live is proof that he is not yet judged by that higher power. Still, we must and will keep our discriminating power at all times.

As to rising above Good and Evil, that does not mean to do evil, of course. But, in fact, there can be no *real* Evil nor Good; if our aim is right, our acts cannot be evil. Now, all acts are dead when done; it is in the heart that they are conceived and are already there done; the mere bodily carrying out of them is a dead thing in itself. So, we may do a supposed good act, that shall outwardly appear good, and yet as our motive perhaps is wrong, the act is naught, but the motive counts.

The great God did all, good and bad alike. Among the rest are what appear Evil things, yet he must be unaffected. So if we follow *Bhagavad-Gîtâ,* second chapter, we must do only those acts we believe right for the sake of God and not for ourselves, and, if we are regardless of the consequences, we are not concerned if they *appear* to be Good or Evil. As the heart and mind are the real planes of error, it follows that we must look to it that we do all acts merely because they are there to be done. It then becomes difficult only to separate ourselves from the act.

We can never as human beings rise above being the instruments through which that called Good and Evil comes to pass, but as that Good and Evil are the result of comparison and are not in themselves absolute, it must follow that we (the real "*we*") must learn to rise internally to a place where these occurrences appear to us merely as changes in a life of change. Even in the worldly man this sometimes happens.

As, say, Bismarck, used to moving large bodies of men and perhaps for a good end, can easily rise above the transient Evil, looking to a greater result. Or the physician is able to rise above pain to a patient, and consider only the good, or rather the result, that is to follow from a painful operation. The patient himself does the same.

So the student comes to see that he is not to do either "Good" or "Evil," but to do any certain number of acts set before him, and meanwhile not ever to regard much his line of conduct, but rather his line of motive, for his conduct follows necessarily from his motive. Take the soldier. For him there is nothing better than lawful war. Query. Does he do wrong in warring or not, even if war is unlawful? He does not unless he mixes his motive. They who go into war for gain or revenge do wrong, but not he who goes at his superior's order, because it is his present duty.

Let us, then, extend help to all who come our way. This will be true progress: the veils that come over our souls fall away when we work for others. Let that be the real motive, and the *quantity* of work done makes no difference.

Z.

It would seem that Good and Evil are not inherent in things themselves, but in the uses to which those things are put by us. They are conditions of manifestation. Many things commonly called immoral are consequences of the unjust laws of man, of egotistic social institutions: such things are not immoral *per se*, but relatively so. They are immoral *only* in point of time. There are others whose evil consists in the base use to which higher forces are put, or to which Life—which is sacred—is put, so that here also evil does not inhere in them, but in ourselves; in our misuse of noble instruments in lower work. Nor does evil inhere in us, but in our ignorance; it is one of the great illusions of Nature. All these illusions cause the soul to experience in matter until it has consciously learned every part; then it must learn to know the whole and all at once, which it can only do by and through reunion with Spirit; or with the Supreme, with the Deity.

If we take, with all due reverence, so much of the standpoint of the Supreme as our finite minds or our dawning intuition may permit, we feel that It stands above, unmoved by either Good or Evil. Our good is relative, and evil is only the limitation of the soul by matter. From the material essence of the Deity all the myriad differentiations of Nature (Prakriti, cosmic substance), all the worlds and their correlations are evolved. They assist the cyclic experience of the soul as it passes from state to state. How, then, shall we say that any state is evil in an absolute sense? Take murder. It seems an evil. True, we cannot *really* take life, but we can destroy a vehicle of the divine Principle of Life and impede the course of a soul using that vehicle. But we are more injured by the deed than any other. It is the fruit of a certain unhealthy state of the soul. The deed sends us to hell, as it were, for one or more incarnations; to a condition of misery. The shock, the natural retribution, our own resultant Karma, both the penalties imposed by man and that exacted by occult law, chasten and soften the soul. It has passed through a most solemn experience which had become necessary to its growth and which in the end is the cause of its additional purification. In view of this result, was the deed evil? It was a necessary consequence of the limitations of matter; for had the soul remained celestial and in free Being, it could not have committed murder. Nor has the immortal soul, the spectator, any share in the wrong; it is only the personality, the elementary part of the soul, which has sinned. All that keeps the soul confined to material existence is evil, and so we cannot discriminate either. The only ultimate good is Unity, and in reality nothing but that exists. Hence our judgments are in time only. Nor have we the right to exact a life for a life. "Vengeance is mine, saith the Lord (Law); I will repay." We become abetters of murder in making such human laws. I do not say that every experience must be gone through bodily, because some are lived out in the mind. Nor do I seek to justify any. The only justification is in the Law.

The innocent man unjustly murdered is rewarded by Karma in a future life. Indeed, any man murdered is reimbursed, so to say; for while that misfortune sprang from his Karma, occult law does not admit of the taking of life. Some men are the weapons of Karma in their wrong-doing, but they themselves have appointed this place to themselves in their past.

The Great Soul needed just that body, whatever the errors of its nature, or its physical environment, and to disappoint the soul is a fearful deed for a man. For it is only man, only the lower nature under the influence of Tamas (the quality of darkness), which feels the impulse to take life, whether in human justice, for revenge, for protection, or so on. "The soul neither kills nor is killed." What we know as ourselves is only the natural man, the lower principles and mind, presided over by the false consciousness. Of the soul we have but brief and partial glimpses—in conscience or intuition—in our ordinary state. There are, of course, psychic and spiritual states in which more is known. Thus nature wars against nature, always for the purpose of bringing about the purification and evolution of the soul. Nature exists only for the purpose of the soul. If we think out the subject upon these lines, we can at least see how rash we should be to conclude that any deed was unmixed evil, or that these distinctions exist in the Absolute. It alone is; all else is phenomenal and transitory; these differences disappear as we proceed upward. Meanwhile we are to avoid all these immoral things and many others not so regarded by the crowd at all, but which are just as much so, because we know to what increased ignorance and darkness they give rise through the ferment which they cause in the nature, and that this impedes the entrance of the clear rays of Truth.

I doubt that the soul knows the moral or immoral. For just consider for a moment the case of a disembodied soul. What is sin to it when freed from that shell—the body? What does it know then of human laws or moralities, or the rules and forms of matter? Does it even see them? What lewdness can it commit? So I say that these moralities are of this plane only, to be heeded and obeyed there, but not to be postulated as final or used as a balance to weigh the soul, which has other laws. The free soul has to do with essences and powers all impersonal; the strife of matter is left behind. Still higher and above as within all, the passionless, deathless spirit looks down, knowing well that, when the natural has once again subsided into its spiritual source, all this struggle and play of force and will, this waxing and waning of forms, this progression of consciousness which throws up coming clouds and fumes of illusion before the eye of the soul, will have come to an end. Even now, while we cannot master these high themes, we can have a patient trust in the processes of evolution and the Law, blaming and judging no man, but living up to our highest intuitions ourselves. *The real test of a man is his motive,* which we do not see, nor do his acts always represent it. J. N.

X

Dear Jasper:

You ask me about the "three qualities sprung from Nature," mentioned in the *Bhagavad-Gîtâ*. They exist potentially (latent) in *Purush* (Spirit), and during that period spoken of in the *Bhagavad-Gîtâ* as the time when He produces all things after having devoured them (which is the same thing as Saturn devouring his children), they come forth into activity, and therefore are found *implicating* all beings, who are said not to be free from their influence.

"Beings" here must refer to formed beings in all worlds. Therefore in these forms the qualities *exist* [for form is derived from Nature=Prakriti=Cosmic Substance.—J. N.], and at the same time *implicate* the spectator (soul) who is in the form. The Devas are gods, that is, a sort of spiritual power lower than the Ishwara in man. They are influenced by the quality of Satwa, or Truth. They enjoy a period of immense felicity of enormous duration, but which having *duration* is not an eternity.

It is written: "Goodness, badness, and indifference—the qualities thus called—sprung from Nature, influence the imperishable soul within the body."

This imperishable soul is thus separated from the body in which the qualities influence it, and also from the qualities which are not it. It is Ishwara. The Ishwara is thus implicated by the qualities.

The first or highest quality is Satwa, which is in its nature pure and pleasant, and implicates Ishwara by connection with pleasant things and with knowledge. Thus even by dwelling in Satwa the soul is implicated.

The second quality is Raja and causes action; it implicates the soul because it partakes of avidity and propensity, and causing actions thus implicates the soul.

The third, Tamo quality, is of the nature of indifference and is the deluder of all mortals. It is fed by ignorance.

Here, then, are two great opposers to the soul—*ignorance* and *action*. For action proceeding from Raja assisted by Satwa does not lead to the highest place, while ignorance causes destruction. Yet when one knows that he is ignorant, he has to perform actions in order to destroy that ignorance. How to do that without always revolving in the whirl of action [Karma, causing rebirths.—J. N.] is the question.

He must first get rid of the idea that he himself really does anything, knowing that the actions all take place in these three natural qualities, and not in the soul at all. The word "qualities" must be considered in a larger sense than that word is generally given.

Then he must place all his actions on devotion. That is, sacrifice all his actions to the Supreme and not to himself. He must either (leaving out indifference) set himself up as the God to whom he sacrifices, or the other real God—Krishna, and all his acts and aspirations are done either for himself or for the All. Here comes in the importance of motive. For if he performs great deeds of valor, or of benefit to man, or acquires knowledge so as to assist man, and is moved to that merely because he thinks *he* will attain salvation, he is acting only for his own benefit and is therefore sacrificing to himself. Therefore he must be devoted inwardly to the All; that is, he places all his actions on the Supreme, knowing that he is not the doer of the actions, but is the mere witness of them.

As he is in a mortal body, he is affected by doubts which will spring up. When they do arise, it is because he is ignorant about something. He should therefore be able to disperse doubt "by the sword of knowledge." For if he has a ready answer to some doubt, he disperses that much. All doubts come from the lower nature, and *never* in any case from the higher nature. Therefore, as he becomes more and more devoted, he is able to know more and more clearly the knowledge residing in his Satwa part. For it says:

"A man who is perfected in devotion (or who persists in its cultivation) finds spiritual knowledge springing up spontaneously in himself in the progress of time." Also: "The man of doubtful mind enjoys neither this world nor the other (the Deva world), nor final beatitude."

The last sentence is to destroy the idea that if there is in us this higher self it will, even if we are indolent and doubtful, triumph over the necessity for knowledge, and lead us to final beatitude in common with the whole stream of man.

The three qualities are lower than a state called Turya, which is a high state capable of being enjoyed even while in this body. Therefore, in that state, there exists none of the three qualities, but the soul sees the three qualities moving in the ocean of Being beneath. This experience is met with not only after death, but, as I said, it may be enjoyed in the present life, though of course consciously very seldom. But there are those high Yogees who can and do rise up to Nirvana, or Spirit, even consciously, while on the earth. This state is the fourth state, called Turya. There is no word in English which will express it. In that state the body is alive though in deep catalepsy. [Self-induced by the Adept.—J. N.] When the Adept returns from it he brings back *whatever he can* of the vast experiences of that Turya state. Of course they are far beyond any expression, and their possibilities can be only dimly perceived by us. I cannot give any description thereof because I have not known it, but I perceive the possibilities, and you probably can do the same.

It is well to pursue some kind of practice, and pursue it either in a fixed place, or in a mental place which cannot be seen, or at night. The fact that what is called Dharana, Dhyana, and Samâdhi may be performed should be known. (See Patanjali's yoga system.)

Dharana is selecting a thing, a spot, or an idea, to fix the mind on.

Dhyana is contemplation of it.

Samâdhi is meditating on it.

When attempted, they of course are all one act.

Now, then, take what is called the well of the throat or pit of the throat.

1st. Select it.—Dharana.

2d. Hold the mind on it.—Dhyana.

3d. Meditate on it.—Samâdhi.

This gives firmness of mind.

Then select the spot in the head where the Sushumna nerve goes. Never mind the location; call it the top of the head. Then pursue the same course. This will give some insight into spiritual minds. At first it is difficult, but it will grow easy by practice. If done at all, the same hour of each day should be selected, as creating a habit, not only in the body, but also in the mind. Always keep the direction of Krishna in mind, namely, that it is done for the whole body corporate of humanity, and not for one's self.

As regards the passions: Anger seems to be the *force* of Nature; there is more in it, though.

Lust (so-called) is the gross symbol of love and desire to create. It is the perversion of the True in love and desire.

Vanity, I think, represents in one aspect the illusion-power of Nature—Maya, that which we mistake for the reality. It is always nearest to us and most insidious, just as Nature's illusion is ever present and difficult to overcome.

Anger and Lust have some of the Rajasika quality; but it seems to me that Vanity is almost wholly of the Tamogunam.

May you cross over to the fearless shore.

Z.

As regards the practices of concentration suggested in this letter, they are only stages in a life-long contemplation; they are means to an end, means of a certain order among means of other orders, all necessary, the highest path being that of constant devotion and entire resignation to the Law. The above means have a physiological value because the spots suggested for contemplation are, like others, vital centers. Excitation of these centers, and of the magnetic residue of breath always found in them, strengthens and arouses the faculties of the inner man, the magnetic vehicle of the soul and the link between matter and spirit. This is a form of words necessary for clearness, because in reality matter and spirit are one. We may better imagine an infinite series of force correlations which extend from pure Spirit to its grossest vehicle, and we may say that the magnetic inner vehicle, or astral man, stands at the halfway point of the scale. The secret of the circulation of the nervous fluid is hidden in these vital centers, and he who discovers it can use the body at will. Moreover, this practice trains the mind to remain in its own principle, without energizing, and without exercising its tangential force, which is so hard to overcome. Thought has a self-reproductive power, and when the mind is held steadily to one idea it becomes colored by it, and, as we may say, all the correlates of that thought arise within the mind. Hence the mystic obtains knowledge about any object of which he thinks constantly in fixed contemplation. Here is the rationale of Krishna's words: "Think constantly of me; depend on me alone; and thou shalt surely come unto me."

The pure instincts of children often reveal occult truths. I heard a girl of fifteen say recently: "When I was a small child I was always supposin'. I used to sit on the window seat and stare, stare, at the moon, and I was supposin' that, if I only stared long enough, I'd get there and know all about it."

Spiritual culture is attained through concentration. It must be continued daily and every moment to be of use. The "Elixir of Life"* *(Five Years of Theosophy)* gives us some of the reasons for this truth. Meditation has been defined as "the cessation of active, external thought." Concentration is the entire life-tendency to a given end. For example, a devoted mother is one who consults the interests of her children and all branches of their interests in and before all things; not one who sits down to think fixedly about one branch of their interests all the day. Life is the great teacher; it is the great manifestation of Soul, and Soul manifests the Supreme. Hence all methods are good, and all are but parts of the great aim, which is Devotion. "Devotion is success in actions," says the *Bhagavad-Gîtâ.* We must use higher and lower faculties alike, and beyond those of mind are those of the Spirit, unknown but discoverable. The psychic powers, as they come, must also be used, for they reveal laws. But their value must not be exaggerated, nor must their danger be ignored. They are more subtle intoxicants than the gross physical energies. He who relies upon them is like a man who gives way to pride and triumph because he has reached the first wayside station on the peaks he has set out to climb. Like despondency, like doubt, like fear, like vanity, pride, and self-satisfaction, these powers too are used by Nature as traps to detain us. Every occurrence, every object, every energy may be used for or against the great end: in each, Nature strives to contain Spirit, and Spirit strives to be free. Shall the substance paralyze the motion, or shall the motion control the substance? The interrelation of these two is manifestation. The ratio of activity governs spiritual development; when the great Force has gained its full momentum, It carries us to the borders of the Unknown. It is a Force intelligent, self-conscious, and spiritual: its lower forms, or vehicles, or correlates may be evoked by us, but Itself comes only of Its own volition. We can only prepare a vehicle for It, in which, as Behmen says, "the Holy Ghost may ride in Its own chariot."

"The Self cannot be known by the *Vedas*, nor by the understanding, nor by much learning. He whom the Self chooses, by him alone can the Self be gained."

"The Self chooses him as his own. But the man who has not first turned aside from his wickedness, who is not calm and subdued, or *whose mind is not at rest,* he can never obtain the Self, even by knowledge."

---

* Originally published in *The Theosophist*, III, 140, 168.—Eds.

The italics are mine; they indicate the value of that stage of contemplation hitherto referred to as that in which the mind has ceased to energize, and when the pure energies of Nature go to swell the fountain of Spirit.

The phrase in the above letter—that the Adept "brings back *what he can*" from Turya—is to be understood as referring to the fact that all depends upon the coördination of the various principles in man. He who has attained perfection, or Mahâtmaship, has assumed complete control of the body and informs it at will. But, of course, while in the body he is still, to some extent, as a soul of power, limited by that body or vehicle. That is to say, there are experiences not to be shared by that organ of the soul called by us "the body," and beyond a certain point its brain cannot reflect or recall them. This point varies according to the degree of attainment of individual souls, and while in some it may be a high point of great knowledge and power, still it must be considered as limited, compared with those spiritual experiences of the freed soul.

The work upon which all disciples are employed is that of rendering the body more porous, more fluidic, more responsive to all spiritual influences which arise in the inner center, in the soul, which is an undivided part of the great Soul of all, and less receptive of the outside material influences generated by the unthinking world and by the qualities in nature. Abstract thought is said to be "the power of thinking of a thing apart from its qualities"; but these qualities are the phenomenal, the evident, and they make the most impression upon our senses. They bewilder us, and they form a part of that trap which Nature sets for us lest we discover her inmost secret and rule her. More than this: our detention as individual components of a race provides time for that and other races to go through evolutionary experience slowly, provides long and repeated chances for every soul to amend, to return, to round the curve of evolution. In this, Nature is most merciful, and even in the darkness of the eighth sphere to which souls of *spiritual* wickedness descend, her impulses provide opportunities of return if a single responsive energy is left in the self-condemned soul.

Many persons insist upon a perfect moral code tempered by social amenities, forgetting that these vary with climate, nationalities, and dates. Virtue is a noble offering to the Lord. But insomuch as it is mere bodily uprightness and mere mental uprightness, it is insufficient and stands apart from uprightness of the psychic nature or the virtue of soul. The virtue of the soul is true Being; its virtue is, to be free. The body and the mind are not sharers in such experiences, though they may afterward reflect them, and this reflection may inform them with light and power of their own kind. Spirituality is not virtue. It is impersonality, in one aspect. It is as possible to be spiritually "wicked" as to be spiritually "good." These attributes are only conferred upon spirituality by reason of its use for or against the great evolutionary Law, which must finally prevail because it is the Law of the Deity, an expression of the nature and Being of the Unknown, which nature is towards manifestation, self-realization, and reäbsorption. All that clashes with this Law by striving for separate existence must in the long run fail, and any differentiation which is in itself incapable of reäbsorption is reduced to its original elements, in which shape, so to say, it can be reäbsorbed.

Spirituality is, then, a condition of Being which is beyond expression in language. Call it a rate of vibration, far beyond our cognizance. Its language is the language of motion, in its incipiency, and its perfection is beyond words and even thought.

"The knowledge of the Supreme Principle is a divine silence, and the quiescence of all the senses." (*Clavis of Hermes.*)

"Likes and dislikes, good and evil, do not in the least affect the knower of Brahm, who is bodiless and always existing." (*Crest Jewel of Wisdom.*)

"Of that nature which is beyond intellect many things are asserted according to intellection, but it is contemplated by a cessation of intellectual energy better than with it." (*Porphyrios.*)

Thought is bounded, and we seek to enter the boundless. The intellect is the first production of Nature which energizes for the experience of the soul, as I said. When we recognize this truth we make use of that natural energy called Thought for comparison, instruction, and the removal of doubt, and so reach a point where we restrain the outward tendencies of Nature, for when these are resolved into their cause and Nature is wholly conquered and restrained, that cause manifests itself both in and beyond Nature.

"The incorporeal substances in descending are divided and multiplied about individuals with a diminution of power; but when they ascend by their energies beyond bodies, they become united and exist as a whole by and through exuberance of power." (*Porphyrios.*)

These hints may suffice for such minds as are already upon the way. Others will be closed to them. Language only expresses the experiences of a race, and since ours has not reached the upper levels of Being we have as yet no words for these things. The East has ever been the home of spiritual research; she has given all the great religions to the world. The Sanscrit has thus terms for some of these states and conditions, but even in the East it is well understood that the formless cannot be expressed by form, nor the Illimitable by the limits of words or signs. The only way to know these states is to *be* them: we never can *really* know anything which we are not. J. N.

XI

Dear Brother:

It has been with regret that I hear of your serious illness, Jasper. While life hangs in the balance, as it would seem yours does and for some time will, you will feel much depression.

Now it is not usual to thus calmly talk to a person of his death; but you do not mind, so I talk. I do not agree with you that death is well. Yours is not a case like that of ———, who *was* to die and decided to accept life from Great Powers and work on for Humanity amid all the throes and anguish of that body.* Why should you not live now as long as you can in the present body, so that in it you may make all the advance possible and by your life do as much good as you can to the Cause and man? For you have not yet as Jasper Niemand had a chance to entitle you to *extraordinary* help after death in getting back again soon, so that you would die and run the chance of a long Devachan and miss much that you might do for *Them*. Such are my views. Life is better than death, for death again disappoints the Self. Death is *not* the great informer or producer of knowledge. It is only the great curtain on the stage, to be rung up next instant. Complete knowledge must be attained in the triune man: body, soul, and spirit. When that is obtained, then he passes on to other spheres, which to us are unknown and are endless. By living as long as one can, one gives the Self that longer chance.

* This doubtless refers to H.P.B. See "Theosophical Mahatmas," *Theosophy*, XXI, 294, and "She Being Dead, Yet Speaketh," *Theosophy*, XXXI, 201.—Eds.

"Atmanam atmana pashya" (Raise the Self by the self—*Gîtâ*) does not seem to be effective after the threshold of death is passed. The union of the trinity is only to be accomplished on earth in a body, and *then* release is desirable.

It is not for myself that I speak, Brother, but for thee, because in death I can lose no one. The living have a greater part in the dead than the dead have in the living.

The doubt which you now feel as to success is morbid. Please destroy it. Better a false hope with no doubt, than much knowledge with doubts of your own chances. "He that doubteth is like the waves of the sea, driven by the wind and tossed." Doubt is not to be guarded solely against when applied to Masters (whom I know you doubt not). It is most to be guarded and repelled in relation to oneself. Any idea that one cannot succeed, or had better die than live, because an injured body seems to make success unattainable, is *doubt*.

We dare not hope, but we *dare* try to live on and on that we may serve Them as They serve the Law. We are not to try to be chelas or to do any one thing in this incarnation, but only to know and to be just as much as we can, and the possibility is not measured. Reflect, then, that it is only a question of being overcome—by what? By something outside. But if you accuse or doubt yourself, you then give the enemy a rest; he has nothing to do, for you do it all yourself for him, and, leaving you to your fate, he seeks other victims. Rise, then, from this despondency and seize the sword of knowledge. With it, and with Love, the universe is conquerable. Not that I see thee too despondent, Jasper, but I fain would give thee my ideas, even did something kill thee against our will next day.

Am glad that although the body is painful, you yourself are all right. We have in various ways to suffer, and I do not doubt it is a great advance if we can in the midst of physical suffering grasp and hold ourselves calm and away from it. Yet, also, the body must be rested. Rest, and let the anxieties to do lie still and dormant. By that they are not killed, and when the body gets stronger more is known.

You have been in storms enough. A few moments' reflection will show you that we make our own storms. The power of any and all circumstances is a fixed, unvarying quality, but as *we* vary in our reception of these, it appears to us that our difficulties vary in intensity. They do not at all. We are the variants.

If we admit that we are in the stream of evolution, then each circumstance must be to us quite right. And in our failures to perform set acts should be our greatest helps, for we can in no other way learn that calmness which Krishna insists upon. If all our plans succeeded, then no contrasts would appear to us. Also those plans we make may all be made ignorantly and thus wrongly, and kind Nature will not permit us to carry them out. We get no blame for the plan, but we may acquire Karmic demerit by not accepting the impossibility of achieving. Ignorance of the law cannot be pleaded among men, but ignorance of fact may. In occultism, even if you are ignorant of some facts of importance you are not passed over by *The Law*, for It has regard for no man, and pursues Its adjustments without regard to what we know or are ignorant of.

If you are at all cast down, or if any of us is, then by just that much are our thoughts lessened in power. One could be confined in a prison and yet be a worker for the Cause. So I pray you to remove from your mind any distaste for present circumstances. If you can succeed in looking at it all as *just what you in fact desired*, then it will act not only as a strengthener of your good thoughts, but will act reflexly on your body and make it stronger.

All this reminds me of H., of whose failure you now know. And in this be not disappointed. It could hardly be otherwise. Unwisely he made his demands upon the Law before being quite ready. That is, unwisely in certain senses, for in the greater view naught can be unwise. His apparent defeat, at the very beginning of the battle, is for him quite of course. He went where the fire is hottest and made it hotter by his aspirations. All others have and all will suffer the same. For it makes no difference that his is a bodily affection; as all these things proceed from mental disturbances, we can easily see the same cause under a physical ailment as under a mental divagation. Strangely, too, I wrote you of the few who really do stay, and soon after this news came and threw a light—a red one, so to say—upon the information of H's retreat. See how thought interlinks with thought on all planes when the True is the aim.

We ourselves are not wholly exempt, inasmuch as we daily and hourly feel the strain. Accept the words of a fellow traveller, these: Keep up the aspiration and the search, but do not maintain the attitude of despair or the slightest repining. Not that you do.

I cannot find the right words; but surely you would know all, were it not that some defects hold you back.

The darkness and the desolation are sure to be ours, but they are only illusionary. Is not the Self pure, bright, bodiless, and free,—and art thou not that? The daily waking life is but a penance and the trial of the body, so that *it*, too, may thereby acquire the right condition. In dreams we see the truth and taste the joys of heaven. In waking life it is ours to gradually distill that dew into our normal consciousness.

Then, too, remember that the influences of this present age are powerful for producing these feelings. What despair and agony of doubt exist to-day in all places! In this time of upturning, the wise man *waits*. He bends himself, like the reed, to the blast, so that it may blow over his head. Rising, as you do, into the plane where these currents are rushing, while you try to travel higher still, you feel these inimical influences, although unknown to you. It is an age of iron. A forest of iron trees, black and forbidding, with branches of iron and brilliant leaves of steel. The winds blow through its arches and we hear a dreadful grinding and crashing sound that silences the still small voice of Love. And its inhabitants mistake this for the voice of God; they imitate it and add to its terrors. Faint not, be not self-condemned. We both are that soundless OM; we rest together upon the bosom of Master.* You are not tired; it is that body, now weak, and not only weak but shaken by the force of your own powers, physical and psychical. But the wise man learns to assume in the body an attitude of carelessness that is more careful really than any other. Let that be yours. You are judge. Who accepts you, who dares judge but yourself? Let us wait, then, for natural changes, knowing that if the eye is fixed where the light shines, we shall presently know what to do. This hour is not ripe. But unripe fruit gets ripe, and falls or is plucked. The day must surely strike when you will pluck it down. You are no longer troubled by vain fears or compromises. When the great thought comes near enough, you will go. We must all be servants before we can hope to be masters in the least.

I have been re-reading the life of Buddha, and it fills me with a longing desire to give myself for humanity, to devote myself to a fierce, determined effort to plant myself nearer the altar of sacrifice.

---

* Originally written: "we rest upon the heart of the Divine." See *Path*, II, 290.—Eds.

As I do not always know just what ought to be done, I must stand on what Master says: "Do what you *can*, if you ever expect to see Them." This being true, and another Adept saying, "Follow the Path They and I show, but do not follow *my* path,"* why then, all we can do, whether great or small, is to do just what we can, each in his proper place. It is sure that if we have an immense devotion and do our best, the result will be right for Them and for us, even though we would have done otherwise had we known more when we were standing on a course of action. A devoted Chela once said: "I do not mind all these efforts at explanation and all this trouble, for I always have found that that which was done in Master's name was right and came out right." What is done in those names is done without thought of self, and motive is the essential test.

So I am sad and not sad. Not sad when I reflect on the great Ishwar, the Lord, permitting all these antics and shows before our eyes. Sad when I see our weakness and disabilities. We must be serene and do what we can. Ramaswamier rushed off into Sikkhim to try and find Master, and met someone who told him to go back *and do his duty*. That is all any of us can do; often we do not know our duty, but that, too, is our own fault: it is a Karmic disability.

You ask me how you shall advise your fellow student. The best advice is found in your own letter to me in which you say that the true monitor is within. This is so. Ten thousand Adepts can do us no great good unless we ourselves are ready, and They act only as suggestors to us of what possibilities there are in every human heart. If we dwell within ourselves, and must live and die by ourselves, it must follow that running here and there to see any thing or person does not in itself give progress. Mind, I do not oppose consorting with those who read holy books and are engaged in dwelling on high themes. I am only trying to illustrate my idea that this should not be dwelt on as an end; it is only a means, and one of many. There is no help like association with those who think as we do, or like the reading of good books. The best advice I ever saw was to read holy books, or whatever books tend to elevate yourself, as you have found by experience. There must be some. Once I found some abstruse theological writings of Plotinus

* H.P.B. wrote: "Follow the path I show, the Masters that are behind—and do not follow me or my PATH." From "She Being Dead, Yet Speaketh," *Theosophy*, XXXI, 299.—Eds.

to have that effect on me—very ennobling, and also an explanation of the wanderings of Ulysses. Then there is the *Gîtâ*. All these *are instinct with a life of their own* which changes the vibrations. Vibration is the key to it all. The different states are only differences of vibration, and we do not recognize the astral or other planes because we are out of tune with their vibrations. This is why we now and then dimly feel that others are peering at us, or as if a host of people rushed by us with great things on hand, not seeing us and we not seeing them. It was an instant of synchronous vibration. But the important thing is to develop the Self in the self, and then the possessions of wisdom belonging to all wise men at once belong to us.

Each one would see the Self differently and yet would never see it, for to see it is to *be* it. But for making words we say, "See it." It might be a flash, a blazing wheel, or what not. Then there is the lower self, great in its way, and which must first be known. When first we see it, it is like looking into a glove, and for how many incarnations may it not be so? We look inside the glove and there is darkness; then we have to *go inside* and see that, and so on and on.

The mystery of the ages is man—each one of us. Patience is needed in order that the passage of time required for the bodily instrument to be altered or controlled is complete. Violent control is not so good as gentle control, continuous and firmly unrelaxed. The Seeress of Prevorst found that a gentle current did her more good than a violent one.* Gentleness is better because an opposition current is always provoked, and, of course, if that which produces it is gentle, it will also be the same. This gives the unaccustomed student more time and gradual strength.

I think your fellow-student will be a good instrument, but we must not break the silence of the future lest we raise up unknown and difficult tribes who will not be easy to deal with.

Every situation ought to be used as a means. This is better than philosophy, for it enables us to know philosophy. You do not progress by studying other people's philosophies, for then you do but get their crude ideas. Do not crowd yourself, nor ache to puzzle

* See "The Seeress of Prevorst," *Path*, II, 332, February, 1888. The writer, "B." (probably for "Brehon," one of Mr. Judge's pen names), referring to this idea of a "gentle current," says: "Herein may lie a valuable hint for medical science; and, indeed, it seems as if it were already tending in this direction. It might be worth while to construct a machine after the pattern given by her. . . ." —Eds.

your brains with another's notions. You have the key to self and that is all; take it and drag out the lurker inside. You are great in generosity and love, strong in faith, and straight in perception. Generosity and love are the abandonment of self. That is your staff. Increase your confidence, not in your abilities, but in the great All being thyself.

I would to God you and all the rest might find peace.

Z.

XII

Dear Jasper:

There are so many questioners who ask about Chelaship* that your letter comes quite apropos to experiences of my own. You say that these applicants must have some answer, and in that I agree with you. And whether they are ready or unready, we must be able to tell them something. But generally they are not ready, nor, indeed, are they willing to take the first simple step which is demanded. I will talk the matter over with you for your future guidance in replying to such questions; perhaps also to clear up my own mind.

The first question a man should ask himself (and by "man" we mean postulants of either sex) is: "When and how did I get a desire to know about chelaship and to become a chela?"; and secondly, "What is a chela, and what chelaship?"

There are many sorts of chelas. There are lay chelas and probationary ones; accepted chelas and those who are trying to fit themselves to be even lay chelas. Any person can constitute himself a lay chela, feeling sure that he may never in this life consciously hear from his guide. Then as to probationary chelas, there is an *invariable* rule that they go upon seven years' trial. These "trials" do not refer to fixed and stated tests, but to all the events of life and the bearing of the probationer in them. There is no *place* to which applicants can be referred where their request could be made, because these matters do not relate to places and to officials: this is an affair of the inner nature. We *become* chelas; we obtain that position in reality because our inner nature is to that extent opened that it can and will take knowledge: we receive the guerdon at the hands of the Law.

* Chela means disciple. It is a Sanscrit word.—J. N.

In a certain sense every sincere member of the Theosophical Society is in the way of becoming a chela, because the Masters do some of Their work with and for humanity through this Society, selected by Them as Their agent. And as *all* Their work and aspiration are to the end of helping the race, no one of Their chelas can hope to remain (or become) such, if any selfish desire for personal possessions of spiritual wealth constitutes the motive for trying to be a chela. Such a motive, in the case of one already a chela, acts instantly to throw him out of the ranks, whether he be aware of his loss or not, and in the case of one trying to become a chela it acts as a *bar*. Nor does a real chela spread the fact that he is such. For this Lodge is not like exoteric societies which depend upon favor or mere outward appearances. It is a real thing with living Spirit-men at its head, governed by laws that contain within themselves their own executioners, and that do not require a tribunal, nor accusations, nor verdicts, nor any notice whatever.

As a general thing, a person of European or American birth has extreme difficulty to contend with. He has no heredity of psychical development to call upon; no known assembly of Masters or Their chelas within reach. His racial difficulties prevent him from easily seeing within himself; he is not introspective by nature. But even he can do much if he purifies his motive, and either naturally possesses or cultivates an ardent and unshakeable faith and devotion—a faith that keeps him a firm believer in the existence of Masters even through years of non-intercourse. They are generous and honest debtors and always repay. How They repay, and when, is not for us to ask. Men may say this requires as blind devotion as was ever asked by any Church. *It does,* but it is a blind devotion to Masters who are Truth itself; to Humanity and to yourself, to your own intuitions and ideals. This devotion to an ideal is also founded upon another thing, which is that a man is hardly ready to be a chela unless he is able to stand *alone* and uninfluenced by other men or events. *For he must stand alone,* and he might as well know this at the beginning as at the end.

There are also certain qualifications which he must possess. These are to be found in *Man: Fragments of Forgotten History,** towards the close of the book, so we will not dwell upon them here.

---

* Long out of print, *Man* was originally published in 1885 by "Two Chelas in the T.S." (Later identified as Mohini M. Chatterji and Mrs. Laura C. Holloway. See *Theosophist,* XIX, 649, Aug., 1898.)—Eds.

The question of the general fitness of applicants being disposed of, we come to the still more serious point of the relations of Guru and Chela, or Master and Disciple. We want to know what it really is to be a pupil of such a Teacher.

The relation of Guru and Chela is nothing if it is not a spiritual one. Whatever is merely outward, or formal, as the relation established by mere asking and acceptance, is not spiritual, but formal, and is that which arises between *teacher* and *pupil*. Yet even this latter is not in any way despicable, because the teacher stands to his pupil, in so far as the relation permits, in the same way as the Guru to his Chela. It is a difference of degree; but this difference of degree is what constitutes the distinction between the spiritual and the material, for, passing along the different shadings from the grossest materiality to as far as we can go, we find at last that matter merges into spirit. (We are now speaking, of course, about what is commonly called *matter*, while we well know that in truth the thing thus designated is not really matter, but an enormous illusion which in itself has no existence. The real matter, called *mulaprakriti* by the Hindus, is an invisible thing or substance of which our matter is a representation. The real matter is what the Hermetists called *primordial earth;* for us, an intangible phase of matter. We can easily come to believe that what is usually called *matter* is not really such, inasmuch as we find clairvoyants and nervous people seeing through thick walls and closed doors. Were this *matter*, then they could not see through it. But when an ordinary clairvoyant comes face to face with *primordial matter*, he or she cannot see beyond, but is met by a dead wall more dense than any wall ever built by human hands.)

So from earliest times, among all but modern western people, the teacher was given great reverence by the pupil, and the latter was taught from youth to look upon his preceptor as second only to his father and mother in dignity. It was among these people a great sin, a thing that did one actual harm in his moral being, to be disrespectful to his teacher even in thought. The reason for this lay then, and no less to-day does also lie, in the fact that a long chain of influence extends from the highest spiritual guide who may belong to any man, down through vast numbers of spiritual chiefs, ending at last in the mere teacher of our youth. Or, to restate it in modern reversion of thought, a chain extends up from our teacher or preceptors to the highest spiritual chief in whose ray or descending line one may happen to be. And it makes no difference whatever, in this occult relation, that neither pupil nor final guide may be aware, or admit, that this is the case.

Thus it happens that the child who holds his teacher in reverence, and diligently applies himself accordingly with faith, does no violence to this intangible but mighty chain, and is benefited accordingly, whether he knows it or not. Nor again does it matter that a child has a teacher who evidently gives him a bad system. This is his Karma, and by his reverent and diligent attitude he works it out, and transcends that erstwhile teacher.

This chain of influence is called the *Guruparampara chain.*

The Guru is the *guide or readjuster,* and may not always combine the function of teacher with it.

Z.

XIII

Dear Jasper:

We now have passed from the mere usual and worldly relations of teacher and pupil to that which we will call the *Lodge* for the nonce.

This Lodge is not to be taken up in the pincers of criticism and analyzed or fixed. It is at once everywhere and nowhere. It contains within its boundaries all real Masters, students, guides, and Gurus, of whatever race or creed or no creed. Of it has been said:

"Beyond the Hall of Learning is the Lodge. It is the whole body of Sages in all the world. It cannot be described even by those who are in it, but the student is not prohibited from imagining what it is like."

So therefore, at any time, any one of its real teachers or disciples will gladly help any other teacher or disciple. But we are not to conclude that, because all are trying to spread the truth and to teach the world, we, who call ourselves chela-aspirants or known chelas of any certain person whom we call Guru, can place ourselves at the same moment under the *direct* tutelage of more than one Guru.

Each man who determines in himself that he will enter the Path has a Guru. But the time between that determination and the hour when he will really know the Master may be long indeed; in some cases it is very short.

We must now occupy a moment in some consideration of divisions.

Just as the merest private in the army has a general who guides the whole, but whom he cannot reach except through the others who are officers, so in this order we find divisions of Gurus as well as divisions of disciples.

There is the Great Guru, who is such to many who never know Him or see Him. Then there are others who know Him, and who are Gurus to a number of chelas, and so on until we may imagine a chela who may be a known Guru to another chela below him.

Then, again, there may be chelas who are acting as Guru—unacknowledged, because *pro tempore* in function—to one or more other chelas.

Now, he who makes the resolution above-mentioned, does thereby make a bond that rests in the highest Law. It is not a thing to be lightly done, because its consequences are of a serious nature. Not serious in the way of disasters or awful torments or such, but serious in respect to the clearness and brilliancy of those rays of Truth which we wish to reach us.

We have thereby in a sense—the degree determined by the sincerity and power of our motive—taken ourselves out of the common, vast, moving herd of men who are living, as to this, like dumb animals, and have knocked at a door. If we have reverenced our teacher, we will now revere our unknown Guru. We must stand interiorly in a faithful attitude. We must have an abiding, settled faith that nothing may shake. For it is to mighty Karma we have appealed, and as the Guru *is Karma* in the sense that He never acts against Karma, we must not lose faith for an instant. For it is this faith that clears up the air there, and that enables us to get help from all quarters.

Then, perhaps, this determinant or postulant or neophyte decides for himself that he will for the time take as teacher or guide some other chela whose teachings commend themselves. It is not necessary that any out-spoken words should pass between these two.

But having done this, even in thought, he should then apply himself diligently *to the doctrine of that teacher,* not changing until he really finds he has another teacher or has gone to another class. For if he takes up one merely to dispute and disagree—whether outwardly or mentally—he is thereby in danger of totally obscuring his own mind.

If he finds himself not clearly understanding, then he should with faith try to understand, for if he by love and faith vibrates into the higher meaning of his teacher, his mind is thereby raised, and thus greater progress is gained.

We now come to the possible case of an aspirant of that royal and kingly faith who in some way has really found a person who has advanced far upon *the Path*. To this person he has applied and said: "May I be accepted, and may I be a chela of either thee or some other?"

That person applied to then perhaps says: "Not to me; but I refer you to some other of the same class as yourself, and give you to him to be his chela: serve him." With this the aspirant goes, say to the one designated, and deliberately both agree to it.

Here is a case where the real Master has recommended the aspirant to a co-worker who perchance is some grade higher than our neophyte, and the latter is now in a different position from the many others who are silently striving and working, learning from any and all teachers, but having no specialized Guru for themselves. This neophyte and his "little guru" are connected by a clear and sacred bond, or else both are mere lying children, playing and unworthy of attention. If the "little guru" is true to his trust, he occupies his mind and heart with it, and is to consider that the chela represents Humanity to him for the time.

We postulated that this "little guru" was in advance of the chela. It must then happen that he says that which is sometimes not clear to his chela. This will all the more be so if his chela is new to the matter. But the chela has deliberately taken that guru, and must try to understand *the doctrine of that teacher.*

The proper function of the Guru is to readjust, and not to pour in vast masses of knowledge expressed in clear and easily comprehended terms. The latter would be a piece of nonsense, however agreeable, and not one whit above what any well-written book would do for its reader.

The faith and love which exist between them act as a stimulus to both, and as a purifier to the mind of the chela.

But if the chela, after a while, meets another person who seems to know as much as his "little guru," and to express it in very easy terms, and the chela determines to take him as a teacher, he commits an error. He may listen to his teaching and admire and profit by it, but the moment he mentally determines, and then, in words, asks the other to be his teacher, he begins to rupture the bond that was just established, and possibly may lose altogether the benefit of both. Not necessarily, however; but certainly, if he acquaints not his "little guru" with the fact of the new adoption of teacher, there will be much confusion in that realm of being wherein both do their real "work"; and when he does acquaint his "little guru" with the fact of the newly-acquired teacher, that older guru will retire.

None of this is meant for those minds which do not regard these matters as sacred. A Guru is a sacred being in that sense. Not, of course, in a general sense—yet, even if so regarded *when worthy,* it is better for the chela—but in all that pertains to the spiritual and real life. To the high-strung soul this is a matter of *adoption:* a most sacred and valuable thing, not lightly taken up or lightly dropped. For the Guru becomes for the time the spiritual *Father* of the chela; that one who is destined to bring him into real life or to pass him on to Him who will do so.

So, as the Guru is the *adjuster* in reality, the chela does not—except where the Guru is known to be a great Sage or where the chela does it by nature—give slavish attention to every word. He hears the word and endeavors to assimilate the meaning underneath; and if he cannot understand he lays it aside for a better time, while he presently endeavors to understand what he can. And even if—as is often so in India—he cannot understand at all, he is satisfied to be near the Guru and do what may properly be done for him. For then his abiding faith will eventually clear his mind—of which there are many examples, regarding which how appropriate is the line:

"They also serve who only stand and wait."

Z.

XIV

Dear Jasper:

What I wrote in my last is what may be properly said to earnest inquirers who show by their perseverance that they are not mere idle curiosity-seekers, desirous of beguiling the tedium of life with new experiments and sensations.

It is not *what* is done, but the spirit in which the least thing is done for Them who are all, that is counted.

You ask the names of the seven rays or lodges. The names could not be given if known to me. In these matters names are always realities, and consequently to give the name would be to reveal the thing itself. Besides, if the names were given, the ordinary person hearing them would not understand them. Just as if I should say that the name of the first is X, which expresses nothing at all to the mind of the hearing person. All that can be said is that there exist those seven rays, districts, or divisions, just as we say that in a town there are legislators, merchants, teachers, and servants. The difference is that in this case we know all about the town, and know just what those names mean. The name only directs the mind to the idea or essential quality.

Again I must go. But Brothers are never parted while they live for the True alone.

Z.

The foregoing letters point clearly to one conclusion concerning that great Theosophist, Madame Blavatsky, though she is unnamed and perhaps unthought of there. Since she sacrificed—not so calling it herself—all that mankind holds dear to bring the glad tidings of Theosophy to the West, that West, and especially the Theosophical Society, thereby stands to her as a chela to his Guru, in so far as it accepts Theosophy. Her relation to these Theosophists has its being in the highest Law, and cannot be expunged or ignored. So those who regard her personality, and, finding it discordant from theirs, try to reach the Masters by other means *while disregarding or underrating scornfully her high services,* violate a rule which, because it is not made of man, cannot be broken with impunity. Gratitude and the common sentiment of man for man should have taught them this, without occult teaching at all. Such persons have not reached that stage of evolution where they can learn the higher truths. She who accepts the pains of the rack in the torments of a body sapped of its life force by superb torrents of energy lavished on her high Cause; she who has braved the laughter and anger of two continents, and all the hosts of darkness seen and unseen; she who now lives on, only that she may take to herself the Karma of the Society and so ensure its well-being, has no need of any man's praise; but even she has need of justice, because, without that impulse in our hearts and souls toward her, she knows that we must fail for this incarnation. As the babe to the mother, as harvest to the earth, so are all those bound to her who enjoy the fruit of her life. May we try, then, to understand these occult connections brought about by the workings of Karma, and bring them to bear upon our diurnal, as well as our theosophical, life. Madame Blavatsky is for us the next higher link in that great chain, of which no link can be passed over or missed.

In further illustration of this letter, I might cite the case of a friend of mine who was at once fired with Theosophy on first hearing of it and ardently desired to become a chela. Certainly he had known these truths in other lives, for all seemed familiar to him, and, though he was what is called "a man of the world," he accepted the philosophy, measured some of its possibilities intuitively, and while careful to do his duty and cause no jars, he ranged his life, especially his inner life, to suit these views. The question of chelaship assumed great prominence in his mind. He knew of no chelas; knew not where to knock nor whom to ask. Reflection convinced him that real chelaship consisted in the inner attitude of the postulant; he remembered magnetic and energic laws, and he said to himself that he could at will constitute himself a chela to the Law, at least so far as his own attitude went, and if this did not satisfy him, it was a proof that he desired some personal reward, satisfaction, or powers in the matter, and that his motive was not pure. He was slow to formulate his desires, even to his own mind, for he would not lightly make demands upon the Law; but he at last determined to put his own motives to the test; to try himself and see if he could stand in the attitude of a faithful chela, unrecognized and apparently unheard. He then recorded in his own mind an obligation to serve Truth and the Law as a chela should, always seeking for light and for further aid if possible; recognizing meanwhile that the obligation was on his side only, and that he had no claims on Masters, and only such as he himself could by the strength of his own purpose institute upon the Law. Wherever he could hear of chelas and their duties he listened or read; he tried to imagine himself in the position of an accepted chela, and to fill, so far as in him lay, the duties of that place, living up to all the light he had. For he held that a disciple should always think and act towards the highest possibilities, whether or not he had yet attained these, and not merely confine himself to that course of action which might be considered suited to his lower class or spiritual estate. He believed that the heart is the creator of all real ties, and it alone. To raise himself by himself was then his task. This attitude he resolved to maintain life after life, if needs were, until at last his birthright should be assured, his claim recognized by the Law.

He met with trials, with coldness from those who felt rather than saw his changed attitude; he met with all the nameless shocks that others meet when they turn against the whirlpool of existence and try to find their way back into the true currents of life. Great sorrows and loneliness were not slow to challenge his indomitable will. But he found work to do; and in this he was most fortunate, for to work for others is the disciple's joy, his share in the Divine life, his first accolade by which he may know that his service is accepted. This man had called upon the Law in faith supreme, and he was answered. Karma sent him a friend, and soon he began to get new knowledge, and after a time information reached him of a place or person where he might apply to become a chela on probation. It was not given him as information usually is; nothing of the sort was told him; but with his extending knowledge and opening faculties a conviction dawned upon him that he might pursue such and such a course. He did so, and his prayer was heard. He said to me afterwards that he never knew whether he would not have shown greater strength of mind by relying wholly upon the reality of his unseen, unacknowledged claim, until the moment should come when Masters should accept and call him. For of course he held the ideal of Masters clearly before his mind all this while. Perhaps his application showed him to be weaker than he supposed, in so far as it might evidence a need on his part for tangible proof of a fact in which his higher nature prompted him to believe without such proof. Perhaps it was but natural and right, on the other hand, that after silent service for some time he should put himself on record at the first opportunity granted him by Karma.

He applied, then. I am permitted to give a portion of the answer he received, and which made clear to him the fact that he was already accepted in some measure before his application, as his intuition had told him. The answer may be of untold value to others, both as clearly setting forth the dangers of forcing one's way ahead of one's race, and also by its advice, admonitions, and evidence that the Great Beings of the Orient deal most frankly and gently with applicants. Also it may mark out a course for those who take the wise plan of testing themselves in silence before pushing their demands upon the Law. For this at once heightens their magnetic vibrations, their evolutionary ratio; their flame burns more brilliantly and attracts all kinds of shapes and influences within its radius, so that the fire is hot about him. And not for him alone: other lives coming in contact with his feel this fierce energy; they develop more rapidly, and, if they have a false or weak place in their nature, it is soon discovered and overthrows them for a time. This is the danger of coming into "the circle of ascetics"; a man must be strong indeed who thus thrusts himself in; it is better as a rule to place oneself in the attitude of a disciple and impose the tests oneself: less opposition is provoked. For forces that are foiled by the Adept may hurl themselves on the neophyte who cannot be protected unless his Karma permits it, and there are always those opposing forces of darkness waiting to thin the ranks of the servitors of the Good Law.

Up to this point, then, we may follow this student, and then we lose sight of him, not knowing whether he progressed or failed, or still serves and waits, because such things are not made known. To tell so much as this is rare, and, since it is permitted, it must be because there are many earnest students in this country who need some such support and information. To these I can say that, if they constitute themselves faithful, unselfish disciples, they are such in the knowledge of the Great Law, so long as they are true, in inmost thought and smallest deed, to the pledge of their heart.

ANSWER TO Y. Says Master:

"Is Y. fully prepared for the uphill work? The way to the goal he strives to reach is full of thorns and leads through miry quagmires. Many are the sufferings the chela has to encounter; still more numerous the dangers to face and conquer.

"May he think over it and choose only after due reflection. No Master appealed to by a sincere soul who thirsts for light and knowledge, has ever turned his face away from the supplicant. But it is the duty of those who call for laborers and need them in their fields, to point out to those who offer themselves in truth and trust for the arduous work, the pitfalls in the soil as the hardship of the task.

*"If undaunted by this warning Y. persists in his determination, he may regard himself as accepted as ———. Let him place himself in such case under the guidance of an older chela. By helping him sincerely and devotedly to carry on his heavy burden, he shall prepare the way for being helped in his turn."**

---

* See p. 271.—Eds.

(Here follow private instructions.)

"Verily if the candidate relies upon the Law, if he has patience, trust, and intuition, he will not have to wait too long. Through the great shadow of bitterness and sorrow that the opposing powers delight in throwing over the pilgrim on his way to the Gates of Light, the candidate perceives that shining Light very soon in his own soul, and he has but to follow it. Let him beware, however, lest he mistake the occasional will-o'-the-wisp of the psychic senses for the reflex of the great spiritual Light; that Light which dieth not, yet never lives, nor can it shine elsewhere than on the pure mirror of Spirit. . . .

"But Y. has to use his own intuitions. One has to dissipate and conquer the inner darkness before attempting to see into the darkness without; to know one's self before knowing things extraneous to one's senses."

And now, may the Powers to which my friend Y. has appealed *be permitted by still greater and much higher Powers* to help him. This is the sincere and earnest wish of his truly and fraternally,

△

This letter also shows incidentally how one Adept may serve another still higher by reporting or conveying His reply.

TO ASPIRANTS FOR CHELASHIP

Sincere interest in Theosophic truth is often followed by sincere aspiration after Theosophic life, and the question continually recurs, What are the conditions and the steps to chelaship; to whom should applications be made; how is the aspirant to know that it has been granted?

As to the conditions and the discipline of chelaship, not a little has been disclosed in *The Theosophist,* Man, Esoteric Buddhism,* and other works upon Theosophy; and some of the qualifications, difficulties, and dangers have been very explicitly set forth by Madame Blavatsky in her article upon "Theosophical Mahatmas" in the *Path* of December, 1886.† To everyone cherishing even a

* Published in India by H.P.B., beginning in October 1879.—Eds.
† Reprinted in *Theosophy,* XIV, 126.—Eds.

vague desire for closer relations to the system of development through which Masters are produced, the thoughtful study of this article is earnestly commended. It will clear the ground of several misconceptions, deepen the sense of the seriousness of such an effort, and excite a healthy self-distrust which is better before than after the gate has been passed.

It is entirely possible, however, that the searching of desire and strength incited by that article may only convince more strongly of sincerity, and that not a few readers may emerge from it with a richer purpose and a deeper resolve. Even where there is not a distinct intention to reach chelaship, there may be an eager yearning for greater nearness to the Masters, for some definite assurance of guidance and of help. In either of these cases the question at once arises before the aspirant. Who is to receive the application, and how is its acceptance to be signified?

The very natural, indeed the instinctive, step of such an aspirant is to write to an officer of a Theosophical Society. None the less is this a mistake. For a Theosophical Society is an *exoteric* body, the Lodge of Masters wholly *esoteric*. The former is a voluntary group of inquirers and philanthropists, with avowed aims, a printed Constitution, and published officers, and, moreover, expressly disavowing any power, as a Society, to communicate with Masters; the latter is an Occult Lodge, of whose address, members, processes, functions, nothing is known. It follows, therefore, that there is no person, no place, no address, to which an aspirant may appeal.

Let it be supposed, however, that such an inquiry is preferred to a person advanced in Occult study, versed in its methods and tests and qualifications. Assuredly his reply would be directly to this effect:

"If you were now fitted to be an accepted chela, you would of yourself know how, where, and to whom to apply. For the becoming a chela *in reality* consists in the evolution or development of certain spiritual principles latent in every man, and in great measure unknown to your present consciousness. Until these principles are to some degree consciously evolved by you, you are not in practical possession of the means of acquiring the first rudiments of that knowledge which now seems to you so desirable. Whether it is desired by your mind or by your heart is still another important question, not to be solved by any one who has not yet the clew to Self.

"It is true that these qualities can be developed (or forced) by the aid of an Adept. And most applicants for chelaship are actuated by a desire to receive instructions directly from the Masters. They do not ask themselves what they have done to merit a privilege so rare. Nor do they consider that, all Adepts being servants of the Law of Karma, it must follow that, did the applicant now merit Their visible aid, he would already possess it and could not be in search of it. The indications of the fulfilment of the Law are, in fact, the partial unfolding of those faculties above referred to.

"You must, then, reach a point other than that where you now stand, before you can even ask to be taken as a chela on probation. All candidates enter the unseen Lodge in this manner, and it is governed by Laws containing within themselves their own fulfilment and not requiring any officers whatever. Nor must you imagine that such a probationer is one who works under constant and known direction of either an Adept or another chela. On the contrary, he is tried and tested for at least seven years, and perhaps many more, before the point is reached when he is either accepted (and prepared for the first of a series of initiations often covering several incarnations), or rejected. And this rejection is not by any body of men just as they incline, but is the natural rejection by Nature. The probationer may or may not hear from his Teacher during this preliminary period; more often he does not hear. He may be finally rejected and not know it, just as some men have been on probation and have not known it until they suddenly found themselves accepted. Such men are those self-developed persons who have reached that point in the natural order after many incarnations, where their expanded faculties have entitled them to an entrance into the Hall of Learning or the spiritual Lodge beyond. And all I say of men applies equally to women.

"When anyone is regularly accepted as a chela on probation, the first and only order he receives (for the present) is to work unselfishly for humanity—sometimes aiding and aided by some older chela—*while striving to get rid of the strength of the personal idea.* The ways of doing this are left to his own intuition entirely, inasmuch as the object is to develop that *intuition* and to bring him to *self-knowledge.* It is his having these powers in some degree that leads to his acceptance as a probationer, so that it is more than probable that you have them not yet save as latent possibilities. In order to have in his turn any title to help, he must work for others, but that must not be his motive for working. He who does not feel irresistibly impelled to serve the Race, whether he himself fails or not, is bound fast by his own personality, and cannot progress until he has learned that *the race is himself* and not that body which he now occupies. The ground of this necessity for a pure motive was recently stated in *Lucifer* to be that 'unless the intention is entirely unalloyed, the spiritual will transform itself into the psychic, act on the astral plane, and dire results may be produced by it. The powers and forces of animal nature can be equally used by the selfish and revengeful as by the unselfish and all-forgiving; the powers and forces of spirit lend themselves only to the perfectly pure in heart.'*

"It may be stated, however, that even those natural forces cannot be discovered by any man who has not obtained the power of getting rid of his personality in some degree. That an emotional desire to help others does not imply this freedom from personality may be seen by the fact that, if you were now perfected in unselfishness in the *real* sense, you would have a conscious existence separate from that of the body and would be able to quit the body at will: in other words, to be free from all sense of self is to be an Adept, for the limitations of self inhibit progress.

"Hear also the words of the Master, taken from Sinnett's *The Occult World*. 'Perhaps you will better appreciate our meaning when told that in our view the highest aspirations for the welfare of humanity become tainted with selfishness if, in the mind of the philanthropist, there lurks the shadow of a desire for self-benefit or a tendency to do injustice, even when these exist unconsciously to himself.'

"While setting forth these facts, as well as the dangers and difficulties—both those set ones appointed by the laws of the Lodge and the more innumerable ones adjudged by Karma and hastened by the efforts of the neophyte—it should also be stated that the Masters desire to deter no man from entering the path. They are well aware, however, from the repeated trials and records of centuries, and from their knowledge of our racial difficulties, how few are the persons who have any clew to their own real nature, which is the foe they attempt to conquer the moment they become pupils of the occult. Hence They endeavor, so far as Karma permits, to hold unfit individuals back from rash ventures, the results of which

* From "Practical Occultism," by H.P.B. See *Theosophy,* XXXI, 102.—Eds.

would recoil upon their unbalanced lives and drive them to despair. The powers of evil, inadequately defied by the ignorant man, revenge themselves upon him as well as upon his friends, and not upon those who are above their reach. Although these powers are not hideous objective shapes coming in tangible ways, they are none the less real and dangerous. Their descent in such instances cannot be prevented: *it is Karma.*

"To lose all sense of self, then, implies the loss of all that ordinary men most value in themselves. It therefore behooves you to seriously consider these points:

"1st. What is your motive in desiring to be a chela? You think that motive is well known to you, whereas it is hidden deep within you, and by that hidden motive you will be judged. It has flared up from unseen regions upon men sure of themselves, has belched out in some lurid thought or deed of which they esteemed themselves incapable, and has overthrown their life or reason. Therefore test yourself ere Karma tests you.

"2d. What the place and duties of a true neophyte are.

"When you have seriously considered both for twenty-one days, you may, if your desire remains firm, take a certain course open to you. It is this.

"Although you do not now know where you can offer yourself to Masters themselves as a chela on probation, yet, in forming that desire in your heart and in re-affirming it (if you do) after due consideration of these points you have then to some extent called upon the Law, and it is within your power to constitute yourself a disciple, so far as in you lies, through the purity of your motive and effort *if both are sufficiently sustained.* No one can fix a period when this effort will bear fruit, and, if your patience and faith are not strong enough to bear you through an *unlimited* (so far as you know) period of unselfish work for humanity, you had better resign your present fancy, for it is then no more than that. But if otherwise, you are to work for the spiritual enlightenment of Humanity in and through the Theosophical Society (which much needs such laborers), and in all other modes and planes as you best can, remembering the word of Masters: 'He who does what he can and all that he can, and all that he knows how to do, does enough for us.' This task includes that of divesting yourself of all personality through interior effort, because that work, if done in the right spirit, is even more important to the race than any outward work we can do. Living as you now are, on the outward plane chiefly, your work is due there and is to be done there until your growth shall fit you to pass away from it altogether.

"In following this course you work towards a fixed point under observation—as is, indeed, the whole Theosophic body, which is now, *as a body,* a chela of Masters—but specialized from other members in the sense that your definite aim and trust are understood and taken into consideration by the unseen Founders and the Law. The Theosophical Society then stands to you, for the time being, as any older chela might who was appointed for you to aid and to work under. *You are not,* understand, a chela on probation, since no one without authority can confer or announce such a privilege. But if you succeed in lifting yourself and others spiritually, it will be known, *no matter what the external silence may seem to be,* and you will receive your full dues from Those who are honest debtors and ministers of the Just and Perfect Law. You must be ready to work, to wait, and to aspire in *silence,* just as all do who have fixed their eyes on this goal. Remember that your truest adviser is to be found, and constantly sought, *within yourself.* Only by experience can you learn to know its voice from that of natural instinct or mere logic, and strengthen this power, by virtue of which the Masters have become what They are.

"Your choice or rejection of this course is the first test of yourself. Others will follow, whether you are aware of them or not, for the first and only right of the neophyte is—*to be tried.* Hence, silence and sorrow follow his acceptance instead of the offer of prompt aid for which he looks. Yet even that shall not be wanting; those trials and reverses will come only from the Law to which you have appealed."

J. N.

XV

Dear Jasper:

I gave your letter to a distressed soul: she returned thanks, saying it was a cooling draught to one athirst. The thanks of course are yours. Now, this lady says it was refreshment to the weary, that letter. True, or she would not say it. But it was not so to me nor to you.

We needed it not. But she illustrates a certain state of progress. She is not yet where we are; but which is happier? She is happier, but poorer in hope. We are not all too happy, but are rich in hope, knowing the prize at the end of time, and not deterred by the clouds, the storms, the miasms and dreadful beasts of prey that line the road. Let us, then, at the very outset wash out of our souls all desire for reward, all hope that we may attain. For so long as we thus hope and desire, we shall be separated from the Self. If in the Self all things *are*, then we cannot wish to be something which we can only compass by excluding something else. Standing where we are, let us purify ourselves to be all things.

So being beyond this lady so grateful, we find that everything we meet on this illusory plane of existence is a lure that in one way or another has power to draw us out of our path. That is the point we are at, and we may call it the point where lures of Maya have omnipresent power. Therefore we must beware of the illusions of matter.

Before we got to this stage we knew well the fateful lure, the dazzling mirror of the elemental Self, here and there in well-defined places, and intrenched as it was, so as to say, in strongly-marked defenses. Those we assaulted; and that was what it desired, for it did think that it then had no need to exercise the enchantment which is hard because so subtle, and so distributed here and there that we find no citadels to take, no battalions in array. But now our dearest friends are unconsciously in league with the deceptive in nature. How strongly do I realize the dejection of Arjuna as he let his bow drop from his hand and sat down on his chariot in despair! But he had a sure spot to rest upon. He used his own. He had Krishna near, and he might fight on.

So in passing along those stages where the grateful lady and others are, we may perhaps have found one spot we may call our own and possess no other qualification for the task. That spot is enough. It is our belief in the Self, in Masters: it is the little flame of intuition we have allowed to burn, and that we have fostered with care.

Then come these dreadful lures. They are, in fact, but mere carcasses, shells of monsters from past existences, offering themselves that we may give them life to terrify us as soon as we have entered them either by fear or love. No matter which way we enter, whether by attachment or by repugnant horror, it is all one: they are in one case vivified by a lover; in the other by a slave who would be free but cannot.

Here it is the lure of enjoyment of natural pleasures, growing out of life's physical basis; there it is self-praise, anger, vanity, what not? Even these beautiful hills and river—they mock one, for they live on untrammelled. Perhaps they do not speak to us because they know the superiority of silence. They laugh with each other at us in the night, amused at the wild struggle of this petty man who would pull the sky down. Ach! God of Heaven! And all the sucklings of Theosophy wish that some great, well-diplomaed Adept would come and open the secret box; but they do not imagine that other students have stepped on the spikes that defend the entrance to the way that leads to the gate of the Path. But we will not blame them, nor yet wish for the things—the special lots—that some of them have abstracted, because now we know the dreadful power that despair and doubt and violated conscience have, we prefer to prepare wisely and carefully, and not rush in like fools where angels do not pass uninvited.

But, Companion, I remind you of the power of the lure. This Path passes along under a sky and in a clime where every weed grows a yard in the night. It has no discrimination. Thus even after weeks or months of devotion, or years of work, we are surprised at small seeds of vanity or any other thing which would be easily conquered in other years of inattentive life, but which seem now to arise as if helped by some damnable intelligence. This great power of self-illusion is strong enough to create a roaring torrent or a mountain of ice between us and our Masters.

In respect to the question of sex. It is, as you know, given much prominence by both women and men to the detriment of the one sex or the other, or of any supposed sex. There are those who say that the female sex is not to be thought of in the spirit; that all is male. Others say the same for the female. Now both are wrong. In the True there is no sex, and when I said "There all men are women and all women are men," I was only using rhetoric to accentuate the idea that neither one nor the other was predominant, but that the two were coalesced, so to say, into *one*. In the same way you might say, "men are animals there and *vice versa*." Mind, this is in regard to Spirit, and not in regard to the psychical states. For in the psychical states there are still distinctions, as the psychical, though higher than the material, is not as high as Spirit, for it still partakes of matter. In the Spirit or Atma *all* experiences of *all* forms of life and death are found at once, and he who is one with the Atma knows the whole manifested Universe at once. I have spoken of this condition before as the Turya or fourth state.

When I say that the female *principle* represents matter, I do not mean *women,* for they in any one or more cases may be full of the masculine principle, and *vice versa.*

Matter is illusionary and vain, and so the female element is illusionary and vain, as well as tending to the *established order.** So in the *Kaballa* it is said that the woman is a wall about the man. A balance is necessary, and that balance is found in women, or the woman element. You can easily see that the general tendency of women is to keep things as they are and not to have change. Woman—not here and there women—has never been the pioneer in great reforms. Of course, many single individual women have been, but the tendency of the great mass of women has always been to keep things as they are until the men have brought about the great change. This is why women always support any established religion, no matter what—Christian, Jewish, Buddhist, or Brahmin. The Buddhist women are as much believers in their religion and averse from changing it as are their Christian sisters opposed in the mass to changing theirs.

Now as to telling which element predominates in any single person, it is hard to give a general test rule. But perhaps it might be found in whether a person is given to abstract or concrete thought, and similarly whether given to mere superficial things or to deep fundamental matters. But you must work that out, I think, for yourself.

Of course in the spiritual life no organ *disappears,* but we must find out what would be the mode of operation of any organ in its spiritual counterpart. As I understand, the spiritual counterparts of the organs are *powers,* and not organs, as the eye is the power to see, the ear the power to hear, and so on. The generative organs would then become the creative power and perhaps the Will. You must not suppose that in the spirit life the organs are reproduced as we see them.

One instance will suffice. One may see pictures in the astral light through the back of the head or the stomach. In neither place is there any eye, yet we see. It must be by the power of seeing, which in the material body needs the specialized place or specializing organ known as the eye. We hear often through the

* Through its negative or passive quality.—J. N.

head without the aid of the auricular apparatus, which shows us that there is the power of hearing and of transmitting and receiving sounds without the aid of an external ear or its inside cerebral apparatus. So, of course, all these things survive in that way. Any other view is grossly material, leading to a deification of this unreal body, which is only an image of the reality, and a poor one, at that.

In thinking over these matters you ought always to keep in mind the three plain distinctions of *physical, psychical, and spiritual, always remembering that the last includes the other two.* All the astral things are of the psychical nature, which is partly material and therefore very deceptive. But all are necessary, for they are, they exist.

The Deity is subject to this law, or rather it is the law of the Deity. The Deity desires experience or self-knowledge, which is only to be attained by stepping, so to say, aside from self. So the Deity produces the manifested universes consisting of matter, psychical nature, and spirit. In the Spirit alone resides the great consciousness of the whole; and so it goes on ever producing and drawing into itself, accumulating such vast and enormous experiences that the pen falls down at the thought. How can that be put into language? It is impossible, for we at once are met with the thought that the Deity must know all at all times. Yet there is a vastness and an awe-inspiring influence in this thought of the Day and Night of Brahman. It is a thing to be thought over in the secret recesses of the heart, and not for discussion. *It is the All.*

And now, my Brother, for the present I leave you. May your restored health enable you to do more work for the world.

I salute you, my Brother, and wish you to reach the terrace of enlightenment.

Z.

BOOK II

In Devotion
TO THE IMMORTALS
and in
The Service of Humanity
This little book
is laid
Upon the Altar
June, 1905

Compiled by
THOMAS GREEN and JASPER NIEMAND

Hitherto I have been an exile from my true country: now I return thither. Do not weep for me: I return to that celestial land where each goes in his turn.

Hermes Trismegistos

FOREWORD

ONE marked difference will be noticed between this, the second volume of LETTERS THAT HAVE HELPED ME, and the earlier volume. That first volume had a unity of purpose and development, setting forth, as it did, in due sequence, the salient points of the Eastern teaching. This unity palpably arose from the fact that the series of letters was written to one individual, and thus followed along a line suited to the unfolding needs and the studies of that individual, as to those of all fellow students pursuing an identical line of thought.

The present volume, on the contrary, consists of letters, and extracts from letters, written to a number of people in different parts of the world. In many instances, an extract only was sent to the compilers by individuals appealed to, that of their store something might be given to their fellow-men. In other instances, the entire letter was sent, but contained personal or other matter, which could not be published. In still other instances, the entire letter is given. It has been thought best to omit all headings and endings to these letters, in order that no discrimination shall be made in respect of the recipients, thus leaving the truths which the letters embody to stand out in their own relief, unmarred by a label and a name. Many of the extracts were published in *The Irish Theosophist,* and still others in the "Tea-Table" of *The Path,* where "Quickly" stood for Mr. Judge. It was the wish of Mr. Judge, expressed in writing to one of the compilers, that the series should be republished (with the addition of other matter) as a second volume of the earlier work. The compilers are thus carrying out the direct wishes of Mr. Judge.

During the lifetime of Mr. Judge, it was possible to rearrange, to suggest excision or amplification, or the grouping of various extracts as one letter; and it was possible as well to annotate, since Mr. Judge read all proof, and was always ready to consider any suggestions, while he was also pleased to see that his annotator had grasped his meaning, or to correct errors in this respect. It is evident that such rearrangement, adding as it would to the completeness and the unity of a series, is much to be desired. It was hoped to continue this method with the present volume; but the death of the writer has made it impossible. We can only publish some letters completely, as they stand, and group together such extracts as remain.

One point more. A great number of letters have thus come up. One compiler alone has many score, all written since the publication of the first volume, and ranging over that period of years in which the trials of Mr. Judge became increasingly heavy, a period to which his unexpected death set a term. How great were these trials, none well knew except the Master Whom he so devotedly served. The last letter of all was written but a very short while before his death. In no single letter out of all these numbers—in no letter that the compilers have seen—is there a harsh or condemnatory word said of the authors of his trials. He accepts the bitter, the profound injustice done him without one word which could impugn the faith he held, the teachings he gave out. Surprise there is; annoyance once or twice at the waste of time, the irrational deeds and words. And then he turns him to that wise compassion which knows that it is not he who is wronged who is in truth the sufferer, but he who inflicts a wrong.

Mr. Judge always taught the truest Occultism, the highest path. When his hour of trial struck, step by step he followed along that path. In the destiny of the crucified, whether Christs, or Christ-disciples, it is always seen that the loudest denial comes from those most helped, most served. It is he who sits "at meat" with them who betrays them. And of all the long line of martyrs, never one has been exonerated to his era, justified to his age. This fact alone should make thinking men pause, remembering further that the crowd always prefers that Barabbas should be released unto them.

The great drama ever follows the same lines. The initiate, be he disciple or be he adept, cannot defend himself; this is the inexorable law. But he has all the tenderest support that his great predecessors along the path of thorns can bestow; all the joy of a battle nobly fought; all the gratitude of those among his fellows whose intuition can follow him behind the veil which screens the initiate from our sight.

So it comes about that these letters breathe the compassion, the patience, the brotherliness their author lived to inculcate. Sorrow, indeed, he felt; but he put it bravely by. His great and kind heart remained sound to the core. He sweetened the hours of bitterness by profound resignation to The Law. He was one of those of whom it is written: "He that loseth his life for My sake shall find it."

For the helping of mankind we publish these letters. To the judgment of posterity we commit them, knowing well that in the eternal spaces the Truth alone prevails. He who is here seen sustaining and consoling his fellows during the saddest hours of his life and down to the doors of the tomb, was in his turn upheld—not alone by a great faith and by an All-Compassionate Hand—but also by the Love enshrined in his own quiet heart. To The Master he left the rest.

THE COMPILERS

LETTERS

I

Dear Brothers and Sisters:

I DO not think you will take it amiss that I again intrude myself before you. I am so far off, and the place where my old friend and teacher—the one who pointed out to me the way that must bring us, if followed, to the light and peace and power of truth—is so dear to me, I would fain speak with those, my fellow-workers, who now live where she worked, and where her mighty soul left the body she used for our advantage. This is surely sufficient reason.

Refer to the Master's letter in *The Occult World* and you will find him saying that the Masters are philanthropists and care only for that. Hence, the very oldest F.T.S. who has been selfish, and not philanthropic, has never come under the notice of the Masters, has never done anything, in fact, toward the development of the soul in his possession, nothing for the race of man. It is not membership in the T.S., nor in any other mystical body, that brings us near the Masters, but just such philanthropic work with pure motive.

Then I know, and say plainly—for as so close to each other we should plainly speak—that some of us, maybe all, have waited and wondered, and wished and hoped, for what? Variously expressed, thus: one wants to go to the Masters, not knowing even if it be fitting; another wants to know what is the vague longing inside; another says, if only the inner senses were developed, and hopes the Master would develop them, and so on; all, however, expressed by what the Master himself has written, "You want to find out about us, of our methods of work, and for that you seek along the line of occultism." Well, it is right for us to seek and to try and to want to reach to Them, for otherwise we never will in any age get where such Beings are. But as wise thinkers we should act and think wisely. I know many of you, and what I am saying should help some as it does me also.

You are all on the road to Masters, but as we are now, with the weak and hereditarily diseased bodies we have, we could not live an hour with Masters did we suddenly jump past space to Them. Some, too, have doubt and darkness—the doubt mostly as to themselves. This should not be harboured, for it is a wile of the lower man striving to keep you back among the mediocre of the race. When you have lifted yourself up over that level of the race, the enemy of man strikes, and strives at all times to bring clouds of doubt and despair. You should know that all, everyone, down to the most obscure, who are working steadily, are as steadily creeping on to a change, and yet on and on to other changes, and all steps to the Master. Do not allow discouragement to come in. Time is needed for all growth, and all change, and all development. Let time have her perfect work and do not stop it.

How may it be stopped? How many have thought of this I do not know, but here is a fact. As a sincere student works on, his work makes him come every day nearer to a step, and, if it be an advance, then it is certain there is a sort of silence or loneliness all around in the forest of his nature. Then he may stop all by allowing despair to come in with various reasons and pretexts; he may thus throw himself back to where he began. This is not arbitrary law but Nature's. It is a law of mind, and the enemies of man take advantage of it for the undoing of the unwary disciple. I would never let the least fear or despair come before me, but if I cannot see the road, nor the goal, for the fog, I would simply sit down and wait; I would not allow the fog to make me think no road was there, and that I was not to pass it. The fogs must lift.

What, then, is the panacea, finally—the royal talisman? It is DUTY, Selflessness. Duty persistently followed is the highest yoga, and is better than mantrams or any posture, or any other thing. If you can do no more than duty it will bring you to the goal. And, my dear friends, I can swear it, the Masters are watching us all, and, without fail, when we come to the right point and really deserve, They manifest to us. At all times I know They help and try to aid us as far as we will let Them.

Why, the Masters are anxious (to use a word of our own) that as many as possible may reach to the state of power and love They are in. Why, then, suppose They help not? As They are Atman and therefore the very law of Karma itself, They are in everything in life, and in every phase of our changing days and years. If you will arouse your faith on this line you come nearer to help from Them than you will recognize.

I send you my love and hope, and best thoughts that you may all find the great light shining around you every day. It is there.

Your brother,

WILLIAM Q. JUDGE

II

Once more, in the absence of Annie [Besant] who is so far away, I send you a word of brotherly greeting. I would ask you to read it impersonally in every part, as I have no reserved thoughts and no ulterior aim in it, and have not had any letters or news from anyone to lead me to write. We are so far away from each other that now and then such a greeting is well, and should be taken in the spirit sent. It is not possible to send to any other household, as none other exists in the Society, you being unique in this—you are the only one. Here we have no such thing, all, nearly, living at other places, and this being merely a centre for work.

Many times have co-operative households been tried and failed. One was tried here and is famous. It was called the Brook Farm, but it had no such high aim and philosophy behind it as you have, and thus the personal frictions, developed at any place of close intimacy, broke it up. That should be a guide to you to enable you to watch and avoid. Yours may alter in number and in personnel, but can never really be broken up if the aim is high and the self-judgment is strict and not self-righteous. I am not accusing you of this, but only stating a common human danger, from which the Theosophist is not at any time exempt. Indeed, he is in danger in your centre from the fact that strong force revolves around it. Hence all must be ever careful, for the personal element is one that ever has a tendency to delude us, as it hides behind various walls and clothes itself in the faults, real or imaginary, of *others*.

Your centre being the only one as yet of such size, it is useful for you to think how you all may best act so as to make it truly international. Each one has a right to his or her particular "crank," of course, but no one ought to think that anyone else is to be judged from not being of the same stripe of "crank." One eats meat, another does not. Neither is universally right, for the kingdom of heaven does not come from meat, nor from its absence. Another smokes and another does not; these are neither universally right nor wrong, as smoke for one is good and for another is bad; the true cosmopolitan allows each to do in such matters as he likes. Essentials are the only things on which true occultism and Theosophy require an agreement, and such temporary matters as food and other habitual daily things are not essentials. One may make a mistake, too, of parading too much his or her particular line of life or act. When this is done the whole world is bored, and nothing effective or lasting is gained except a cranky impression.

In a place like yours, where so many of all sorts of nature are together, there is a unique opportunity for gain and good in the chance it gives one for self-discipline. There friction of personality is inevitable, and if each one learns the great "give and take," and looks not for the faults of the others but for the faults he sees in himself, because of the friction, then great progress can be made. The Masters have said that the great step is to learn how to get out of the rut each one has by nature and by training, and to fill up the old grooves. This has been misconstrued by some who have applied it only to mere outer habits of life, and forgotten that its real application is to the mental grooves, and the astral ones, also. Each mind has a groove, and is not naturally willing to run in the natural groove of another mind. Hence often comes friction and wrangle. Illustrate it by the flanged wheel of the steam-engine running on a track. It cannot run off nor on a track of broader or narrower gauge, and so is confined to one. Take off the flange and make the face of the wheel broader, and then it can run on any track that is at all possible. General human nature is like the engine—it is flanged and run for a certain size of track—but the occultist, or the would-be one, should take off the flange and have a broad-faced wheel that will accommodate itself to the other mind and nature. Thus in one life, even, we might have the benefit of many, for the lives of other men are lived beside us unnoticed and unused because we are too broad and flanged in wheel, or too narrow and flanged also. This is not easy, it is true, to change, but there is no better opportunity in the whole world, than is hourly presented to you to make the alteration. I would gladly have such a chance, which Karma has denied me, and I see the loss I incur each day by not having it there nor here. You have it, and from there should go out to all the earth, soon or late, men and women who are broad and free and strong for the work of helping the world. My reminding you of all this is not a criticism, but is due to my own want of such an opportunity, and, being at a distance, I can get a clearer view of the case, and of what you have for your own benefit and also for all others.

It is natural for one to ask: "What of the future, and what of the defined object, if any, for our work?" That can be answered in many ways.

There is, first, our own work, in and on ourselves, each one. That has for its object the enlightenment of oneself for the good of others. If that is pursued selfishly, some enlightenment comes, but not the amount needed for the whole work. We have to watch ourselves, so as to make of each a centre from which, in our measure, may flow out the potentialities for good that from the adept come in large and affluent streams. The future, then, for each, will come from each present moment. As we use the moment, so we shift the future up or down for good or ill; the future, being only a word for the present, not yet come, we have to see to the present more than all. If the present is full of doubt or vacillation, so will be the future; if full of confidence, calmness, hope, courage and intelligence, thus also will be the future.

As to the broader scope of the work, that comes from united effort of the whole mass of units. It embraces the race, and as we cannot escape from the destiny of the race, we have to dismiss doubt and continue at work. The race is as a whole in a transition state, and many of its units are kept back by the condition of the whole. We find the path difficult, because, being of the race, the general race-tendencies very strongly affect us. This we cannot do away with in a moment. It is useless to groan over it; it is also selfish, since we in the distant past had a hand in making it what it now is. The only way we can alter it is by such action now as makes of each one a centre for good, a force that makes "for righteousness," and that is guided by wisdom. From the great power of the general badness, we each one have a greater fight to wage the moment we force our inner nature up beyond the dead level of the world. So, before we attempt that forcing, we should on the lower plane accumulate all that we can of merit by unselfish acts, by kind thoughts, by detaching our minds from the allurements of the world. This will not throw us out of the world, but will make us free from the great force which is called by Bœhme the "Turba," by which he meant the immense power of the unconscious and material basis of our nature. That material base being devoid of soul is more inclined on this plane to the lower things of life than to the higher.

Hence, until we have in some degree conquered that, it is useless for us to be wishing, as so many of us do, to see the Masters and to be with Them. They could not help us unless we furnished the condition, and a mere desire is not the needed condition. The new condition calls for a change in thought and nature.

So the Masters have said this is a transition age, and he who has ears to hear will hear what has thus been said. We are working for the new cycles and centuries. What we do now in this transition age will be like what the great Dhyan Chohans did in the transition point—the midway point in evolution—at the time when all matter and all types were in a transition and fluid state. They then gave the new impulse for the new types, which resulted later in all the vast varieties of nature. In mental development we are now at the same point; and what we now do in faith and hope for others, and for ourselves, will result similarly on the plane to which it is all directed. Thus in other centuries we will come out again and go on with it. If we neglect it now, so much the worse for us then. Hence we are not working for some definite organization of the new years to come, but for a change in the Manas and Buddhi of the Race. That is why it may seem indefinite, but it is, nevertheless, very defined and very great in scope. Let me refer you to that part of *The Secret Doctrine,** penned by Master Himself, where the midway point of evolution is explained in reference to the ungulate mammals. It should give you a glimpse of what we have to do, and remove all vain longings for a present sojourn with our unseen guides and brothers. The world is not free from superstition, and we, a part of it, must have some traces left of the same thing. They have said that a great shadow follows all innovations in the life of humanity. The wise one will not bring on that shadow too soon—not until some light is ready to fall at the same time for breaking up the darkness.

Masters could give now all the light and knowledge needed, but there is too much darkness that would swallow up the light, except for a few bright souls, and then a greater darkness would come on. Many of us could not grasp nor understand all that might be given, and to us would result a danger and new difficulty for other lives,

* By H. P. Blavatsky. (Orig. Pub., 1888. A photographically reprinted edition is in print.)—Eds.

to be worked out in pain and sorrow. It is from kindness and love that Masters do not blind us with the electric flash of truth complete.

But, concretely, there is a certain object for our general work. It is to start up a new force, a new current in the world, whereby great and long-gone Gnanis, or wise ones, will be attracted back to incarnate among men here and there, and thus bring back the true life and the true practices. Just now a pall of darkness is over all that no Gnani will be attracted by. Here and there a few beams strike through this. Even in India it is dark, for there, where the truth is hid, the thick veil of theological dogma hides all; and, though there is a great hope there, the Masters cannot pierce through to minds below. We have to educate the West so that it may appreciate the possibilities of the East, and thus on the waiting structure in the East may be built up a new order of things for the benefit of the whole. We have, each one of us, to make ourselves a centre of light—a picture gallery from which shall be projected on the astral light such scenes, such influences, such thoughts, as may influence many for good, shall thus arouse a new current, and then finally result in drawing back the great and the good from other spheres, from beyond the earth. This is not spiritualism at all, for it has no reference to the denizens of spook-land in any way.

Let us then have great faith and confidence. See how many have gone out from time to time from your centre to many and distant parts of the world, and how many will continue to go for the good and the gain of man of all places. They have gone to all parts, and it must be that even if the centre should be disrupted from causes outside of you, its power and reality will not be destroyed at all, but will ever remain, even after all of it may have gone, so far as bricks and mortar are concerned.

I give you my best wishes and brotherly greeting for the new year and for every year that is to come.

Affectionately yours,

WILLIAM Q. JUDGE

III

I send you this, and you keep it, using it later on when I give the word. It is to be headed by me later.

The Theosophical movement was begun as a work of the Brotherhood of which H. P. B. is a member, and in which the great Initiate, who was by her called Master, is one of the Chiefs.

It was started among Western people by Western people, the two chief agents being H. P. B., a Russian, and H. S. Olcott, an American. The place where it was started was also Western—the City of New York.

But notwithstanding that the Brotherhood thus had it begun, it must, as a Society, be kept with a free platform, while at the same time its members are individually free to take and hold what belief they find approved by conscience, provided that belief does not militate against Universal Brotherhood. Hence they are at perfect liberty to believe in the Lodge of that Brotherhood and in its messengers, and also to accept their doctrines as to man, his nature, powers and destiny as given out by the messengers on behalf of the Lodge.

The fact is significant that the Theosophical movement was thus, as said, begun in the Western world, in the country where the preparations for the new root race are going on, and where that new root is to appear. This was not to give precedence to any one race or country over another, or to reduce any race or country, but was and is according to the law of cycles, which is a part of evolution. In the eye of that great Law no country is first or last, new or old, high or low, but each at the right time is appropriate for whatever the work is that must be performed. Each country is bound up with all the others and must assist them.

This movement has, among others, an object which should be borne in mind. It is the union of the West with the East, the revival in the East of those greatnesses which once were hers, the development in the West of that Occultism which is appropriate for it, so that it may, in its turn, hold out a helping hand to those of older blood who may have become fixed in one idea, or degraded in spirituality.

For many centuries this union has been worked towards and workers have been sent out through the West to lay the foundations. But not until 1875 could a wide public effort be made, and then the Theosophical Society came into existence because the times were ripe and the workers ready.

Organizations, like men, may fall into ruts or grooves of mental and psychic action, which once established are difficult to obliterate. To prevent those ruts or grooves in the Theosophical movement, its guardians provided that necessary shocks should now and then interpose so as to conduce to solidarity, to give strength such as the oak obtains from buffeting the storm, and in order that all grooves of mind, act, or thought, might be filled up.

It is not the desire of the Brotherhood that those members of the Theosophical movement who have, under their rights, taken up a belief in the messengers and the message should become pilgrims to India. To arouse that thought was not the work nor the wish of H. P. B. Nor is it the desire of the Lodge to have members think that Eastern methods are to be followed, Eastern habits adopted, or the present East made the model or the goal. The West has its own work and its duty, its own life and development. Those it should perform, aspire to and follow, and not try to run to other fields where the duties of other men are to be performed. If the task of raising the spirituality of India, now degraded and almost suffocated, were easy, and if thus easily raised it could shine into and enlighten the whole world of the West, then, indeed, were the time wasted in beginning in the West, when a shorter and quicker way existed in the older land. But in fact it is more difficult to make an entry into the hearts and minds of people who, through much lapse of time in fixed metaphysical dogmatism, have built in the psychic and psycho-mental planes a hard impervious shell around themselves, than it is to make that entry with Westerners who, although they may be meat eaters, yet have no fixed opinions deep laid in a foundation of mysticism and buttressed with a pride inherited from the past.

The new era of Western Occultism definitely began in 1875 with the efforts of that noble woman who abandoned the body of that day not long ago. This does not mean that the Western Occultism is to be something wholly different from and opposed to what so many know, or think they know, as Eastern Occultism. It is to be the Western side of the one great whole of which the true Eastern is the other half. It has, as its mission, largely entrusted to the hands of the Theosophical Society, to furnish to the West that which it can never get from the East; to push forward and raise high on the circular path of evolution now rolling West, the light that lighteth every man who cometh into the world—the light of the true Self, who is the one true Master for every human being; all other Masters are but servants of that true One; in it all real Lodges have their union.

Woe is set apart—not by Masters but by Nature's laws—for those who, having started in the path with the aid of H. P. B., shall in any way try to belittle her and her work, still as yet not understood, and by many misunderstood. This does not mean that a mere person is to be slavishly followed. But to explain her away, to belittle her, to imagine vain explanations to do away with what is not liked in that which she said, is to violate the ideal, is to spit back in the face of the teacher through whom the knowledge and the opportunity came, to befoul the river which brought you sweet waters. She was and is one of those brave servants of the universal Lodge sent to the West to take up the work, well knowing the pain and obloquy and the insult to the very soul—worst of all insults—which were certain from the first to be hers. "Those who cannot understand her had best not try to explain her; those who do not find themselves strong enough for the task she plainly outlined from the beginning had best not attempt it." She knew, and you have been told before, that high and wise servants of the Lodge have remained with the West since many centuries for the purpose of helping it on to its mission and destiny. That work it would be well for the members of the Theosophical Movement to continue without deviating, without excitement, without running to extremes, without imagining that Truth is a matter of either longitude or latitude: the truth of the soul's life is in no special quarter of the compass, it is everywhere round the whole circle; and those who look in one quarter will not find it.

(This letter is marked in red pencil, by the hand of Mr. Judge, "unfinished." In fact, it ends with the word "will," as above, but in publishing earlier some extracts from this letter, the owner had the permission of the writer to supply the last three words, which he had intended to place there when called away, and in his haste for the post, in returning, had omitted to add.)

IV

To The Theosophical Publication Society

It is with great regret that I learn from recent London advices that the Managers of the Society there think that the Tract, "Epitome of Theosophy," which appeared in *The Path*, is "too advanced to be reprinted now, and that what is needed is 'a stepping-stone from fiction to philosophy'."

Permit me to say that I cannot agree with this opinion, nor with the policy which is outlined by it. The opinion is erroneous, and the policy is weak as well as being out of accord with that of the Masters. Those Masters have approved the project of the new Society and are watching the unfolding of its policy.

If I had made up that Epitome wholly myself I might have some hesitation in speaking in this way, but I did not. The general idea of such a series of tracts was given to me some two years ago, and this one was prepared by several students who know what the people need. It is at once comprehensive and fundamental. It covers most of the ground, and if any sincere reader grasps it he will have food for his reflection of the sort needed.

If, however, we are to proceed by a mollified passage from folly (which is fiction) to philosophy, then we at once diverge from the path marked out for us by the Masters; and for this statement I can refer to letters from Them in my hands. I need only draw your attention to the fact that when those Masters began to cause Their servants to give out matter in India, They did not begin with fiction, but with stern facts such as are to be found in the *Fragments of Occult Truth,** which afterwards became Mr. Sinnett's *Esoteric Buddhism.* We are not seeking to cater to a lot of fiction readers and curiosity hunters, but to the pressing needs of earnest minds. Fiction readers never influenced a nation's progress. And these earnest minds do not desire, and ought not to be treated to, a gruel which the sentence just quoted would seem to indicate as their fate.

Then again, I beg to remind my English brothers in this enterprise that they should remember that the United States contain more theosophists and possible subscribers and readers than the whole of Europe. They do not want fiction. They want no padding in their search for truth. They are perfectly able to grasp that which you call "too advanced." The Master some years ago said that the U. S. needed the help of the English body of theosophists. That they did not get, and now do not require it so much, and their ideas and needs must be considered by us. We have twenty-one Branches to your three in Great Britain, and each month, nearly, sees a new Branch. Several have written me that they understand the T.P.S. is to give them *good* and *valuable* reprints and not weak matters of fiction.

* First published in *The Theosophist,* at intervals from October, 1881, to July, 1883. The first three "Fragments" are by H.P.B., the others being signed "Lay Chela" (A. P. Sinnett). The series is reprinted in *Theosophy,* II.—Eds.

I therefore respectfully urge upon you that the weak and erroneous policy to which I have referred shall not be followed, but that strong lines of action be taken, and that we leave fiction to the writers who profit by it or who think that thus people's minds can be turned to the Truth. If a contrary line be adopted, then we will not only disappoint the Master (if that be possible) but we will in a very large sense be guilty of making false representations to a growing body of subscribers here as well as elsewhere.

I am, fraternally yours,
WILLIAM Q. JUDGE

V

It is a relief to turn from these eternal legal quibbles (of my business) to say a word or two on eternal matters.

Now and then there are underlined sentences occurring in *The Path*. These ought to be studied. One about one yogee not doing anything not seen in another yogee's mind will open up a subject.* Reticence does not always mean ignorance: if we dig out the knowledge we drag down at the same time rocks and debris of other sorts, whereas, if a miner hands us the nugget, that is all we get at the time. So a slight reticence often results in our going at the digging ourselves.

In September *Path* is another. Getting back the memory of other lives is really the whole of the process,† and if some people don't understand certain things it is either because they have not got to that point in their other lives or because no glimmer of memory has yet come.

The communion of saints is a reality, and it often happens that those brought up in the same school speak the same language. While not being one, such are very like co-scholars, no matter when or where. Furthermore, there are some peculiar natures in this world who, while they are like mirrors or sponges that reflect and absorb from others certain information, still retain a very strong individuality of their own. So it is with this gentleman whose letter you enclose. There is scarcely any doubt that he, if he tells

* From the second installment of "A Hindu Chela's Diary," published by Mr. Judge in the *Path,* July, 1886, and reprinted in *Theosophy,* III, 265. The quotation, *"no Yogee will do a thing unless he sees the desire in another Yogee's mind,"* occurs on page 268.—Eds.

† From the third installment of the "Diary," *Theosophy,* III, 359.—Eds.

true tales, sees in the astral light. The description of things "moving about like fishes in the sea" is a real description of one of the manners in which many of these elemental forms are seen. So, as premised above, it may be settled that he sees in the astral light.

He should know that that astral light exists in all places and interpenetrates everything, and is not simply in the free air alone. Further should he know that to be able to see as he sees in the light is not *all* of the seeing thus. That is, there are many sorts of such sight, *e.g.*, he may see now certain airy shapes and yet not see many others which at the same time are as really present there as those he now sees. So it would seem that there are "layers" or differences of states in the astral light. Another way to state it is that elementals are constantly moving in the astral light—that is, everywhere. They, so to say, show pictures to him who looks, and the pictures they show will depend in great part upon the seer's thoughts, motives and development. These differences are very numerous. It therefore follows that in this study *pride* must be eliminated. That pride has disappeared from ordinary life does not prove that it has done any more than retreat a little further within. So one must be careful of becoming even inwardly vain of being able to see any such things; for, if that happens, it will follow that the one limited plane in which one may be a seer will be accepted as the whole. That, then, will be falsity. But if recognized as delusive, because partial, then it remains true—so far as it goes. All true things must be total, and all totalities exist at once, each in all, while these partial forms exist partially in those that are total. So it follows that only those that are total reveal entire truth, and those that partake of lower nature—or are partial—receive but a limited view of truth. The elementals are partial forms, while the man's individual soul is total, and according to the power and purity of that form which it inhabits, "waits upon the Gods."

Now our bodies, and all "false I" powers up to the individual soul, are "partial forms," in common with the energic centres in astral light. So it must follow that, no matter how much we and they participate in each other, the resulting view of the one Truth is partial in its nature because the two partial forms mingling together do not produce totality. But it intoxicates. And herein lies the danger of the teaching of such men as P. B. Randolph, who advocates participation with these partial beings by means of sensual excesses glorified with a name and gilded with the pretence of a high purpose—*viz.*, knowledge: KNOWLEDGE MUST BE CAREFULLY OBTAINED WITH A PURE MOTIVE.

This motive is the point for this gentleman to study. He says that he "will know," and that he "desires to escape from present limitations of this personality, which is all loneliness."

As he did go forward on the path of knowledge, he would find that this imaginary loneliness of which he speaks is, by comparison with the utter loneliness of that path, a howling mob, a tramping regiment.

As he is fighting alone his own fight, let him carefully note his motive in seeking to know more, and in seeking to escape from his present "loneliness." Must it not be true that loneliness cannot be escaped from by abhorrence of it or even by its acceptance, but by its recognition? What next? Well, this—and perhaps it is too simple. He ought to assure himself that his motive in knowing and being is that he may help all creatures. I do not say that this is not now his motive, but, for fear it should not be, I refer to it. For as he appears to be on the borderland of fearful sights and sounds, he ought to know the magic amulet which alone can protect him while he is ignorant. It is that boundless charity of love which led Buddha to say: "Let the sins of this dark age fall on me that the world may be saved," and not a desire for escape or for knowledge. It is expressed in the words: "THE FIRST STEP IN TRUE MAGIC IS DEVOTION TO THE INTERESTS OF OTHERS." It was expressed by Krishna when he said: "Near to Renunciation is salvation" (or the state of a Jivanmukta).

But he naturally will ask if he should cultivate his powers. Well, of course, he should at some time or other; but he ought to begin at motives and purification of thought. He may, if he chooses, abandon the ideas of this large-hearted charity and yet make great progress in "powers," but surely then death and ashes will be the result. That does not concern me.*

[Latterly a friend related a strange experience to the Tea Table. He had been brought up among the Welsh, and was a firm disbeliever in the "supernaturalism" so rife among that people, until occultism explained to him so many of the strange occurrences and

* The substance of the letter to which Mr. Judge is replying is given in the "Tea Table Talk," *Path*, June, 1887, followed by a portion of his answer. This last, being less condensed than that published in the original LETTERS, is here substituted.—Eds.

sights he had hitherto defied. From childhood he had been used to seeing "strange things moving about like fishes in the sea," to hearing strange sounds and seeing distant places or objects, though his sturdy attitude of negation, and his attributing them to optical or nervous defects, had of late years somewhat lessened the number of those phenomena. One day recently, he had been reading of some psychometric experiments, and fell to thinking of some place to which he desired to go. Closing his eyes, he thought strongly of this place, determined to see, if possible, a person who was there. All at once an indescribable lightness seemed to pervade his whole person. He thought—"I can go there!" and rising, was half across the room in a moment, when turning his head, he beheld himself seated in the chair he had left. At this a nameless horror seized him, a dreadful fear; he rushed back into his body—how, he knew not—overcome with terror at his own involuntary act.

This fact of his undue alarm and its possible cause excited some discussion around the Tea Table. Finally it was agreed to write to an eminent occultist on the subject. His reply will interest all students of this important branch of occultism.]

Why did he have a horror when he nearly succeeded in getting away from his body—in being for a moment free? That is an important question. Its solution may be found in many ways. I will mention one. If the place, or person, he wished to go to was one to which he ought not then to have gone, or if his motive in desiring to go there was not pure, then a horror might result that drove him back. Motive is highly important, and must be examined and tested countless times. The meaning of the word *motive* must not here be limited to what is called bad or improper motive. I will just as willingly examine into bad as into good motives, and, no matter how lurid the light on them, I will still examine them impartially. If one has a bad motive, then the results are his own Karma, and not that of any other, except those who willingly take it on themselves.

In the above case, indifference of motive is just as much to be guarded against as any other sort. In leaving the body without motive, we leave it under the impressions of Tamoguna (Darkness) and when set free we are very likely to be caught in a whirl which is far from pleasant. Horror may then result. I do not say it always will result. But great forces are not to be set in motion with impunity. We must be able to put down and control an equal opposition, and good motive alone affords us this balance of power by setting the Law on our side. The highest possible motive must be laid at the bottom, or else we will meet trouble which only power can overcome. Yet again, if even with a bad motive he had attempted to go to a place where a similar motive existed, then no horror would have come. If he will tell himself, or me, just where he was wanting to go, I may say why he had a horror. But I do not want to know.

It is not necessarily a horror-producing thing to leave the body. Only lately I know of a friend who went out of his body a distance of 10,000 miles and had no horror. In that case he desired to see a friend on a common purpose which had in view the amelioration of this dark age; and again, he left his body and saw the surrounding sweeps of wood and vale, and had no horror in either case. Similarity of motive creates an electric or magnetic current along which we may possibly proceed in safety provided it is not crossed by a still stronger current. If one is sure of motive, and that is pure, then going out of the body is not detrimental.

This inquirer lays much stress upon the fact that he was "rushing back" to his body of his own accord. That does not prove that he was not pushed back. When the saturated solution in a glass is disturbed, *itself, by its own volition, crystallizes,* but it had first to have the predisposing cause in the shape of the blow on the glass. So although he "rushed back," it was because of the push he received from something he cannot describe nor understand.

An illustration will show the dangers. Take the case of one who determines to leave the body merely to go to another who is admired by him, or whom he desires to see. This other, however, is protected by high motives and great purity. The first is mixed in motive in waking life, but, as soon as the disengaged state comes on, the motive is changed into a mere will or curiosity to see the second, combined perhaps with more or less sensuality, *e.g.,* a desire to see a woman much admired and to pour into her unwilling ear pretended or real human love. The elementals and other guardians of the second protect that soul, and hurl vague horrors at the first, who, if he is not a skilled black magician is—

a. Either merely pushed back into the body, or

b. Is assailed with fears that prevent him from finding or entering his body, and that may be occupied by an elementary, good, bad or indifferent, and his friends say he waked up suddenly insane!

Motive is then the main point for this and every inquirer to study. If he is sure of his motives, and that they are neither indifferent, curious, selfish, nor imprudent, and he trusts in the Unity of the Supreme Soul, he cannot be in much danger.

Well—enough!

VI

The letters proposed by your friend are a device of the enemy, as you may have supposed, and which you were warned to expect in unexpected quarters and ways. Therefore they should not be written. It is the small rift in the lute that destroys it; in human history small and unexpected events alter the destiny of nations.

On this plane the dark powers rely upon their ability to create a maya. They have seen that you are not to be trapped in the prominent lines of work and so try their hands where your currents exist in a prominent place but with a very small matter. Let me point out.

If you issue these letters they would be an endorsement of all that your friend might think to do, and neither you nor Y. are free from mistakes yet. They would amount to a declaration, to the perception of others, that you were guiding Y. in everything and were at all times conscious of it. Do you or Y. know where this would end? Do you see the possibilities flowing from the acceptance in full of those letters by the others? And what would their action be? Are they free from the curse of superstition; are they clear in the co-ordination of psychic with brain thought? No. The result would not only be different from what you and Y. can see, but worse. Now further.

It is true—and humanly natural—that the others (like you and *your* friends) indulged in some slight critiques on your friend, but they were small and coupled with sincere and kind thoughts up to their lights, no matter how large and bitter all this was made by maya to appear. The dark powers seized on them, enlarged them, dressed them up, assumed the images of the thinkers, enlivened the thoughts with elementals, all with an object, *viz.*, to make your friend think it all came from the others. Why, if that were so then those others (poor weak mortals) are fiends. But are they? No. It was wished by the dark ones to irritate your friend and you, so as by the irritation to split a breach forever unhealable. In Y.'s very weak state they found it easy, and hoped by distance to make you blind.

Tell your friend to remember what was long ago said—that the Master would manage results. You must not manage, precipitate, nor force. Beware. Let Y. assume that the others do not think harshly nor critically, but put it all against the dark powers, and the results will be managed by Master. As chelâs and students conceal rather than give out your inner psychic life, for by telling of it your proper progress is hindered. There must be silence in heaven for a time or the dark ones rejoice to so easily get good, malleable images for annoying you. It will be tried again either that way or some other. By gentleness, detachment, strict attention to duty, and retiring now and then to the quiet place, bring up good currents and keep back all evil ones. Remember it is the little things the work is done through, for they are not noticed, while the larger ones draw the eyes and minds of all.

I think of you always as the brave soldier, made not of mud and soft things, but made of long pieces of steel and strips of diamond and flashes of long light that has no harshness, and a big, big spring all the way through. That is you. And your eyes laugh now and then, even if you do have a pain in your head. Inside you are all right, as you know very well, don't you? Then if you are that soldier, it means that he will spring back as soon as the body has had time to get some better. The body is like the heart; it has to have time to get to some other condition. But you will get there. A steady mind and heart stands still and quiet until the muddy stream rolls clear. Now sleep, I say; I command you to sleep. I have tried to help you to sleep, and I wish you to sleep, for sleep will do you good as nothing else can. I hope to see you drop all when ——— comes, and go to sleep for a while, and far enough from the row to be quiet. It is sleep your tired nature on the outside wants, for sleep knits up the ravelled thread of life and makes us young again. You have been so awake, that the power of equilibrium between life and the body is disturbed and needs a chance. This is fact. One can get wrought up, and then Prana is too strong; so little children sleep much. *Be a child once.*

Well, I'm near home, or rather the centre spot, for pilgrims like you and me have no real house and don't want it; it's too dull and usual for such to want a home. And perhaps the little brother is good and well? He shall be ever present, as he always has been, in those little songs and tales told to oneself in the dark, and is, too, the lone warrior seen on the plain of stupid infantry, and he rides a horse whose blood is electricity. Au revoir. Tell ——— I can stand alone; it is the best way to stand, and what I always was and shall be. Let the ripples and the foam go on coming and going; the old river and the bed of the river do not move for all that is on the top. Is it not so? Well, good-bye, and good luck, and may the devas help you, and also karma. Love to all, as usual.

As forevermore,

VII

I was very glad indeed to get your letter, but sorry to read of your troubles. Strangely, too, a similar trouble with a very dear friend of mine is now uppermost in my mind, and I would like to crave the favour from you that you would tell me what kind of place the asylum is you speak of. The only accessible one here is a mere prison, where men do nothing, and where I do not think the influence would be other than depressing. Do you think that, at the one you have in mind, a man of active mind, who merely wishes to get rid of his present trouble, would be able to occupy himself?

I am indeed sorry that you have to tell me such matters, but they will rest in my confidence; and I thank you and ——— for your renewed invitation.

It is best not to inquire into some of the mysteries of life, but surely a full reliance upon the Spirit within and upon the law that the hands that smite us are our own, will relieve the pressure of some events that seem mysteries. I find the greatest consolation in these reflections, and then I see that each moment is mine, and that when gone it is passed and merged into the sum of my being; and so I must strive to Be. Thus I may hope to become in time the conscious possessor of the whole of Being. So I do not strive after mystery. The great struggle must be to open up my outer self, that my higher being may shine through, for I know that in my heart the God sits patient, and that his pure rays are merely veiled from me by the many strivings and illusions that I bring on outwardly. This being so, I can only look at the Society and its work (under my lights) as the best available channel for my actions in the effort to help others. Its methods, then, as far as I am concerned, will be only mine, and thus I cannot attach to it the methods of any other person.

Believe me sincerely yours,

VIII

As for me, all that is the matter is my health, not yet full and good. If that were all right, I would have nothing. What do I care for all the row? It will soon be over; some will be dead; the sooner the better, and then we shall have other fun. I look at it all as so much fun and variety, sure; I am not joking. It is variety, and without that what would life be? As all these asses bray we learn new notes of the scale not known before. A heap of letters I got; but I am O.K.—fragile, perhaps, but not brittle. I would like to be with you both and have some sweet fun without tears or spite, but we have to be apart, to meet now and then. Poor ———! Don't be hard on him. He had to be silent, you know. A small matter, but more important than he knew for him. Let up on him, and don't jeer. He has a hard enough time with himself, to have any added by massage from others.

C———'s allusion to "suffering" opens up a vein of thought which I have had. I have examined myself for the "uses" of this rumpus, to see if I am properly "suffering." Well, I can't find it. Down in the deeps I may be; but I find myself cheerful, happy, and anything but morose or sad. Ergo: can I be suffering? Do you know? Positively, I do not know. Ought I? Am I a wretch because I do not suffer, or because, being in actual suffering, I am insensate and do not perceive it? But, on the other hand, I feel no anger and no resentment. Really, it puzzleth me. Many nights I do not sleep, and have used the hours (as I now do), when all is still, in looking over all, and yet I feel all right—everywhere. Of course, I have committed my human faults and sins, but I mean, on the Grand Round-Up, I find nothing to "suffer me"; nothing that I shall rush out to amend by taking the ridiculous and nasty world to my bosom in confidence upon.

As for myself. Well. What? Nothing. I know not and care not. I am joyful and glorious that the work thus goes. My desires are not here, and all the racket sounds to me far off, as if miles from my ear. I am acting as a pump-engine, and trying to force a lot on. This is not for myself. I must find myself alone, as we all are, and then the Law will say: "Next!" But what next I do not care and don't want to know, for when "Next" is said I will see what it is to do. Just now the best and biggest work by us poor children is on this plane with the great aid of Master, Whose simple single will keeps the whole organization [in being], and acts as its support and shield. We are not big enough yet to handle the Akasa, but we may help Them to, and that is all I want to do. I have used the present affairs to be as a lesson to me, for it may be used as a test to me as to pride and ambition; and I find that, no matter how I turn it, the same result comes. I am seeking other things while working in this. Try as I may to raise an ambition for power, and to raise a desire to change a supposed case (non-existent in fact), I can't do it. So you see, my dear Comrade, I am all right.

These questions you ask me:

When the self is first seen, it is like looking into a glove; and for how many incarnations may it not be so? The material envelope throws up before the eye of the Soul waving fumes and clouds of illusion.

The brain is only the focus through which are centralized the forces and thoughts that are continually coming in through the solar plexus of the heart. Many such thoughts, therefore, are lost, just as millions of seeds in nature are lost. It behooves us to study them and to guard them when there; but can we call them our own? Or weep over them? Let us be as wide as great Nature concerning them, and let each go on to its own place without colouring them with our own colour and acceptance or adhesion.

The spiral movement is the double movement of the astral light, one spiral inside the other. The diastole and systole of the heart are caused by that double movement of the Akasa. But do not presumptuously grasp the movement too soon, for often even the heart moving too rapidly destroys the life.

The brutes unconsciously are aware of the general human opposition, which in each human being they see focalized.

It is easier to sink back into the Eternal than to dive. The diver must needs have the power to retain breath against the rush caused by diving, while to sink gives time to get and keep the breath.

Nothing else greatly new. Am waiting to hear of your completer health. Sustained on the wave you will come in with the tide in time. Best love to ——— and to ——— and to thee. May you all be well sustained. I think I have now given you all there is. Salute most noble, brave, and diamond-hearted! May we meet after the dust settles, and we will meet forever in the long, long manvantaras before us all. Peace! Peace! the path of peace and not of war: such are the words.

As forevermore,

IX

I do not know what to write, for I've been so occupied with people. I am anxious about my lectures; still unprepared. I cannot naturally reply to many of your points, because I have a retiring feeling, and so shall not reply. Indeed, I often think how nice it would be not to speak or write. I am no hand at those nice phrases that people like. Of course, that does not alter my real feelings, but chickens are chickens and often think nonsense. I want to forget and forgive all those children and childish acts. Let us do it, and try as much as possible to be real brothers, and thus get nearer the truth. And by work we will defeat the enemy of Master: by still silently working.

I hope still you will emerge sooner or later all the better and the stronger. I know you will, and I do not see you dead by any means. You are less hopeful for yourself than for others. But you have the will and the fire to fight on to the last bone and the last moment. I only wish I could see you all to hearten you up a little more: that is, to talk with you, for you do not need much of the grit. . . .

I often hear from Him now. That terrible racket cleared me up. He says that much haste must be avoided. And that I must not let the flood carry me off. He asks me to say to you that you have a natural rapidity that must be guided by yourself and the best way is to wait after a letter and to sleep on a plan. He also says that . . . (I am not aware of this, but He must be right), that you have a subtle desire to be the first to make or propose a good plan or act. Do not let this carry you off, but be slower as to that. It is good advice, I think, for the additional reason that one can now and then take a plan from the head of another.

I see the clans have been gathering. Keep it up and see to it as far as possible that partisanship is at a low ebb and that only good, steady loyalty and work are the main motive. *And cast no one out of your heart.*

I must ask for a calmer motion at this time. It is absolutely necessary.

A word of love to ______ ? I sent it. I sent many. I sent it not only visibly but also the other way. What could I say? I do not know. In what I sent my whole heart was put. Does not ______ forever stand for me and with me? How can I use words when the fibres of my heart are involved? And what good is my philosophy if, when the actual taking of ______ off seemed so near, I indulged in mere words? I cannot do it. If I try, then the words are mere rubbish, lies and unreal, as I am not able to do this, no matter how much others can. Our real life is not in words of love or hate or coldness but in the fiery depths of the heart. And in those depths ______ is and was. Could I say more? No; impossible. And even that is small and badly said.

It is true that day by day the effect of my philosophy is more apparent on me, as yours is and will be on you, and so with us all. I see it myself, let alone all I hear of it from others. What a world and what a life! Yet we are born alone and must die alone, except that in the Eternal Space all are one, and the One Reality never dies.

If ambition slowly creeps up higher and higher it will destroy all things, for the foundations will be weak. In the end, the Master will win, so let us breathe deep and hold fast there, as we are. And let us hurry nothing. Eternity is here all the time. I cannot tell you how my heart turns to you all. You know this, but a single word will do it: *Trust!* That was what H. P. B. said. Did she not know? Who is greater than our old and valiant "old Lady"? Ah, were she here, what a carnage! Wonder, anyhow, how she, or he, or it, looks at the matter? Smiling, I suppose, at all our struggles.

Again, in storm and shine, in heat and cold, near or afar, among friends or foes, the same in One Work.

X

My Dear Companion (Campanero),

Your long letter and message received. All I can say is that it is gigantically splendid, marvelously accurate. And let me then return to you this message . . . that this must prove to you that you are not standing still. . . . It's all well enough to be out in the rapids as you say I am, but what of it when I don't hear such a message as yours myself? Thank you. It is a bugle blast from the past. Perhaps in some other age I taught you that and now you give it to me again. When I said in mine that in Kali Yuga more could be done than in any other age in the same period, I stated all you say but I didn't know it. Now your clear light falls upon it and I see it well. But fear not. You got so familiar to me that I permitted myself to let out some of the things that I now and then feel. But I swear to you that I do not always so let them rush before me. Truly, you have proved that your place is "where the long roll finds you standing."

Now, don't you begin to see more and more things? Don't you feel things that you know without anyone to tell you?

My friend Urban* has shown me a letter from ——— in which the latter, feeling dark in consequence of various causes, sees no light. This is merely the slough of despond, I tell him. We know the light is ahead, and the experience of others shows that the darkest hour is just before the dawn. I tell him also that strong souls are thus tried inevitably because they rush ahead along the road to the light. In the *Finnish Epic* [the *Kalevala*] it is said that guarding a certain place are hideous serpents and glittering spears. And so it really is.

But although such is the truth, I have also to tell him that he ought, as far as possible, to try to ameliorate the circumstances. I will make my meaning clear. He is living now, as you know, among people of an opposite faith. Around them are elementals who would, if they could, implant suspicion and distrust about those whom he reveres, or, if they fail there, will try to cause physical ills or aggravate present ones. In his case these have succeeded in part in causing darkness. . . . Now ———, while not just in that case, is surrounded, while not strong, by those who inwardly deplore his beliefs . . . and hence the elementals are there and they quarrel with those of ——— and bring on despair, reduce strength, and so on. I tell ——— those circumstances ought to be ameliorated every now and then, for I know he would at once, if changed to a better place, get better. And so I have written to him to make a change as soon as he can.

It is highly important that no replies should be made to attacks. Get the people to devote themselves to work and to ignoring attacks. The opposing forces strain every nerve to irritate some or all of us so

* Eusebio Urban was one of Mr. Judge's pen names in the *Path*.—Eds.

that we may reply in irritation and precipitate more follies. Consider solely how to improve old work, get up new work and infuse energy into work. Otherwise the beneficent influences intended for all F.T.S. will be nullified.

Cheer up ———, and from your standpoint tell him how to know the distinction between the intellect and the spiritual mind. Tell him how to find out his spirit-will and to ignore a little the mental attitude he takes. Do not point to particular instances of his own failure but detail your own inner experience. It will do him good.

Upanishads: "Subsisting" here means, not that the self *exists* by reason of food, but that as a manifestation, as one causing the body to be visible and to act, the self subsists in that state by means of the food which is used. It is really a reversed translation, and ought to read—as I think—"The self exists in close proximity to the heart and causes the body to exist by reason of the food which it takes in for its subsistence." That is, continual reference is had to the doctrine that if the self were not there the body would not exist. Yes: it also means that the self procures vital airs from the food which the one life causes to be digested. For note that which you know: did we not take food, the material unit of the trinity would die, and the self be disappointed, and then [the self] would get another body to try in again. For is it not permitted to each one to try to set up a habit in that material unit whereby we may as incarnated beings know the self? Then when that is done we do not live as others; but all the same, even then, the self must subsist, so to say, while in manifestation, by means of food, no matter if that food be of a different character, corresponding to the new state. Even the Devas subsist by food. You know "they enter into that colour, or sound, or savour, at the sacrifice; they rise in that colour, etc., and by it they live." Watch words, ——— dear; they are traps. Catch ideas, and I will understand by the context that you are not confined to the ordinary meanings.

I am swamped in work, but my courage is up, and I feel the help sent from the right place.

Let us go on from place to place and from year to year; no matter who or what claims us outwardly, we are each the property of the self.

As forevermore and after,

XI

To ______

There is a sentence in your letter not explained by J. Niemand, which, however, needs explaining, for it is the outgrowth of an erroneous idea in you. You say: "Can I help these ignorant elementals with mental instruction? I tried it, but not successfully."

In all cases where trouble or mental distress is caused by the elementals, you *cannot*. Elementals are not ignorant. They know just as much and just as little as you do. Most generally more. Do you not know that they are reflectors? They merely mirror to you either your own mind, or the mental strata caused by the age, the race, and the nation you may be in. Their action is invariably automatic and unconscious. They care not for what is called by you "mental instruction." They hear you not.

Do you know how they hear, or what language they understand? Not human speech; nor ordinary human thought clothed in mental speech. That is a dead letter to them altogether.

They can only be communicated with through correlations of colours and sounds. But while you address yourself to them, those thoughts assume life from elementals rushing in and attaching themselves to those thoughts.

Do not, then, try to speak to them too much, because did you make them know [you] they might demand of you some boon or privilege, or become attached to you, since in order to make them understand they must *know* you—and a photographic plate forgets not.

Fear them not, nor recoil in horror nor repulsion. The time of trial must be fulfilled. Job had to wait his period until all his troubles and diseases passed away. *Before* that time he could do naught.

But we are not to idly sit and repine; we are to bear these trials, meanwhile drawing in new and good elementals so as to have, in Western phrase, a capital on which to draw when the time of trial has fully passed away. . . .

On all other points, Niemand has well explained. Read both together.

Lastly, know this law, written on the walls of the temple of learning.

"Having received, freely give; having once in thought devoted your life to the great stream of energy in which elementals and souls alike are carried—and which causes the pulse beat of our hearts—you can never claim it back again. *Seek, then, that mental devotion which strains to give.* For in the Law it is written that we must give away all or we lose it; as you need mental help, so do others who are wandering in darkness seeking for light."

XII

To-day I got your wire, "——— very low." This is a shock to me. I hardly believe it is the end at all. I cannot believe it, there is so much fire there. But I wired you to ask if I was to tell ———. Also to read 2nd ch. *Bhag. Gîtâ.* That, my dear follow, solves all these troubles for me, though it doesn't kill out immediate pain. Besides, it is Karma, just and wise. Defects are in us all, and if this is the taking off, why, it means that a lot of obstructive Karma is thus at once and forever worked off, and has left ——— free for greater work in better places. I would I were there with you. Tell him how much I love him and that in this era of Kali Yuga no sincere one, such as he, remains long away from the work there is to do. Words are of no use. I have sent thoughts, and those are useful, whether we are in the body or out of it. I sent every night lately all the help I could and continued through the day, not only to ———, but also you. It reached there, I know, but I can't overcome Karma if it is too strong.

Tell ——— if it should come to the worst, that no regrets about the work are needed. What has already been accomplished there will last, and seethe and do its work for several years to come. So in that direction there could be nothing to regret. I cannot write ——— directly; but if able to hear this—or maybe when it arrives —then head it as if it were to him, and not to you.

So, dear ———, in the presence of your wire this is all I can write. You know my feelings, and I need not say any more.

As ever,

XIII

You did right to send me that letter. Of course, I am sorry to hear from you in that way, but am glad that you wrote. Let me tell you something—will you believe it? You are not in nearly such a bad way as you think, and your letter, which you sent me unreservedly, shows it. Can you not, from the ordinary standpoint of worldly wisdom, see it so? For your letter shows this—a mind and lower nature in a whirl, not in the ordinary sense, but as though, figuratively speaking, it were whirling in a narrow circle, seemingly dead, yet kept alive by its own motion. And above it, a human soul, not in any hurry, but waiting for its hour to strike. And I tell you, I know it will strike.

If so far as your personal consciousness goes you have lost all desire for progress, for service, for the inner life—what has that to do with it? Do you not think that others have had to go through with all of that, and worse—a positive aversion, maybe, to everything connected with Theosophy? Do you not know that it takes a nature with some strength in it to sink very low, and that the mere fact of having the power to sink low may mean that the same person may in time rise to a proportionately greater height? This is not the highest path to go, but it is one that many have to tread. The highest is that which goes with little variation, but few are strong enough to keep up the never-ceasing strain. Time alone, and many ages of service, can give them that strength. But meanwhile there is that other to be traveled. Travel it bravely.

You have got the ______. Which of the hells do you think you are in? Try to find out and look at the corresponding heaven. It is very near. And I do not say this to try to bolster you up artificially, for that would be of no use and would not last, even if I were to succeed in doing it. I write of facts, and I think that somewhere in your nature you are quite well aware that I do so.

Now what is to be done: * * * * In my opinion you should deliberately give yourself a year's trial. Write and tell me at the end of that year (and meantime as often as you feel called upon to do so, which will not be very often) how you then feel, and, if you do not feel inclined to go on and stick to it, I will help you all I can. But you must do it yourself, in spite of not wanting to do it. You can.

Make up your mind that in some part of your nature, somewhere, there is that which desires to be of use to the world. Intellectually realize that that world is not too well off and probably wants a helping hand. Recognize mentally that you should try to work for it sooner or later. Admit to yourself that another part of your nature—and if possible see that it is the lower part—does not care in the least about the world or its future, but that such care and interest should be cultivated. This cultivation will, of course, take time—all cultivation does. Begin by degrees. Assert constantly to yourself that you intend to work and that you will do so. Keep that up all the time. Do not put any time limit to it, but take up the attitude that you are working towards that end. Begin by doing ten minutes' work every day of any sort—study, or the addressing of envelopes, or anything, so long as it be done deliberately and with that object in view. If a day comes when this is too irksome, knock it off for that day. Give yourself three or four days' rest, and do it deliberately. Then go back to your ten minutes' work. At the end of six or seven weeks, you will know what to add to that practice; but go slowly, do nothing in a hurry; be deliberate.

Don't try to feel more friendly to this or that person—more actively friendly, I should have said. Such things must spring up of their own accord and will do so in time. But do not be surprised that you feel *all* compassion die out of you in some ways. That, too, is an old story. It is all right because it does not last. Do not be too anxious to get results from the practice I have outlined above. Do not look for any: you have no concern with them, if you do all that as a duty. And finally, do not forget, my dear fellow, that the dead do come to life and that the coldest thing in the world may be made hot by gentle friction. So I wish you luck, and wish I could do more for you. But I will do what I can.

XIV

Now, this is, as I said, an era. I called it that of Western Occultism, but you may give it any name you like. But it is Western. The symbol is the well-intended American Republic, which was seen by Tom Paine beforehand as "a new era in the affairs of the world." It was meant to be, as nearly as possible, a brotherhood of nations, and that is the drift of its Declaration and Constitution. The T.S. is meant to be the same, but has for many years been in a state of friction. It has now, if possible, to come out of that. It cannot be a brotherhood unless each, or some, of its units becomes a brother in truth. And *brother* was the noble name given in 1875 to the Masters. Hence you and I and all of us must cultivate [brotherhood]. We must forgive our enemies and those who assail us, for only thus can the great brothers properly help by working through us. There seems to be a good deal to forgive, but it is easily done, inasmuch as in fifty years we'll all be gone and forgot.

Cut off, then, thoughts about those "foolish children" until harmonious vibrations ensue to some extent. That absurdity . . . let go. I have deliberately refrained from jumping at such a grand chance. So, you see, forgive, forgive and largely forget. Come along, then, and with me get up as fast as possible the feeling of brotherhood.

Now then, you want more light, and this is what you must do. You will have to "give up" something. To wit: have yourself called half an hour earlier than is usual and devote it *before* breakfast to silent meditation, in which brood upon all great and high ideas. Half an hour! Surely, that you can spare. And don't eat first. If you can take another half *before* you go to bed, and without any preliminaries of undressing or making things agreeable or more comfortable, meditate again. Now don't fail me in this. This is much to give up, but give it up, recollecting that you are not to make all those preparations so often indulged in by people. . . . "The best and most important teacher is one's seventh principle centered in the sixth. The more you divest yourself of the illusionary sense of personal isolation, and the more you are devoted to the service of others, the more Maya disappears and the nearer you approach to Divinity." Good-bye, then, and may you find that peace which comes from the Self.

XV

In answer to your questions:

(1) Clothes and astral form.

Answer.—You are incorrect in assuming that clothes have no astral form. Everything in nature has its double on other planes, the fact being that nothing visible in matter or space could be produced without such a basis. The clothes are seen, as well as the person, because they exist on the astral plane as well as he. Besides this, the reason why people are seen on the astral plane with clothes of various cut and colour, is because of the thought and desire of the person, which clothes him thus. Hence a person may be seen in the astral light wearing there a suit of clothes utterly unlike what he has on, because his thought and desire were on another suit, more comfortable, more appropriate, or what not.

(2) What can true and earnest Theosophists do against the Black Age or Kali Yuga?

Answer.—Nothing *against* it, but a great deal *in* it; for it is to be remembered that the very fact of its being the iron, or foundation, age, gives opportunities obtained in no other. It is only a quarter as long as the longest of the other ages, and it is therefore crammed four times as full of life and activity. Hence the rapidity with which all things come to pass in it. A very slight cause produces gigantic effects. To aspire ever so little now will bring about greater and more lasting effects for good than at any other time. And, similarly, evil intent has greater powers for evil. These great forces are visibly increased at the close of certain cycles in the Kali Yuga. The present cycle, which closes Nov. 17th, 1897—Feb. 18th, 1898, is one of the most important of any that have been. Opportunities for producing permanent effects for good, in themselves, and in the world as a whole, are given to Theosophists at the present time—opportunities which they may never have again if these are scattered.

XVI

The Masters have written that we are all bound together in one living whole. Hence the thoughts and acts of one react upon all.

Experience has shown that it is true, as said by Masters, that any sincere member in any town can help the T.S. and benefit his fellow townsmen. It is not high learning that is needed, but solely devotion to humanity, faith in Masters, in the Higher Self, a comprehension of the fundamental truths of Theosophy, and a little—only a little—sincere attempt to present those fundamental truths to a people who are in desperate need of them. That attempt should be continuous. No vain striving to preach or prove phenomena will be of any value, for, as again Masters have written, one phenomenon demands another and another.

What the people want is a practical solution of the troubles besetting us, and that solution you have in Theosophy. Will you not try to give it to them more and more and save ——— from the slough it is in?

I would distinctly draw your attention to Brother ———. There is not that complete sympathy and toleration between him and you which there ought to be, and, for the sake of the work, it should be otherwise. You may say that it is his fault. It is not wholly, for you must, also, be somewhat to blame, if not in this life, then from another past one. Can you deny that for a long period he has held up the Branch there? For if he had not, it would have died out, even though you also were necessary agents.

Have any of you had unkind or revengeful feelings to him? If so, ought you not to at once drive them out of your hearts? For I swear to you on my life that if you have been troubled or unfortunate, it is by the reaction from such or similar thoughts about him or others. Drive them all out of your hearts, and present such kindliness and brotherliness to him that he shall, by the force of your living kindness, be drawn into full unity and co-operation with you.

Discussion or proofs to show that you are all right and he wrong avail nothing. We are none of us ever in the right—there is always that in us that causes another to offend. The only discussion should be to the end that you may find out how to present to the world, in your district, one simple, solid, united front.

As to the expression "seeing sounds," this you understand, of course, so far as the statement goes. It records the fact that, at one time, the vibrations which now cause a sound were capable of making a picture—and this they do yet on the astral plane.

XVII

In reply to your question:

Neither the general law nor the Lodge interferes to neutralize the effect of strain upon the disciple's physical energies when caused by undue exertion or want of regularity, except in certain cases. Hence the Theosophist is bound to see that his hours for sleep, work, and recreation are properly arranged and adjusted, since he has no right to live so as to break himself down, and thus deprive the cause he works for of a useful and necessary instrument.

Your friend's energies have been disarranged and somewhat exhausted by irregularities as to rest and recreation, since work has been hard and required rest—whether asleep or awake—has not been had. This causes excitement, which will react (or has) in many different ways in the system and upon the organs. It causes mental excitement, which again raises other disturbance. He, like anyone else, should take measures to insure regularity as to rest, so that what work he does shall be better, and the present excitement subside in his system. It is not wise to remain up late unless for a good purpose, and it is not that to merely remain with others to late hours when nothing good or necessary can be accomplished. Besides other reasons, that is a good one.

Excitement is heat; if heat be applied to heat, more is produced. Coolness must be applied so as to create an equilibrium. This applies in that case, and the establishment of regularity in the matter of rest is the application of coolness. Second, the various exciting and "wrongful" acts or thoughts of others are heat; coolness is to be produced by discharging the mind of those and ceasing to refer to them in words; otherwise the engendered heat will continue. It is needless to refer to reasons resting on points of conduct and example, for those anyone is capable of finding and applying.

As there is no hurry, it is easy to divest the mind of anxiety and the irritation arising from hurry. Again, comparison of one's own work or ways of doing things better than others is wrong and also productive of the heat above spoken of.

XVIII

You are right in thinking that the essential principles of Theosophy are often stated without the use of that name, for it is the universal fundamental system which underlies the religions of every age. The New Testament, rightly understood, teaches Theosophy, and we know that both Jesus and St. Paul were initiates. Of course, in Theosophy, as in any other Science, one understands more as one reads more, and I recommend you to read and digest such of our books as you can conveniently procure.

Now in respect to the questions you ask, let me say that Theosophy requires no man to abandon a mode of life which is not in itself wrong. The use of meat diet is not a sin; it is not even an offence; it is a habit which the race has now largely conformed to, and is not a question of morals or right. At a certain stage of advance as a chela or disciple, the use of meat food has to be abandoned because of its psychical and physiological effects. But you have not reached that stage, nor is it likely that you will for a long time. As the use of meat is not an offence, so neither can be the supply of it to others, so that your assisting in killing hogs for market is in no way opposed to your duty as a man or as a Theosophist. That being your duty in present circumstances, I should recommend you to perform it without hesitation.

Men and women are complementary in character, and therefore adapted to each other. It is natural that each sex should enjoy the company of the other, and what is natural cannot be wrong. Moreover, it is perfectly proper that when a suitable mate is found, a man should marry and settle down as a householder, bringing up a family with right views and high purposes. He contributes a service to humanity, who puts [leaves] children to take his place after his death, and to reproduce his true and altruistic life. Consequently, if you find a suitable match and desire matrimony, there can be no possible reason why you should not carry out such a purpose. Like the abstention from meat, celibacy is essential to advance after a certain stage, but that stage has not yet been reached by you, and you cannot, therefore, be subjected to its conditions. There can be no one rule laid down for all human beings, inasmuch as the temperaments and desires are so different. Each must work out the problem of life in his own way. If your aspirations are so set on higher things that you find the lower a hindrance, it is evident that you should not indulge in the latter; but if you are not so hindered, then no less a duty is yours. You are right in thinking that the essential to all true progress is a wish to conform utterly to the Divine Will, we being certain that we shall be helped in proportion—as is our need.

XIX

Yes, you are right. I am in danger, but that danger is not on the outside, although it is on the outside that attempts are brought forward. And in some sense all those with me are in danger too. It is a danger from ______ which ever tries to forestall the steps of those who travel forward. So, too, my dear, you are in the same sort of danger. But while the danger is there, there is yet encouragement in the fact itself. For we would not be so placed if we had not been so fortunate as to have progressed through work and patience to the point where ______ sees enough in us to try and stop progress and hinder our work. Hence, if they see they cannot stop us, they try all plans to get up strife, so as to nullify our work.

But we will win, for knowing the danger we take measures against it. I am determined not to fail. Others may; but ——— and I will not. Let us, then, await all suffering with confidence and hope. The very fact that you suffer so much is objective evidence of progress, even though so painful, not only to you but to those who love you. So, while I do not say "suffer on," I am comforted by the knowledge that it will be for great good in the future. So I am writing this, instead of machining it, in order that you may feel the force of my love and comradeship.

Let us all draw closer together in mind and heart, soul and act, and try thus to make the true brotherhood through which alone our universal and particular progress can come.

To thee, oh holder of the flame, my love I send. Well, I go again, but never do I forget. My best love and blessing to thee. I cannot speak of these things, but thou knowest.

And now, as formerly, and as now, and as forever and forevermore,

XX

To those I love and who work with me.

My last words before going to the Convention.*

Doubts and questions have arisen as to some things since the present cloud gathered. Among others it has been said it were better that Olcott had left the chair; it would be well for him to go and so on. These views should not be held. If held, they should be dismissed. There are two forces at work in the T.S., as well as in the world and in man. These are the good and the bad. We cannot help this: it is the Law! But we have rules and we have preached of love and truth and kindness; and above all, we have spoken of gratitude, not only of Masters, but among us. Now this applies to these questions as to Olcott, and as well there come in principles of policy. Now let me tell you what one has said to me in whom I believe and whose words I endorse. Thus:

"He retains the position for two reasons: (*a*) To pay a debt of gratitude, (*b*) The T.S. must not *seem* to the outside world to split or to become separate entities. It must remain *one undivided whole solid* from side to side and retaining even its 'incompetent

* Evidently the Convention of 1892. We have completed the text of this letter by reference to the *Theosophical Forum*, August, 1933.—Eds.

president.' It must not be known that he is wholly incapable. He is capable of going on with his small portion of work to the end if well assisted. The work must not fail because here and there *personalities* fall and sin and are unwise. TRUTH remains and IT IS, whoever falls, but the multitude look to the visible leader. If he falls apart like an unjointed puzzle, at once they say, 'there is no truth, nothing which IS'; and the work of a century is ruined and must be again rebuilt from its foundations, and years of backward tendency must come between the wreck of one undertaking and the beginning of another. The same power that overruled his intended resignation and frustrated it, will overrule the present trouble.

"Let me say one thing that I KNOW: Only the feeling of true brotherhood, of true love toward humanity, aroused in the soul of some one strong enough to stem this tide, can carry us through. For LOVE and TRUST are the only weapons that can overcome the REAL enemies against which the true theosophist must fight. If I or you go into this battle from pride, from self-will, from desire to hold our position in the face of the world, from anything but the purest motives, we will fail. Let us search our souls well and look at it as we never looked before. See if in us is the reality of the brotherhood which we preach and which we are supposed to represent."

Let us remember those famous words: "Be ye wise as serpents but harmless as doves." Let us remember the teaching of the Sages that death in the performance of our own duty is preferable to the doing by us of the duty of another, however well we may do the latter: the duty of another is full of danger. Let us be of and for peace, and not for war alone.

Sincerely as ever,
WILLIAM Q. JUDGE

XXI

It is true ______ suffered through my cold and hard feelings. But it was her fault, for I say now as then to ______ that she, absorbed in ______, neglected my members, who are my children, and for whom I wanted her best and got her worst. That made me cold, of course, and I had to fight it, and didn't care if ______ did not like it. I have no time to care. I am glad she has gone to ______.

It is her trial and her chance and when she gets back she can see for herself if she is able to prevent the "big head" from coming on as has happened with others. If she does, then she will have stood the reaction and I have faith she will stand; but still it has to be met. Time comes on sure, and with it trial. H. P. B. was her preparer and comfort, but men are not made into steel by comfort, and note that H. P. B. then died off.

My trip all over this country shows me that it is of more consequence that I should now work up the U. S., where the Masters first worked in this century. It needs all I can do. . . . So, when I have fulfilled my engagement on the English stage, I shall skip back here quickly and do this work. The field is even greater than I thought, although I had a big idea of it. From the United States we can affect the world and they will come to us from all places either for solid work or for help in their need. . . .

Well now, of you: I feel it all. It is up, and down. It is well you are courageous, and to endure you are able. Indeed, endure is the best word, for that is what the oak does when the storms rage: it is better to endure when we can do nothing than to faint and fall. The facts are to be faced. I hope they may turn out otherwise, but if not, it is Karma. Aside from pain, it is the same as anything else. If it comes, it will not last long. Still, I hope it cometh not. I think much of it, but know the bravery of you and the high soul that dwells there. All the time of pain and dogged fighting I know your real self sits up above it all unaffected, and so does mine, and from that let us take comfort. All things in this age move like lightning and so with all our Karma, though mine has so often seemed slow, so far as concerns me. Well, I cannot go on with this. I feel as you do: I stand by you in heart and have often of late sent you messages of hope and power to help you.

I advised ——— to do her part to lessen the constant bringing forward of the name of H. P. B., instead of independent thought on Theosophy. We have too much of it and it is no proof of loyalty, and it gives rise to much of the foolish talk of our dogmatism. You will understand, and may be able to influence some to a more moderate though firm attitude that will not lessen their loyalty and devotion. One good point is that the true chêla does not talk much of his Master and often does not refer to that Master's existence. It has almost become the same as unnecessarily waving the red flag at a bull. Those of us who have experience do not do it; but the younger ones do. X ——— does it here in his speeches and I am going to speak to him of it. If it be not avoided, the first thing we know there will be a split between the H. P. B.'ers and the theosophists *pur sang,* the latter claiming to be the real thing because devoid of any personal element. You and I and ——— do not find it necessary all the time to be flinging her (H. P. B.) in the faces of others, and it is well now to take the warning offered from the outside. Besides, I have had a very strong inside warning on it. My best love, now that we are near Christmas and New Year, and may there be some sunshine to light the path. I send you my love unsullied by a mere gift.

I hope ——— will be firm and proceed as indicated, but she, like us all, must meet her own old enemies in herself.

Again I go, as for evermore,

XXII

Great excitement last night. It was the regular night of ——— T.S. and ——— was to speak. We got there at 8:15, and the hall was full. He began, and had just been fifteen minutes, when it was discovered that the building was on fire. We stopped and let 1,000 people in the various halls get out, then quietly went and none were hurt, only two, ——— and ———, getting a few quarts of water from a burst hose.

It was a queer exit, for we went downstairs beside the elevator, and glass, bricks and water were falling down the light well, while the fire on the top stories of it roared and made a fine light, and streams of fire ran down the oily elevator pipes on the other side; and firemen pulled up hose neck or nothing as we got away. It was ———'s own meeting, and it ended in fire! None of the great psychics present had had the remotest premonition, but one invented afterwards an *ex post facto* sense of terror.

Tell ——— the time has passed for him to vacillate; he knows his guru—she was and is H. P. B. Let him reflect ere he does that which, in wrecking her life and fame, will wreck his own life by leaving him where nothing that is true may be seen. . . . Silence is useful, now and then, but silence sometimes is a thing that speaks too loud. I am his friend and will help. No one can hurt him but himself; his work and sacrifice were noble and none can point at him.

See what I said in the opening volume of *The Path:* the study of what is now called "practical occultism" was not the object of that journal. "We regard it as incidental to the journey along the path. The traveller, in going from one city to another, has perhaps to cross several rivers; maybe his conveyance fails him and he is obliged to swim, or he must, in order to pass a great mountain, know engineering in order to tunnel through it, or is compelled to exercise the art of locating his exact position by observation of the sun: but all that is only incidental to his main object of reaching his destination. We admit the existence of hidden, powerful forces in nature, and believe that every day greater progress is made towards an understanding of them. Astral body formation, clairvoyance, looking into the astral light, and controlling elementals is all possible, but not all profitable. The electrical current, which when resisted in the carbon produces intense light, may be brought into existence by any ignoramus who has the key to the engine-room and can turn the crank that starts the dynamo, but is unable to prevent his fellow man or himself from being instantly killed, should that current accidentally be diverted through his body. The control of these hidden forces is not easily obtained, nor can phenomena be produced without danger, and, in our view, the attainment of true wisdom is not by means of phenomena, but through the development which begins within.

"True occultism is clearly set forth in the *Bhagavat Gita* and *Light on the Path,* where sufficient stress is laid upon practical occultism, but, after all, Krishna says, the kingly science and the kingly mystery is devotion to and study of the light which comes from within. The very first step in true mysticism and true occultism is to try to apprehend the meaning of Universal Brotherhood, without which the very highest progress in the practise of magic turns to ashes in the mouth.

"We appeal, therefore, to all who wish to raise themselves and their fellow creatures—man and beast—out of the thoughtless jog-trot of selfish everyday life. It is not thought that Utopia can be established in a day; but, through the spreading of the idea of Universal Brotherhood, the truth in all things may be discovered. What is wanted is true knowledge of the spiritual condition of man, his aim, and destiny. Such a study leads us to accept the utterance of Prajapati to his sons: 'Be restrained, be liberal, be merciful; it is the death of selfishness'."

This is the line for us to take and to persevere in, that all may in time obtain the true light.

EXTRACTS

ON THEOSOPHY AND THE T.S.

All the work that any of us do anywhere redounds to the interest and benefit of the whole T.S., and for that reason we know that we are united.

The Self is one and all-powerful, but it must happen to the seeker from time to time that he or she shall feel the strangeness of new conditions; this is not a cause for fear. If the mind is kept intent on the Self and not diverted from it, and comes to see the Self in all things, no matter what, then fear should pass away in time. I would therefore advise you to study and meditate over the *Bhagavad Gita,* which is a book that has done me more good than all others in the whole range of books, and is the one that can be studied all the time.

This will do more good than anything—if the great teachings are silently assimilated and put into action, for it goes to the very root of things and gives the true philosophy of life.

If you try to put into practice what in your inner life you hold to be right, you will be more ready to receive helpful thoughts and the inner life will grow more real. I hope with you that your home may become a strong centre of work for Theosophy.

You want to know the inner situation of the T.S. Well, it is just this: we have all worked along for eighteen years, and the T.S. as a body has its karma as well as each one in it. Those in it who have worked hard, of course, have their own karma, and have brought themselves to a point ahead of the T.S. Now, if the branches are weak in their knowledge of Theosophy, and in their practise of its precepts and their understanding of the whole thing, the body is in the situation of the child who has been growing too fast for its strength; if that be the case it is bound to have a check. For my part I do not want any great rush, since I too well know how weak even those long in it are. As to individuals, say you, ——— and so on. By reason of hard and independent work you have got yourselves in the inner realm just where you may soon begin to get the attention of the Black Magicians, who then begin to try to knock you out, so beware. Attempts will be silently made to arouse irritation, and to increase it where it now exists. So the only thing to do is to live as much as possible in the higher nature, and each one to crush out the small and trifling ebullitions of the lower nature which ordinarily are overlooked; thus strength is gained in the whole nature, and the efforts of the enemy made nil. This is of the highest importance, and if not attended to it will be sad. This is what I had in view in all the letters I have sent to you and others. I hope you will be able to catch hold of men, here and there, who will take the right, true, solid view, and thus be left behind you as good men and good agents.

———

When I was in ——— I broached to you and others the plan of getting Theosophy to the working people. Has anything been done? It must be simply put. It can be understood. It is important. Let us see if this thing cannot be done—you all promised to go to work at it. Why not, like the Bible man, turn from all these people who will not come, to the byways and hedges? Then I feel sure that, if managed right, a lot of people who believe in Theosophy but don't want to come out for it, would help such a movement, seeing that it would involve talking to the poor and giving them sensible stuff. If need be, I'd hold a meeting every night, and not give them abstractions. Add music, if possible, etc. Now let me hear your ideas. Time rolls on, and many queer social changes are on the way.

———

I have your long letter from ——— and you are right as to conduct of Branches. No Branch should depend on one person, for if so, it will slump, sure; nor on two or three either. Here they depended on me for a long time, and my bad health in voice for a year was a good thing as it made the others come forward. ——— is right enough in his way, but certainly he ought to be fitting himself for something in addition to speaking, as the T.S. has to have a head as well as a tongue; and if a man knows he is bad at business, he should mortify himself by making himself learn it, and thus get good discipline. We sadly need at all places some true enthusiasts. But all that will come in time. The main thing is for the members to study and know Theosophy, for if they do not know it how can they give any of it to others? Of course, at all times most of the work falls upon the few, as is always the case, but effort should be made, as you say, to bring out other material.

. . . I am abundantly sure that you are quite correct in saying that it is the Branches which work that flourish, and that those addicted to "Parlour Talks" soon squabble and dwindle. You have gone right to the root of the matter. So, also, I agree with you, heart and soul, in what you say as to the policy of a timid holding and setting forth of Theosophy. Nothing can be gained by such a policy, and all experience points to energy and decision as essential to any real advance.

You are, I think, quite right to attempt to get all members to work for their individual advance, by working for their Branches. By doing things in this way, they provide an additional safeguard for themselves, while forming a centre from which Theosophical thought can radiate out, to help and encourage others who are only beginning their upward way.

I find that you state my view exactly. That view is that the A B C of Theosophy should be taught all the time, and this, not only for the sake of outsiders, but also for the sake of the members who are, I very well know, not so far along as to need the elaborate work all the time. And it is just because the members are not well grounded that they are not able themselves to get in more inquirers. Just as you say, if the simple truths practically applied as found in Theosophy are presented, you will catch at last some of the best people—real workers and valuable members. And Theosophy can best be presented in a simple form by one who has mastered the elements as well as "the nature of the Absolute." It is just this floating in the clouds which sometimes prevents a Branch from getting on. And I fully agree, also, that if the policy I have referred to should result temporarily in throwing off some few persons it would be a benefit, for you would find others coming to take their places. And I can agree with you, furthermore, out of actual experience.

You by no means need to apologize for asking my attention to the matter of your joining the Theosophical Society. It is my great desire and privilege to give to all sincere enquirers whatever information I may possess, and certainly there can be no greater pleasure than to further the internal progress of any real student and aspirant. I think you quite right in wishing to identify yourself with the Theosophical Society, not only because that is the natural and obvious step for anyone sincerely interested; but also because each additional member with right spirit strengthens the body for its career and work.

In taking advantage of an opportunity to introduce Theosophy into the secular press, you are doing exactly the work which is so invaluable to the Society, and which I so constantly urge upon our members. It is in this way that so very many persons are reached who would otherwise be quite inaccessible, and the amount of good which seed thus sown can accomplish is beyond our comprehension. You have my very hearty approval of and encouragement in your work, and I am very sure that that work will not be without fruit.

NEW YORK, *October 11th, 1892.*—This is the era of *Western* Occultism. We are now to stand shoulder to shoulder in the U.S. to present it and enlarge it in view of coming cussedness—attacks which will be in the line of trying to impose solely Eastern disciples on us. The Masters are not Eastern nor Western, but universal.

I shall be glad to give you any information possible respecting Theosophy and the Theosophical Society, but I think you err in supposing that the purpose of either is to encourage the study of what is known as the Occult Arts. Knowledge concerning, and control of, the finer forces of nature are not things which should be sought after at our elementary stage of progress; nor would such attainment be appropriate, even if possible, to anyone who had not thoroughly mastered the principles of Theosophy itself.

Mere desire for powers is a form of selfishness, and receives no encouragement from our Teachers. Mme. Blavatsky stated this matter very clearly indeed in an article published in *Lucifer,* entitled "Occultism *versus* the Occult Arts."* When persons without a large preliminary training in the real Wisdom-Religion seek knowledge on the Occult plane, they are very apt, from inexperience and inadequate culture, to drift into black magic. I have no power to put you into communication with any adept to guide you in a course of Occult study, nor would it be a service to you if the thing were possible. The Theosophical Society was not established for any such purpose, nor could anyone receive instructions from an adept until he was ripe for it. In other words, he must undergo a long preliminary training in knowledge, self-control, and the subjugation of the lower nature before he would be in any way fit for instruction on the higher planes. What I recommend you to do is to study the elementary principles of Theosophy, and gain some idea of your own nature as a human being and as an individual, but drop entirely all ambition for knowledge of powers which would be inappropriate to your present stage, and to correct your whole conception of Theosophy and Occultism.

On Masters

I think the way for all western theosophists is through H. P. B. I mean that as she is the T.S. incarnate—its mother and guardian, its creator — the Karmic laws would naturally provide that all who drew this life through her belonged to her, and if they denied her, they need not hope to reach ———, for how can they deny her who gave this doctrine to the western world? They share her Karma to little purpose, if they think they can get round this identification and benefit, and ——— want no better proof that a man does not comprehend their philosophy. This would, of course, bar him from ——— by natural laws (of growth). I do not mean that in the ordinary business sense she must forward their applications or their merits; I mean that they who do not under-

* *Lucifer,* May, 1888. Reprinted in *Theosophy,* XXXI, 149.—Eds.

stand the basic mutual relation, who undervalue *her* gift and *her* creation, have not imbibed the teaching and cannot assimilate its benefits.

She must be understood as being what she is to the T.S., or Karma (the law of compensation, or of cause and effect) is not understood, nor the first laws of occultism. People ought to *think* of this: we are too much given to supposing that events are chances, or have no connection with ourselves—each event is an effect of the Law.

What should be done is to realize that "the Master-Soul is one," with all that that implies; to know the meaning of the old teaching, "Thou art That." When this is done we may with impunity identify our consciousness with that of anything in nature; not before. But to do this is a lifetime's work, and beforehand we have to exhaust all Karma, which means duty; we must live for others and then we will find out all we *should* know, not what we would *like* to know.

Devotion and aspiration will, and do, help to bring about a proper attitude of mind, and to raise the student to a higher plane; also, they secure for the student help which is unseen by him, for devotion and aspiration put the student into a condition in which aid can be given to him, though he may, as yet, be unconscious of it. But conscious communication with one's Master can only be accomplished after *long* training and study. What a student has to do, and is able to do, is to fit himself to receive this training.

The recognition from a Guru will come when you are ready, and my advice to you is that, if possible, you put away from yourself the desire for such recognition, for such desire will hinder you. If you will read the *Bhagavad Gîtâ,* especially chapters ii. and iii., I think you will find much to help you. There it says: "Let, then, the motive for action be in the action itself, not in the event. Do not be incited to actions by the hope of their reward . . . perform thy duty . . . and laying aside all desire for any benefit to thyself from action, make the event equal to thee, whether it be success or failure." It is but natural that a student should hope for recognition from a Master, but this desire is to be put aside, and that work is to be done which lies before each. At the same time, each one knows that the effect follows the cause; hence, whatever our due, we shall receive it at the right time.

Every Chêla (and we are all that once we determine to be) has these same difficulties. Patience and fortitude! For an easy birth is not always a good one. The kingdom of heaven is taken only by violence, and not by weakness of attack. Your constant aspiration preserved in secret has led you to that point where just these troubles come to all. Console yourself with the thought that others have been in the same place and have lived through it by patience and fortitude. . . . Fix your thoughts again on Those Elder Brothers, work for Them, serve Them, and They will help through the right appropriate means and no other. To meditate on the Higher Self is difficult. Seek, then, the bridge—the Masters. "Seek the truth by strong search," by doing service, and by enquiry, and Those who know the Truth will teach it. Give up doubt, and arise in your place with patience and fortitude. Let the warrior fight, the gentle yet fierce Krishna, who, when he finds thee as his disciple and his friend, will tell thee the truth and lighten up the darkness with the lamp of spiritual knowledge.

Attacks cannot hurt: they must needs come, but all we have to do is to keep right on, working steadily, and Masters will see after the rest. For, that which is done in Their name will come right; and this whole thing has arisen because I have chosen to proclaim my personal belief in the existence of these beings of grandeur. So, let us shake again with the confidence born from the knowledge of the wisdom of the Unseen Leaders, and we go forth once more, separately, again to the work, even if not to meet until another incarnation is ours. But, meeting then, we shall be all the stronger for having kept faith now.

I am glad that you have such a faith in the Great Workers who are behind us. They *are* behind us, to my personal knowledge, and not behind me only, but behind all sincere workers. I know that their desire is that each should listen to the voice of his inner self and not depend too much on outside people, whether they be Masters, Eastern disciples or what not. By a dependence of that kind you become at last thoroughly independent, and then the unseen helpers are able to help all the more.

We are all human, and thus weak and sinful. If, in one respect, we are better than others, then, in some other way, they are better than we are. We would be self-righteous to judge others by our own standard. . . . Are we so wise as never to act foolishly? Not at all. . . . Indeed I have come to the conclusion that in this nineteenth century a pledge is no good, because everyone reserves to himself the right to break it, if he finds after a while that it is galling, or that it puts him in some attitude inconsistent with something he may have said or done at some other time. . . . In ———'s case, . . . everyone should never think but the very best, no matter what the evidences are. Why, if the Masters were to judge us exactly as They must know we are, then good-bye at once! We would all be sent packing. But Masters deal kindly with us in the face of greater knowledge of our faults and evil thoughts from which none are yet exempt. This is my view, and you will please me much if you are able to turn to the same [view], and to spread it among those on the inside who have it not. It is easy to do well by those we like; it is our duty to make ourselves do and think well by those we do not like. Masters say we think in grooves, and but few have the courage to fill those up and go on other lines. Let us who are willing to make the attempt try to fill up these grooves, and make new and better ones.

. . . Keep up your courage, faith, and charity. *Those who can to any extent assimilate the Master, to that extent they are the representatives of the Master, and have the help of the Lodge in its work.* . . . Bear up, firm heart, be strong, be bold and kind, and spread your strength and boldness.

H. P. B. then said that it is by falling and by failing that we learn, and we cannot hope to be at once great and wise and wholly strong. She and the Masters behind expected this from all of us; she and They never desired any of us to work blindly, but only desired that we work unitedly.

H. P. B. wrote me in 1890: "Be more charitable for others than for yourself, and more severe on yourself than on others." This is good advice. A strain always weakens the fibres and produces friction. I hope all misunderstandings will fly away.

On Occult Philosophy

Begin by trying to conquer the habit, almost universal, of pushing yourself forward. This arises from personality. Do not monopolize the conversation. Keep in the background. If someone begins to tell you about himself and his doings, do not take first chance to tell him about yourself, but listen to him and talk solely to bring him out. And when he has finished, suppress in yourself the desire to tell about yourself, your opinions and experiences. Do not ask a question unless you intend to listen to the answer and inquire into its value. Try to recollect that you are a very small affair in the world, and that the people around do not value you at all and grieve not when you are absent. Your only true greatness lies in your inner true self and it is not desirous of obtaining the applause of others. If you will follow these directions for one week you will find they will take considerable effort, and you will begin to discover a part of the meaning of the saying, "Man, know thyself."

It is not necessary to be conscious of the progress one has made. Nor is the date in any sense an extinguisher, as some have styled it.* In these days we are too prone to wish to know everything all at once, especially in relation to ourselves. It may be desirable and encouraging to be thus conscious, but it is not necessary. We make a good deal of progress in our inner, hidden life of which we are not at all conscious. We do not know of it until some later

* The "date" rumored (wrongly) to be the "extinguisher" was 1897. (Compare LETTERS, p. 97.) See two articles by Mr. Judge: "Will Master's Help be Withdrawn in 1898 till 1975?" in the *Path*, November, 1894, and "The Closing Cycle," in the *Irish Theosophist*, January, 1895. Both articles were republished, under the second title, in *Theosophy*, XXXII, 81.—Eds.

life. So, in this case, many may be quite beyond the obstacles and not be conscious of it. It is best to go on with duty, and to refrain from this trying to take stock and measuring of progress. All of our progress is in the inner nature, and not in the physical where lives the brain, and from which the present question comes. The apparent physical progress is evanescent. It is ended when the body dies, at which time, if the inner man has not been allowed to guide us, the natural record against us will be a cipher, or "failure." Now, as the great Adepts live in the plane of our inner nature, it must follow that they might be actively helping every one of us after the date referred to, and we, as physical brain men, not be conscious of it on this plane.

. . . I strongly advise you to give up all yoga practices, which in almost all cases have disastrous results unless guided by a competent teacher. The concussions and explosions in your head are evidences that you are in no fit condition to try yoga practices, for these effects result from lesions of the brain, *i.e.*, from the bursting of the very minute brain cells. I am glad you have written to me upon this matter, that I may have an opportunity of warning you. Also, I advise you to discontinue concentration on the vital centres, which again may prove dangerous unless under the guidance of a teacher. You have learnt, to a certain degree, the power of concentration, and the greatest help will now come to you from concentration upon the Higher Self, and aspiration toward the Higher Self. Also, if you will take some subject or sentence from the *Bhagavad Gîtâ,* and concentrate your mind upon that and meditate upon it, you will find much good result from it, and there is no danger in such concentration.

As to the question about the disintegration of the astral body and the length of time beforehand when it could be seen: My answer was not meant to be definite as to years, except that I gave a period of two years as a long one before the death of the physical body. There are cases—perhaps rare—in which five years before the death of the physical, a clairvoyant has seen the disintegration of the astral beginning. The idea intended to be conveyed is that, regardless of periods of time, if the man is going to die naturally (and that includes by disease), the corruption, disintegrating or breaking up of the astral body may be perceived by those who can see in that way. Hence the question of years is not involved. Violent deaths are not included in this, because the astral in such cases does not disintegrate beforehand. And the way of seeing such a death in advance is by another method altogether. Death from old age—which is the natural close of a cycle—is included in the answer as to death by disease, which might be called the disease of inability to fight off the ordinary breaking-up of the cohesive forces.

You cannot develop the third eye. It is too difficult, and until you have cleared up a good deal more on philosophy it would be useless, and a useless sacrifice is a crime of folly. But here is advice given by many Adepts: every day and as often as you can, and on going to sleep and as you wake—think, think, think, on the truth that you are not body, brain, or astral man, but that you are THAT, and "THAT" is the Supreme Soul. For by this practice you will gradually kill the false notion which lurks inside that the false is the true, and the true, the false. By persistence in this, by submitting your daily thoughts each night to the judgment of your Higher Self, you will at last gain light.

Now as to *The Voice of the Silence,** and the cycles of woe (undergone by the Arhan who remains to help mankind), it is easy to understand. You must always remember, when reading such things, that terms must be used which the reader will understand. Hence, speaking thus, it must be said that there are such cycles of woe—from our standpoint—just as the fact that I have no amusements, and nothing but work in the T.S., seems a great penance to those who like their pleasures. I, on the contrary, take pleasure and peace in the "self-denial," as they call it. Therefore, it must follow that he who enters the secret Path finds his peace and pleasure in endless work for ages for Humanity. But, of course, with his added sight and knowledge, he must always be seeing the self-inflicted miseries of men. The mistake you make is to give the person thus "sacrificed" the same small qualities and longings as we now have, whereas the wider sweep and power of soul make what we call sacrifice and woe seem something different. Is not this clear, then? If it were stated otherwise than as

* By H. P. Blavatsky. (Orig. Pub., 1889.)—Eds.

the *Voice* has it, you would find many making the vow and then breaking it; but he who makes the vow with the full idea of its misery will keep it.

If we can all accumulate a fund of good for all the others we will thus dissipate many clouds. The follies and the so-called sins of people are really things that are sure to come to nothing if we treat them right. We must not be so prone as are the people of the day, of whom we are some, to criticize others and forget the beam in our own eye. The *Bhagavad Gîtâ* and Jesus are right in that they both show us how to do our own duty and not go into that of others. Every time we think that someone else has done wrong we should ask ourselves two questions:

(1) Am I the judge in this matter who is entitled to try this person?

(2) Am I any better in my way? Do I, or do I not offend in some other way just as much as they do in this?

This will settle the matter, I think. And in . . . there ought to be no judgments and no criticism. If some offend, then let us ask what is to be done, but only when the offence is against the whole. When an offence is against *us*, then let it go. This is thought by some to be "goody-goody," but I tell you the heart, the soul, and the bowels of compassion are of more consequence than intellectuality. The latter will take us all sure to hell if we let it govern only. Be sure of this and try as much as you can to spread the true spirit in all directions, or else not only will there be individual failure, but also the circle H. P. B. made as a nucleus for possible growth will die, rot, fail, and come to nothing.

It is not possible to evade the law of evolution, but that law need not always be carried out in *one* way. If the same result is produced, it is enough. Hence, in any one hour or minute, the being attaining adeptship could pass through countless experiences *in effect*. But, as a fact, no one becomes an adept until he has in some previous time gone through the exact steps needed. If you and I, for instance, miss adeptship in this *Manvantara*, we shall emerge again to take up the work at a corresponding point in the much higher development of the next, although then we may seem low down in the scale—viewing us from the standard then to prevail.

The law is this. No man can rush on and fail to escape the counter current, and in proportion as he rushes, so will be the force of the current. All members who work hard come at last to the notice of the Lodge, and the moment they do so, the Black Lodge also takes notice; hence, questions arise, and we are tried in subtle ways that surpass sight, but are strong for the undoing of him who is not prepared—by right thought and sacrifice to the higher nature—for the fight. I tell you this. It may sound mysterious, but it is the truth, and at this time we are all bound to feel the forces at work, for as we grow, so the other side gets ready to oppose.

Be sure that you understand me right about the Black side. I mean this: when men work along a good while, and really raise themselves up by that, they get the attention of the Black if they are of sufficient importance for it. I have their attention, and it makes a trouble now and then. What we all want to have, then, is the best armour for such a fight, and that is patience. Patience is a great thing, and will work in more ways than one, not only in personal life, but in wider concerns.

The difficulty of remembering the things you read, and the like, may be due to one or many causes. First, it indicates the need of mental discipline in the way of compelling yourself to serious reading and thinking, even though for a short time each day. If persisted in, this will gradually change the mental action, just as one can alter the taste for different sorts of food taken into the body. Again, if you have been dealing in what is known as Mind Cure or Metaphysical Healing, you should avoid it, because it will increase the difficulty you mention. It is different from good, ordinary, mental discipline. And also if you have been in any way following Spiritualism or indulging in psychic thoughts or visions or experiences, these would be a cause for the trouble, and should be abandoned.

There is no need for you to be a despairer. Reflect on that old verse, "What room is there for sorrow and what room for doubt in him who knows that the Self is one, and that all things are the

Self, only differing in degree." This is a free rendering, but is what it means. Now, it is true that a man cannot force himself at once into a new will and into a new belief, but by thinking much on the same thing—such as this—he soon gets a new will and a new belief, and from it will come strength and also light. Try this plan. It is purely occult, simple, and powerful. I hope all will be well, and that as we are shaken up from time to time we shall grow strong.

_______'s article strove to show that H. P. B. did not teach the doctrine of reincarnation in '77, as she did later, which is quite true so far as the public was then concerned. But she did teach it to me and others, then as now.* Further, it seems clear what she meant, to wit, that there is no reincarnation for the astral monad, which is the astral man; and, it being a theosophical doctrine that the astral man does not reincarnate save in exceptional cases, she taught then the same thing as she did later. H. P. B. told me personally many times of the real doctrine of reincarnation, enforced by the case of the death of my own child, so I know what she thought and believed.

I am not able to give you the definition which you ask for, as it seems to me, spirit cannot be defined except in this way, that the whole universe is made of spirit and matter, both constituting together the Absolute. What is not in matter is spirit, and what is not in spirit is matter; but there is no particle of matter without spirit, and no particle of spirit without matter. If this attempted definition is correct, you will see that it is impossible to define the things of the spirit, and that has always been said by the great teachers of the past.

What a petty lot of matter we spend time on, when so much is transitory. After a hundred years what will be the use of all this? Better that a hundred years hence a principle of freedom and an

* See " 'Isis Unveiled' and Reincarnation," a *Forum* answer by W.Q.J. in October, 1893 (reprinted in *Theosophy*, XV, 132) and also H.P.B.'s own statements: " 'Isis Unveiled' and the 'Theosophist' on Reincarnation," in the *Theosophist*, August, 1882, and "Theories About Reincarnation and Spirits," the *Path*, November, 1886 (reprinted in *Theosophy*, II, 243).—Eds.

impulse of work should have been established. The small errors of a life are nothing, but the general sum of thought is much. . . . I care everything for the unsectarianism that H. P. B. died to start, and which is now threatened in its own house. Is it not true that Masters have forbidden Their chelâs to tell under what orders they act, for fear of the black shadow that follows innovations? Yes. . . .

Am very sorry to hear that your health is not good. In reply to your question: A sound body is not expected, because our race is unsound everywhere. It is Karma. Of course a correct mental and moral position will at last bring a sound body, but the process may, and often does, involve sickness. Hence sickness may be a blessing on two planes: (1) the mental and moral, by opening the nature, and (2) on the physical, as being the discharge into this plane of an inner sickness of the inner being.

The question of sex is not the most difficult. The personal one is still harder. I mean the purely personal, that relating to "me." The sexual really relates only to a low plane gratification. If Nature can beat you there, then she need not try the other, and *vice versa;* if she fails on the personal she may attempt the other, but then with small chance of success.

We all differ and must agree to disagree, for it is only by balancing contrary things that equilibrium (harmony) is obtained. Harmony does not come through likeness. If people will only let each other alone and go about their own business quietly all will be well. . . . It is one's duty to try to find one's own duty and not to get into the duty of another. And in this it is of the highest importance that we should detach our *minds* (as well as our tongues) from the duties and acts of others whenever those are outside of our own. If you can find this fine line of action and inaction you will have made great progress.

Do not stop to consider your progress at all, because that is the way to stop it; but take your mind off the question of your progress and do the best you can. I hope you will be able to acquire in no long time that frame of mind which you so much desire. I think you will acquire it if you will take your mind off yourself as much as possible, and throw it into something for someone else, which would, in course of time, destroy the self impression.

I regret exceedingly all your troubles and difficulties. They are all, it goes without saying, matters of Karma, and must right themselves in process of time. Meantime, your work and duty lie in continuing patient and persevering throughout. The troubles of your friends and relatives are not your Karma, though intimately associated with it by reason of the very friendship and relation. In the lives of all who aspire to higher things there is a more or less rapid precipitation of old Karma, and it is this which is affecting you. It will go off shortly, and you will have gained greatly in having gotten rid of a troublesome piece of business.

As it will take many a life for one to overcome the personal nature, there is no good in imagining what things and thoughts would then be like. It is certain that, in the long journey, the whole nature changing, it is adjusted to all conditions. Many of those matters which we call the woes of others are really nothing at all, and only "skin deep"; the real woe of the race is not that.

By setting apart a *particular* time for meditation, a habit is formed, and, as the time comes round, the mind will after a while become trained, so that meditation at the particular time will become natural. Hence, it will be well for you to keep to the same hour as far as possible.

You ask if I was at —— where you saw me. Let me tell you something in confidence. I am around at all places, but, of course, most at such as where you, ——, and others like that are, but, it is not necessary for me to remember it at all, as it is done without that, since this brain has enough to do here. To remember, I should have to retire and devote myself to that, and it would make things no better.

A college course is not necessary for occultism. One of the best occultists I know was never in college. But if a man adds good learning to intuition and high aspiration he is naturally better off than another. I am constantly in the habit of consulting the dictionary and of thinking out the meanings and the correlations of words. Do the same. It is good.

The old mission of the Rosicrucians, though dead on the outside, is not dead, for the Masters were in that as They are in this, and it may be possible to usher in a new era of western occultism devoid of folly. We should all be ready for that, if it be possible.

In regard to the pictures which you see, observe them with indifference, relying always on the Higher Self, and looking to it for knowledge and light—pictures or no pictures.

On Work

Yes, that business is already a "back number," stale and unprofitable. I have found that work tells. While others fume and fret and sleep, and now and then start up to criticize, if you go right on and work, and let time, the great devourer, do the other work, you will see that, in a little while, the others will wake up once more to find themselves "left," as they say in the land of slang. Do, then, that way. Your own duty is hard enough to find out, and by attending to that you gain, no matter how small the duty may be. The duty of another is full of danger. May you have the light to see and to do! Tell ——— to remember to work to the end to make himself an instrument for good work. Times change, men go here and there, and places need to be filled by those who can do the best sort of work, who are full of the fire of devotion, and who have the right basis, and a sure and solid one for themselves. My love to all.

I am very sorry that so many efforts on your part to influence the public press have been unsuccessful, but I feel sure that you will ultimately be successful. I am inclined to think that you will almost certainly find that articles written by Theosophists on the spot will obtain more ready admission than if you send them articles which have already been printed.

They have a more local colouring, and therefore a greater local interest. . . . I feel sure that by persistent and steady work, such as you are doing, you will win your way, and that even the most conservative papers will find it to their interest to insert articles.

Both ———— and ———— are two weak, half-corroded spots. It is due to (*a*) gossip about others, including me and others in the three lands; (*b*) to the personal element; (*c*) most of all to the absence of real faith in the Masters, for wherever that is not strong the work goes down; (*d*) to a sort of fear of public opinion; (*e*) to incomplete grasp of the elementary truths; and so on.

Stick to it that the way is to do all you can and let the results go. You have nothing to do with results; the other side will look out for that. This is really the culmination of the work of ages, and it would be a poor thing, indeed, if the Lodge had to depend alone on our puny efforts. Hence, go on and keep the spirit that you have only to proceed, and leave the rest to time and the Lodge. If all the other members had the same idea, it would be better for the old T.S. But let us hope on, for we have some any way, and that is more than none.

You are right, too, about *The Secret Doctrine*: it is a mine, and is the magazine for the warrior Theosophists, which is the description of you and me and some others.

Let us all be as silent as we may be, and work, work; for as the enemy rages, they waste time, while work shines forth after all is over, and we will see that as they fought we were building. Let that be our watchword. . . . I hope no weak souls will be shaken off their base. If they get on their *own* base they will not be shaken off.

On Wisdom in Action

This is the right conclusion, to let all talk and other people's concerns slip by and not meddle. No one should be taking information to another, for it fans a flame, and now we have to ignore everything and just work on, be good and kind and, like St. Paul's charity, overlook all things. Retire into your own silence and let all others be in the hands of Karma, as we all are. "Karma takes care of its own." It is better to have no side, for it is all for the Master and He will look out for all if each does just right, even if, to their view, another seems not to do so. By our not looking at their errors too closely, the Master will be able to clear it all off and make it work well. The plan of quiet passive resistance, or rather, laying under the wind, is good and ought to work in all attacks. Retreat within your own heart and there keep firmly still. Resist without resisting. It is possible and should be attained. Once more, *au revoir* only, no matter what may happen, even irresistible Death itself. Earthquakes here yesterday: these signify some souls of use have come into the world somewhere; but where?

Well, now, just at this minute I do not know exactly what to say. Why not take up an easy and fluidic position in the matter? An occultist is never fixed on any particular mortal plan. So do not fix your mind as yet on a plan. Wait. All things come to him who waits in the right way. Make yourself in every way as good an instrument for any sort of work as you can. Every little thing I ever learned I have now found out to be of use to me in this work of ours. Ease of manner and of speech are of the best to have. Ease of mind and confidence are better than all in this work of dealing with other men—that is, with the human heart. The more wise one is the better he can help his fellows, and the more cosmopolitan he is the better, too. . . . When the hour strikes it will then find you ready; no man knows when the hour will strike. But he has to be ready. You see, Jesus was in fact an occultist, and in the parable of the foolish virgins gave a real occult ordinance. It is a good one to follow. Nothing is gained, but a good deal is lost, by impatience—not only strength, but also sight and intuition. So decide nothing hastily. Wait; make no set plan.

Wait for the hour to make the decision, for if you decide in advance of the time you tend to raise a confusion. So have patience, courage, hope, faith, and cheerfulness.

The very first step towards being positive and self-centered is in the cheerful performance of duty. Try to take pleasure in doing what is your duty, and especially in the *little* duties of life. When doing any duty put your whole heart into it. There is much in this life that is bright if we would open our eyes to it. If we recognize this, then we can bear the troubles that come to us calmly and patiently, for we know that they will pass away.

. . . You can solidify your character by attending to small things. By attacking small faults, and on every small occasion, one by one. This will arouse the inner attitude of attention and caution. The small faults and small occasions being conquered, the character grows strong. Feelings and desires are not wholly of the body. If the *mind* is deliberately taken off such subjects and placed on other and better ones, then the whole body will follow the mind and grow tractable. This struggle must be kept up, and after a while it will be easier. Old age makes only this difference—the machine of body is less strong; in old age the thoughts are the same, if we let them grow without pruning.

There is never any need to worry. The good law looks out for all things, and all we have to do is our duty as it comes along from day to day. Nothing is gained by worrying about matters and about the way people do not respond. In the first place, you do not alter people, and in the second, by being anxious as to things, you put an occult obstacle in the way of what you want done. It is better to acquire a lot of what is called carelessness by the world, but is in reality a calm reliance on the law, and a doing of one's own duty, satisfied that the results must be right, no matter what they may be. Think that over, and try to make it a part of your inner mind that it is no use to worry; that things will be all right, no matter what comes, and that you are resolved to do what you see before you, and trust to Karma for all the rest.

I am sorry to hear that you are passing through what you mention. Yet you knew it would have to come, and one learns, and the purpose of life is to learn. It is all made up of learning. So, though it is hard, it is well to accept it, as you say.

Do you know what it is to resist without resistance?

That means, among other things, that too great an expenditure of strength, of "fortitude," is not wise. If one fights, one is drawn into the swirl of events and thoughts, instead of leaning back on the great ocean of the Self which is never moved. Now you see that. So, lean back and look on at the ebb and flow of life that washes to our feet and away again many things that are not easy to lose nor pleasant to welcome. Yet they all belong to Life, to the Self. The wise man has no personal possessions.

Anyway, you are right that struggling is wrong. Do it quietly—that is the way the Masters do it. The reaction the other way is just as you say, but the Master has so much wisdom He is seldom, if ever, the prey of reactions. That is why He goes slowly. But it is sure. . . . I know how the clouds come and go. That is all right; just wait, as the song says, till they roll by.

Arouse, arouse in you the meaning of "Thou art That." Thou art the Self. This is the thing to think of in meditation, and if you believe it, then tell others the same. You have read it before, but now try to realize it more and more each day, and you will have the light you want. . . . If you will look for wisdom you will get it sure, and that is all you want or need. Am glad all looks well. It would always look well if each and all minded their own things and kept the mind free from all else.

Patience is really the best and most important thing, for it includes many. You cannot have it if you are not calm and ready for the emergency, and as calmness is the one thing necessary for the spirit to be heard, it is evident how important patience is. It also prevents one from precipitating a thing, for by precipitation we may smash a good egg or a good plan, throw the Karma off for the time, and prevent certain good effects flowing. So, keep right on, and try for patience in all the very smallest things of life every day, and you will find it growing very soon, and with it will come greater strength and influence on and for others, as well as greater and clearer help from the inner side of things.

For the love of heaven do not take any tales or information from any person to any other. The man who brought news to the king was sometimes killed. The surest way to make trouble out of nothing is to tell about it from one to another. Construe the words of the *Gîtâ* about one's own duty to mean that you have nothing to do in the smallest particular with other people's fancies, tales, facts, or other matters, as you will have enough to do to look out for your own duty. . . . Too much, too much, trying to force harmony. Harmony comes from a balancing of diversities, and discord from any effort to make harmony by force. . . . In all such things I never meddle, but say to myself it is none of my affair at all, and wait till it *comes to me*—and thank God if it never arrives! And that is a good rule for you.

Think of these points:

(*a*) Criticism should be abandoned. It is no good. Co-operation is better than criticism. The duty of another is dangerous for one whose duty it is not. The insidious coming of unbrotherly criticism should be warned against, prevented, stopped. By example you can do much, as also by word in due season.

(*b*) Calmness is now a thing to be had, to be preserved. No irritation should be let dwell inside. It is a deadly foe. Sit on all the small occasions that evoke it and the greater ones will never arise to trouble you.

(*c*) Solidarity.

(*d*) Acceptation of others.

It is not wise to be always analyzing our faults and failures—to regret is waste of energy. If we endeavour to use all our energy in service of the Cause, we shall find ourselves rising above our faults and failures, and though these must perhaps occur, they will lose their power to drag us down. Of course, we do have to face our faults and fight them, but our strength for such a struggle will increase with our devotion and unselfishness. This does not mean that vigilance over one's thoughts and acts is ever to be relaxed.

If you will rely upon the truth that your inner self is a part of the great Spirit, you will be able to conquer these things which annoy, and if you will add to that a proper care of your bodily health, you will get strength in every department. Do not look at things as failures, but regard every apparent failure after real effort as a success, for the real test is in the effort and motive, and not in the result. If you will think over this idea on the lines of *The Bhagavad Gîtâ,* you will gain strength from it.

As before, so now, I will do all I can for you, which is not much, as each must do for himself. Just stay loyal and true, and look for the indications of your own duty from day to day, not meddling with others, and you will find the road easier. It is better to die in one's own duty than to do that of another, no matter how well you do it. Look for peace that comes from a realization of the true unity of all and the littleness of oneself. Give up all, in mind and heart, to the Self, and you will find peace.

The deadening dullness you speak of is one of the trials of the age, but we have some good and earnest people, and they may act as the righteous men in the cities of old, for our ideas are more mighty than all the materialism of the age, which is sure to die out and be replaced by the truth. You will have to take care that the spirit of the time, and the wickedness and apathy of the people, do not engender in you a bitter spirit. This is always to be found in the beginning, but now, being forewarned, you are forearmed.

Do not allow bitterness to come up; keep off all personalities all the time; let the fight be for a cause and not against anyone. Let no stones be thrown. Be charitable. Do not let people be asked to step out, no matter what they do; when they want to go they may go, but don't have threats nor discipline, it does no good but a lot of harm.

Say, look here, never growl at anything you have to do. If you have to go, just take it as a good thing you have to do, and then it will redound to the good of them and of yourself, but if it is a constant cross then it does no good and you get nothing. Apply your theories thus. . . . It is a contest of smiles if we really know our business. . . . Never be afraid, never be sorry, and cut all doubts with the sword of knowledge.

I think that you will be helped if you will try to aid some poor, distressed person by merely talking and expressing your sympathy, if you are not able to help in money, though the very fact of giving five cents to someone who needs it is an act which, if done in the right spirit—that of true brotherliness—will help the one who gives. I suggest this because you will, by doing so, set up fresh bonds of sympathy between you and others, and by trying to alleviate the sorrows or sufferings of others, you will find strength come to you when you most need it.

Let them croak, and if we keep silent it will have no effect; as there has been trouble enough, it is better not to make it any worse by referring to it. The only strength it has is when we take notice. It is better policy for all of us who are in earnest and united to keep still in every matter that has any personal bearing.

Silentio, my dear, is almost as good as patience. He laughs best who does it last, and time is a devil for grinding things. . . . Use the time in getting calmness and solid strength, for a big river is not so because it has a deep bed, but because it has VOLUME.

Rely within yourself on your Higher Self always, and that gives strength, as the Self uses whom it will. Persevere, and little by little *new ideals* and thought-forms will drive out of you the old ones. This is the eternal process.

Troubles are ahead, of course, but I rather think that the old war-horse of the past will not be easily frightened or prevented from the road. Do your best to make and keep good thought and feeling of solidarity. . . . Our old lion of the Punjab is not so far off, but all the same is not in the place some think, nor in the condition, either.

The way gets clearer as we go on, but as *we* get clearer we get less anxious as to the way ahead.

There is service objective and its counterpart within, which being stronger will at last manifest without.

Do not judge in anger, for though the anger passes the judgment remains.

The promises I made to myself are just as binding as any others.

Be true lovers, but of God, and not of each other. Love each the other in that to one another ye mirror God, for that God is in you each.

We all are; I, too. We never *were* anything, but only continually are. What we are now determines what we will be.

In order to off-set the terribly cold effect of perceiving the littleness of human affairs, one must inculcate in oneself a great compassion which will include oneself, also. If this is not done, contempt comes on, and the result is dry, cold, hard, repellent and obstructive to all good work.

I know that his absence is a loss to you, but I think if you will regard all things and events as being in the Self and It in them, making yourself a part of the whole, you will see there is no real cause for sorrow or fear. Try to realize this, and thus gain confidence and even joy.

There are valleys in which the greatest shadows are due to old lives in other bodies, and yet the intensity of universal love and of aspiration will dissipate those in an instant of time.

THE LIGHT OF THE EYE FADETH, THE HEARING LEAVETH THE EAR, BUT THE POWER TO SEE AND TO HEAR NEVER DESERTETH THE IMMORTAL BEING, WHICH LIVETH FOREVER UNTOUCHED AND UNDIMINISHED.

Book of Items

BOOK III

To all
Who have discovered
in the Writings of W.Q.J.
Advice, Guidance and Encouragement
at every Turn and
for every Circumstance of Life

March 21, 1946

Compiled by
EDITORS, "THEOSOPHY"

FOREWORD

WILLIAM Q. JUDGE once said of a Theosophical essay that it would be "profitable for doctrine, for reproof, for correction, for instruction in righteousness." There could be no more fitting epitome of the influence of Mr. Judge's own writings, whether magazine articles or letters to his friends and theosophical associates. Nor was there ever a title more felicitous than "Letters that Have Helped Me," for it expresses at once the simplicity and the power of W. Q. J.

The "exquisite modesty" to which Jasper Niemand (then Mrs. Julia Campbell VerPlanck) referred in her Preface to Book I has concealed much from the careless reader, whose indifference prevents his understanding. Indeed, the "help" that proceeds through these simple, direct words of Mr. Judge finds its way only to the heart that is open, to the mind that is eager and free. He appealed, as was his mission, to the "subtle sight of the subtle-sighted," and in his seventh letter to Jasper he confided: "Many have I halted, and spoken the exact words to them, have exposed to them my real heart, and they heard nothing; they thought that heart was something else."

But some have heard and have understood, then as now, and to them Mr. Judge declares himself, more truly and intimately, it sometimes seems, than might be the case if they had contacted anything other than the essence, or the *presence,* of Mr. Judge, as it inheres in his written word. W. Q. J. the Teacher is a vivid figure, W. Q. J. the Friend, a most sympathetic companion, and W. Q. J. the Great Soul—an Ideal and a Fact.

It is now half a century since he left the scene—"on what high mission bent we know not." What he wrote on the occasion of H. P. B.'s passing, we might repeat, in turn, of him:

> It must not be forgotten that the part played by H. P. Blavatsky can never be rightly given to the world, because it would not be understood. Her service and efforts can never be estimated, but they may be glimpsed by intuitional natures.

That a more complete picture may be glimpsed of William Q. Judge, the LETTERS THAT HAVE HELPED ME have been carefully edited and somewhat enlarged, by reference to the original publications, chiefly to Mr. Judge's own *Path* Magazine. Certain obvious corrections of style have been made in these letters—so hurriedly written—and occasional footnotes added, so that the book might not hold surface obscurities for the new reader, as well as to facilitate reference to old theosophical magazines now long out of print. Where possible, reference has also been made to reprints of the articles mentioned, in the more accessible *Theosophy* Magazine.

"Theosophy" was the name which the *Path* assumed, at Mr. Judge's direction, in its eleventh volume—a change which may be regarded as a line of direction for the future. The first number, however—*Theosophy* for April, 1896—carried the announcement of his death. Sixteen years later, in 1912, Robert Crosbie, a student and co-worker of Mr. Judge's, established, with his associates in the newly-formed United Lodge of Theosophists, a "reincarnation" of the *Path,* in a new magazine, using the title Mr. Judge had selected. That magazine is still published, and fills a great need for those who wish to study the magazine articles of Mme. Blavatsky and Mr. Judge.

In this semicentennial edition of the LETTERS, some more "Gleanings" have been added, following the method described by the editors in the second foreword. The ten volumes of the *Path* have been most carefully gone over, and all the quotations from Judge letters, whether long or short, are here gathered together. Several "Tea Table Talks" (a *Path* series contributed by Jasper over the pseudonym, "Julius"—for *Julia* Campbell VerPlanck) have been reproduced entire, for their wealth of Judge material, and also to illustrate the way students of that day were provided with the comments of Mr. Judge, his identity concealed under a variety of disguises.

Jasper's articles were frequently spiced with quotations "from a letter of a friend"—always Mr. Judge—and so several excerpts are from this source. It may be noticed in passing that Jasper's "Letters on the True," in the second volume of the *Path,* contain some of the statements on which Mr. Judge comments in Book I. Also, in several instances, Jasper has interjected paragraphs from Mr. Judge's letters without the formality of quotation marks. Mr. Judge had no pride of authorship—as appears from the variety of names he himself used in writing—and he was too intent upon getting *ideas before people's minds* to be much concerned about whose name was signed to them. It can readily be imagined how a conversation with him must have fired the genius of a writer, the real "authorship" of the resultant article being then a moot question!

Another group of *Path* excerpts, the sayings of "Quickly" (Mr. Judge, as Jasper tells us), suggests the character of his "psychic experiences," some of manifestly deep meaning. The "Tea Table Talks," as will be seen, were rich in explanation by Mr. Judge of dreams and dreaming. There were several natural "psychics"—Jasper among them—in the Society in those days, and Jasper's writings helped to establish a commonsense attitude toward the psychic, giving as well some philosophical basis for experiences that some people have quite frequently, and almost everyone has at least once.

As to phenomena generally, it has been stated that "in W. Q. J.'s presence H. P. B. caused more phenomena to happen than could be described in a volume." Mr. Judge himself wrote in the *Path* that the "phenomena were those amazing feats of magic, hundreds of which I witnessed in broad daylight or blazing gaslight, from 1875 to 1878." If for no other reason, he was qualified by such experiences to discuss the broad question of phenomena with authority. Some of these happenings he described in "Conversations on Occultism with H. P. B." (*Theosophy,* III, 36), and his series, "Conversations on Occultism" (*Theosophy,* I and II), will suggest reasons why H. P. B. so favored him with demonstrations of occult powers.

The letters written by W. Q. J. while in London and Paris, in 1884, introduce a phase of his life which is of profound importance to the determined student of occultism, for Mr. Judge's account of these ordeals, as he observed their workings in his own nature, contains many hints for disciples who must some day face for themselves these universal experiences of the Path. It may seem, on the surface, as if Mr. Judge was "overwhelmed" by the conflict and the turmoil of that hour, yet intrinsic evidence—for example, the constant iteration that *he will stand*—shows that not once was he shaken from his spiritual centre, whatever the harassments and sufferings of the personal man. Another aspect of his life, during this crucial period, is brought out in the second part of "A Weird Tale," in which Mr. Judge tells of meeting an Adept in London, and of the instructions given him. Most of all, however, these London and Paris letters confirm what has already been divined by the intuitive reader of the letters to Jasper—that in writing of the tests and trials of disciples, W. Q. J. knew whereof he spoke.

Mr. Judge's "stories" have long been out of print, and are now presented for the first time in book form. These tales—"truer" than allegories—belong quite literally to the story of W. Q. J., and they illustrate his use of pseudonyms when he desired to present statements for consideration on their merits, apart from any question of personalities or authority. Mr. Crosbie, whose friendship with Mr. Judge began in the year of the *Path's* founding, 1886, has suggested:

> It is well known that Wm. Q. Judge used pen names for many articles published in his magazine, "The Path," in order to conceal his identity, especially in the case of articles of occult significance intended to convey information to the earnest observant student. The reader would do well to consider all such writings to be recitals of facts and events in which the author was directly concerned. Those who understand the cyclic return of individuals into physical existence with all of their acquired tendencies and relations to others, will find both warning and prophecy for the then future in many of the articles, the proofs of which may be obtained by comparing what was then written with what subsequently occurred in the history of the Movement. *Truly* "history repeats itself."

In reading the LETTERS, Mr. Judge's own statement (*Path*, IX, 57) should be kept in mind, that "The LETTERS [to Jasper] were written by me in the regular course of correspondence with the persons to whom they were sent, and were not then intended for publication, nor did I even dream of subsequent publication." How Mr. Judge came to write this series of letters is told by Bertram Keightley in the *Path* (IX, 14). Mrs. VerPlanck was so deeply impressed by the first talk she heard on the Teaching "that she joined the T. S. within two weeks, and thenceforward began her unceasing work for Theosophy." The account continues:

> Living with her parents at a distance from New York she wrote for the PATH under the names of "Julius," "August Waldensee," "J," and later on as "Jasper Niemand," as

well as unsigned articles, and also corresponded with T.S. enquirers. In those days writers were so few in the Society that they had to take several names, and often one would write up the notes or finish the articles of another.

In answer to some enquirers as to the "Jasper Niemand" writings, Mrs. Keightley [Mrs. VerPlanck had married Dr. Archibald Keightley in 1891] writes: ". . . The *Letters that Have Helped Me* were received at my Pennsylvania home. They were written for me and for Dr. Keightley—and for the use of others later on—by Mr. Judge, at the express wish of H.P.Blavatsky. The letter which is the source of this request [by H.P.B.], and which conveys assurance of Mr. Judge's qualifications for the office of instructor, purported to be written *through* Madame Blavatsky (it begins 'Says Master' [see Letter XIV, Book I, and p. 271 for the omitted "private instructions"—Eds.]), and is one of those so ably described by Col. H. S. Olcott in the *Theosophist* for July, 1893, where he says that communications from high occult sources received through H.P.B. always resembled her handwriting."

This modification of H.P.B.'s handwriting is decidedly interesting in the above mentioned letter, whose data amply justify the manner in which "Z" is spoken of in Niemand's preface. Moreover, H.P.B. spoke of her friend Mr. Judge as the "exile," and Annie Besant wrote later on, "You are indeed fortunate in having W.Q.J. as Chief. Now that H.P.B. is gone, it is the Americans who have as immediate leader the greatest of all exiles."

The technical meaning of these titles, "Greatest of the Exiles" and "Friend of all Creatures," as employed in the East, is totally unknown in the West; the latter being a phrase that has more than once been applied, half in jest, to W.Q.J. by his intimates on account of his often enforced doctrine of "accepting all men and all things"—provided they *work* for Theosophy.

Book II presents letters and extracts written from 1891 to 1894 —the years immediately following Mme. Blavatsky's death—when Mr. Judge, as H.P.B. before him, had to meet the full force of the storm brewed by enemies of Theosophy and the T.S. These letters, according to those who received them, "were written on a basis of some intimacy, during times of storm and difficulty for the most part, and when the writer was nearly always being attacked either openly or privately. They are peculiar, inasmuch as from first to last they do not contain an uncharitable remark about any person, dead or living." (*Irish Theosophist,* December, 1894.)

A correspondent has recorded of that period: "In the first hour of the attack he wrote, 'Be kind, be charitable, and throw no stones'." Mr. Judge took his own advice, from the first hour to the last, determined always to be "of and for peace, and not for war alone." He saved his strength for the real battles—with wrong ideas, and wrong courses of action—and his victory in this Holy War may be seen from some words of H.P.B., written in 1889 (see pp. 277-8).

To one of his associates on the *Path,* who asked what the students would do without him—how could they manage if he died, Mr. Judge said, "Go to the pages of the *Path* Magazine. Study what I have written there, and you will know what I would do." The letters of Mr. Judge, no less than his more formal writings, convey that timeless guidance which only great souls know to give, and the lines of direction therein are as eternal as the truths from which they stem.

As a star, seen brilliantly out of the corner of the eye, flickers out and disappears when focussed upon, so the Being called "W.Q.J." fades and flickers by ordinary light, alternately dazzling and bewildering those who attempt to fix his position in the theosophical galaxy. But, as with all matters bearing on the real and eternal Theosophical Movement, or on the inner life of any true theosophical effort, the status of Mr. Judge—whether student, guide, friend, teacher, Master's Agent or Adept—is finally clarified, not by dogmatic assertions, hard and fast theories, personal testimonies and imaginings, but by Theosophy itself, when found, studied, understood and adhered to by the individual for himself.

—EDITORS

March 21, 1946

TEA-TABLE TALKS

The Tea Table witnessed a strange discussion last week, between Didymus and Quickly. I have not hitherto alluded to the latter, who is a man of remarkable will power, to which his psychic development and training have not a little contributed. He sat chatting with the ladies on this occasion, when Didymus, walking in, remarked to him:—"Ah! old man, I've just come from your office."

"You mean at noon, when you left me to go to the Stewart sale with Miss Polly."

"Oh! but I changed my mind," said she.

"Of course! Why mention it?" said I, and got that rare thing from a woman, a natural (as well as expressive) look.

"So," continued Didymus, to Quickly, "I went back to your den. It was just 3:20 by Old Trinity as I entered."

"Well! I've been there since 2 o'clock," said Quickly.

"You weren't though, for I stood at your door looking straight in, and I'll swear you were not there."

"My dear boy, I sat down at my desk at 3 P. M., noting that I had just three-quarters of an hour to spare, and never rose till 3:40 when I came up here."

"But I say, how could I be mistaken? I passed your clerks in the outer office and went right to your den. It's small, rather bare, no books, no closets, bright sunlight streaming in. There was your chair standing empty, I looked all over the place; a cat couldn't have hidden there."

Quickly was silent. His color changed slightly. The two men eyed each other; then Quickly diverted the conversation. With all due modesty, I may say I have the quickness of a Gordon setter on an occult trail, and, as the laws of the Tea Table provide that all such experiences, once broached, must be held as common property among this little band of earnest seekers, I called the meeting to order and Quickly to account.

"Well," said he slowly, "Didymus bade me farewell for the day at noon, as he was going to the sale. At 3:10 P. M. I was reading some very private letters—in fact—they related to high themes in occultism. As I read, I suddenly thought of Didymus, and the strange idea flashed through my head that he might perhaps return and see the letters in my hands. In my then frame of mind—for I am a queer chap that way sometimes—I had a positive throb of horror lest he might come in and see them, and I mentally went over a little farce of dropping them out of sight."

"You needn't have done that, old man," said Didymus.

"I know it," rejoined the other, with his shrewd nod, "but the whole thing passed through me as I tell you. The letters related to matters which went to the very roots of my life, and it seemed as if I couldn't stand their being seen just at first."

A sympathetic movement ran like a wave through the group and showed that Quickly was understood by all.

"I was in a direct line from my door," resumed he. "It was 10 feet off, and the light very bright. At 3:25 I finished reading them, and had seen no one. I wrote a letter, finished it at 3:40 and came straight up here. I can swear I never left my room from 3 to 3:40 P. M."

"And if the lives of those dearest to me depended on it, I would have sworn that you were not there. I stood in front of your chair at 3:20 for several moments; your clerks saw me come and go."

Of course this strange occurrence was discussed at more length, but the facts remained the same. Can we explain them? I think so. We know that Adepts possess the power of becoming invisible at will, and that one of the methods employed consists in mesmerizing the lookers-on, so that they do not perceive him who so wills it. All that is required is the institution of a certain vibration through a strong *self-conscious* will. This Quickly has not.* But reading those letters relating to the higher self had so raised his vibrations and intensified his psychic perception, that when the inner self raised a note of alarm at the approach of Didymus, and the idea of discovery was conveyed to the normal consciousness of Quickly, the will to remain unseen was so intense that, unknown to his mind, his soul emitted or employed that vibration necessary to set up such an akasic disturbance as would perturb the sight of a looker-on. This sight depended upon the transmission of certain vibrations to the optic nerve, and these were wanting. Many such incidents

* Or, it would probably be more correct to say, he did not desire to to be known as possessing it.—Eds.

happen to those whose psychic senses are gradually unfolding, and, when well attested, as in this case, are useful hints to fellow students.

—From *The Path,* May, 1887

Even Quickly, the grim, the saturnine, has been beguiled by summer. He writes: "I am doing fairly well with the trout, thanks, old man; but I've had a queerish, nervous shock. Serves me right, too. Jolting along in one of those beastly Wagner cars, I saw great hollows in the banks, where land slides had taken place. I got to thinking of them intently; wished hard to examine them; found *myself* out on the bank at such a place. Suddenly the 'limited' came along in the contrary direction from the train my astral self had left. It roared down on me: I got startled and confused. Although it could not strike me, it yet struck me full and square—*I felt the headlight hurled against my head!* Jupiter! It sent me plunging back into my body (on my own train) with a nervous tremor and jar from which I haven't yet recovered. See the dangers of leaving the body for puerile purposes, before you are fully poised and self-centered. True, I was out before I was aware, but an occultist should always be aware of all things. I knew well that no catapult could injure or even disperse those fine molecules, or do aught more than pass through them. Yet so strong are the illusions of matter, that I lost my presence of mind in the uproar. Even mystics commit folly! Let me tell you, Julius; it's been a lesson to me."

—July, 1887

Quickly one night dreamed that he went out into an adjoining street and saw that several houses had been altered with new stoops and cherry doors. Next day he went there, but found no alteration. A month after, they were all altered as he dreamed, with new stoops and cherry doors. There was a blue door he used to see in the astral light, when awake, about which the Tea Table chaffed him. Now he writes exultant: "The blue door I told you I saw turns out to be a piece of second-sight. The door across the street that I see every morning and evening, has been so altered. I believe I saw the picture just when the owner had determined to paint it over in a few months to come. His thought and determination made a strong picture which I got and thus saw the thing occur. Most men make up their minds nearly every day in general what they will do weeks ahead and thus the ether is full of such pictures at all times. Those pictures of things so well founded that they must soon eventuate, are seen by us."

—August, 1887

Speaking of pictures of future events in the astral light, when with the Tea Table recently, Quickly gave an excellent reply to some rather nervous queries from the ladies regarding such "omens" as visions of death scenes or funerals passing by. Said he: "They are, of course, compounded; there are other elements in them than those of thought. But the causes must already exist, for if I died now, my relatives have a fair, general idea of the kind of funeral I should have," (shudders from the ladies) "and so the whole scene might easily be pictured and suddenly seen by a person in a tense nervous condition. Then again, in most cases, a train of similar causes will always produce similar effects or pictures. The soul, having an enormous power of induction, can begin with a known cause; its effect becomes another cause. Unthinking men, acting blindly, will always be moved in known and easily premised ways; thus all the elements can be calculated in an instant and a long-distant event be seen. It appears in some cases to be an extension of the power of cause calculation possessed by many. There are various methods in life which show that all this can be done. See the doctrine of least squares, and others."

—September, 1887

An inquirer writes: "I want to tell you of a little experience I had last week. I would call it a dream, but it is unlike any dream I ever had. It was in the night, of course, and I thought that I—the real I—was standing by the bedside, looking down at my sleeping form. The whole room was light, yet it did not seem like sunlight; it came from no particular point, it cast no shadows; it seemed to be diffused from, or to pervade, all things equally; it was not colored, like sunlight or gaslight—it seemed white, or silvery. Everything was clearly visible: the furniture, the mosquito bar, the brushes on the toilet-table. The form on the bed I recognized distinctly. It was lying as usual, on the right side, the right arm curved under the pillow, my favorite attitude. I seemed to see it even more clearly, more distinctly than the ordinary reflection in the mirror, for whereas there one only has the reflection of a plane surface, here I saw it as a solid, just as I do other people and could also observe the breathing. This did not last more than, perhaps, thirty seconds, but long enough for me to see the body distinctly, to observe and comment upon the fact that the face had an expression of weariness, to note the light as before remarked and some objects in the room. Then all faded away, and afterwards—tho' how long, of course I don't know—I awoke and it was day. Was this a dream, or did I remember that much of the excursion of my 'Astral,' and was the light I saw the Astral Light? C."

This inquirer was answered, "I believe that what you saw was the remembrance of what really happened. Your astral self got out—as it always does—and looked back at the body. It is more than likely that all that you saw occurred when you were returning to the body, and that is why it was short. We remember distinctly only that which is nearest to us. I think you went out when you fell asleep and then on coming back to wakefulness you kept a recollection of the last few seconds. You do not really forget what you saw and thought while away. It sinks into your upper, or sub-conscious, or super-conscious mind, from which it will all percolate into the thoughts of your waking state. To remember what happens during sleep, is to be a conscious seer. So we only get these useless glimpses of our returning to the body.

"We go away in deep dreamless sleep to other spheres and states, where we get ideas and so forth, and the way back is through many different states, all having their denizens and obstructions. Besides that, there are two ways to ascend and descend: the direct and indirect. So, much is lost and mixed up on those two roads. Now I talk of actualities and not sentimentally.

"We must be patient, because it takes time to find out how to walk, and much time is spent in getting hold of clues. A great deal depends on purity of thought and motive, and breadth of view."

—October, 1887

Quickly thought he could beat that dream: he generally does go us one better, and I don't know that any one envies him some of his occult adventures at least. He was living in New York, and had an acquaintance who was better known to the family of his uncle than to himself. He went to Washington and put up in a private house in R. Street. On the second night he dreamed he was at home and was going in by the basement way in company with the above-named gentleman and his own deceased sister. As they were about entering, the gentleman put his hand on the overhanging stoop, which at once fell upon him, and he disappeared beneath it. Every one in the dream seemed to feel very badly about him. Next day Quickly made a note of the dream in his diary and dismissed it from his mind. Not writing home, he heard nothing about the gentleman, but when he returned to New York he learned that his acquaintance had had a severe fall which brought on an old trouble, and that he had died on the night of the dream. The Professor listened with the genuine "I-know-all-about-it" air, and remarked at the close that the dream was doubtless caused by the events of the man's life passing rapidly through his dying mind, and when he came to his relations with Quickly, that recollection vibrated in connection with Quickly and caused his dream, reaching him all the more rapidly because his physical nature was at the moment quiescent in sleep. I do not doubt myself that this suggestion is a correct clue to all *similar* occurrences.

—March, 1888

The student * was prevailed on the other night to say something about dreams and dreaming.

"Yes, although the greater number of dreams are foolish, we must not despise them utterly, but should discriminate. If we rely on dreams we shall at last become verily superstitious and amenable to punishment by our friends. The fact that nearly all people dream is an enormous fact. For in these dreams, foolish, sad, grave, or prophetic, there is some ego or person or individual who experiences the feelings that we note in dreams and remember afterwards. The same sort of cognitions and sensations is perceived in dreams as when we are awake. *Who* feels, *who* suffers and enjoys? is the question. That is what we should consider. But it is true that

* By this time, the name "Quickly" was no longer used, Mr. Judge being henceforth referred to simply as "Student" or "X."—Eds.

one may learn the meaning of his own dreams; rare is the man who can say what, if any, meaning the dreaming of another has."

—May, 1891

The student remarked, "Dreams are not understood generally, and most of those we have are forgotten in five minutes after waking up. Job truly said that in the visions of the night man is instructed. That this [the Bishop's dream under discussion] was a day-dream does not alter the case. Bulwer Lytton shows that the first initiations come in dreams. They are nearly always in symbols, for the inner man has no such language as ours. He sees and speaks by pictures. He throws out a thought as a picture. It is for us to grasp it and remember. Each picture is modified by the changing methods of our waking hours of thought. Your friend has well dreamed and well interpreted, and if we were to act upon our dream-teaching when it gives high motive, then we could encourage, as it were, the inner dreamer so that oftener we might get instruction. The Bishop's impulse is to slightly sniff at his relative because he is so practical. Yet he, even, dreams and a great fact is therefore present in his experience—the fact of dreaming. Our dreams present an opportunity to us as waking men and women to so live that the Inner Self may more easily speak to us. For, as with new acquaintances and strange languages, it is necessary to become accustomed to the new forms of speech and thought, so that out of the great confusion reigning at first we may bring order with instruction. The lesson of this dream is for all; it is to throw off the hold of self upon us each in his own way—for all differ—and to abandon all fear. But we cannot do either while we remain impure; as we purify, so we succeed."

—March, 1892

"What good are dreams, anyway?" said the Professor the other day. "Is there any use in our paying the slightest attention to them? I have been dreaming that the duck we ate at dinner the other day had grown to the size of an elephant and threatened me with a wave of his web foot. It was really terrifying."

"Oh!" said the student, who had been looking steadily at the Professor, "then it terrified? Do you see nothing in the fact that someone was appalled by this imaginary duck?"

"It was only an image in my brain," responded the Professor.

"Yes, very true, it was an image produced by bad digestion; but you ignore an immense fact connected with the image. That great point is that this unexisting duck gave a shock to the perceiver within. The person and faculties that cause your body to shrink from what you call real danger in waking life are the same person and faculties which were terrified by the duck of your dream."

"Really," said the Professor, "I never regarded it in that light. You mean that even in this foolish instance I had an introspective experience, showing, by means of the dream state, the actual existence and functioning of myself as a real person within?"

Here the widow, who had stopped in town *en route* for a new seaside, interrupted with, "Ah, Professor, you are at least learning something. Perhaps you will not be so ready hereafter to laugh at my dream of my new bonnet."

"Why, what was that?"

"Well, I dreamed I was tying on a new one before the glass and thinking what a lucky person I was in getting the first of the new style, when in walked Lady Eleanor, who appeared at once to grow green with envy at my success."

"Yes," remarked the student, "it was just the opposite of his elephantine duck. Yours was not caused by indigestion. It was pleasant. It gratified your love of personal decoration, not unmixed with a desire to stand ahead of the others, unmarried or not. But the person within perceived the event which your mind brought up, and was thereupon pleased. That inner person never sees material objects. It only cognizes the idea of the objects, whether presented by the waking senses or by the mind in dreams. It is a thinker who looks on these ideas. And whether the dream be folly or not in itself, the great fact remains that some one perceived it. In our waking moments we run after folly just as much as we do in dreams. We call it experience, whether it be wise or unwise, whether it be the pursuit of great things or their opposite. Why should we refuse to use our dreams as experience appropriate to that state? For the thinker the experience is the same, whether obtained from what the waking eye sees or from the mind's own motions in a dream."

The Professor looked serious a moment and then he said, "You have thrown some light on the matter, but what about dreams of other sorts? Are they all equally foolish, and all only for the use you mention?"

"No, they are not all alike. But there are dreamers and dreamers. Not every person is a real dreamer in the old sense of that term. Some dreams are visions of the night. The real man then sees many facts of life, of history, of family, of nations. He is not bound by the body then, and so makes immediate conclusions. He may see a war that is to come, because he sees all the facts that must lead to a war; and so he impresses on the brain the pictures of battles, of armies, of standards. He can also perceive the coming of single events connected with himself or others. This is because no fact can come without an antecedent cause. He looks on the causes, instantly calculates results down to exact dates even, and then throws the picture upon the receptive brain. If he be a king, and at the same time a good dreamer of this class, his dream-visions have relation to the kingdom, and so may be of more importance than those of the peasant. And yet sometimes such dreamers are obscure men, and often dream that which relates to the whole kingdom. Every idea except those of purest mathematics is presented as a picture or drama to the mind and not in words. Hence often the brain distorts the picture, with confusion as a consequence.

"Sometimes, too, we dream of people we do not know to be alive or dead, or that they ever were. These sometimes are caused by our inner self in dream meeting the self of another whom we had known in a prior life, and then we are unable to identify them with our present brain experience. But they are not nonsense or imagination.

"Then, again, there is the dream that often comes to those who are striving to live the higher life and to develop their inner faculties. In this, one is often apparently attacked and pursued. It is the struggle between the higher and the lower nature in which sometimes terror supervenes in consequence of old passions and tendencies seeming to get the upper hand. That fear produces a picture of pursuit or battle, and the dreamer wakes up in the condition brought on by an ordinary nightmare. If the aspiration towards a higher life is kept up, but a corresponding change in daily thought and act does not take place, the dream will be repeated, varying perhaps in detail, and cease to come only when the fight is given up and one re-plunges into the lower sort of conduct, or when the battle is won by the opposite course of life and thought."

The Professor thanked the student, promising more questions some other evening. We all then gathered in another room to discuss the Theosophical prophecies so often made, that our selfish civilization is sure to bring on very serious struggles in society.

—September, 1892

I had just finished reading aloud a letter from one of our circle sent from the West the other day, when the Professor arrived, and seeing the student sitting at the end of the table cried, "Oh, my dear fellow, you are just the man I wanted. Your talk about dreams the other day gave me so many new ideas I think I have hit on a poser for you this time."

We all became at once very much interested at the prospect of the student's being posed. He is seldom put to flight, for he has a way of waiting until you have said all you wish, and then gives the matter such a turn that his expected defeat is your own Sedan day. This time he looked at the Professor quite straight and laconically ejaculated, "Letters and their forerunners, I presume."

A sort of falling of the jaw came to the Professor, and then I knew that again our dear student had posed the other man, and at the same time the voice of the widow whispered in my ear, "I saw a blue light go out of his eyes when old 'Prof.' first spoke."

"Why," exclaimed the Professor, "that's it exactly, though I don't quite give it just that title. But how did you know? Pshaw, it was only a guess! It is this way. When I am thinking of a man, and the same day or the same hour receive a letter from him, is there any necessary connection between my thoughts and the getting of the letter?"

"There may be, and there may not. It all depends. Perhaps as much connection as between our listening here to a letter being read, your coming in just then, and my putting your query for you, 'by guess' as you say. A close connection is quite possible, and exists in the greater number of such cases. You have heard of the so-called superstition of the 'forerunner' in Scotland and other countries? No, you paid no attention to that? Well, they think that some people have what they call a 'forerunner.' This is often a fleeting image of the person which comes to the house or place to which the original is actually travelling, as if to give warning of the approaching person, but which does not speak. In other cases it is a knock or number of knocks sent on ahead as a kind of courier in advance. It does not forbode death, but is simply a forerunner, the person's own familiar herald. Well, it is the same thing with letters. They have their forerunners which travel on in advance, some at a long distance, others not far before. It is a sort of pressure of aura, an aura full of the characteristics of the writer, and given impulse and direction from the very definite thoughts and ideas of the correspondent toward the person written to. But really this is preaching; I don't wish to monopolize the evening."

We all drew in our breaths, for this was exactly what we had been talking about one day in the student's absence, and now he provokingly proposed to cut off the explanation at the beginning. So there was chorus of "Go on! Don't do like that. This is not a tea in Society. You can have the evening."

"Do you mean," questioned the Professor, with an "I'll-draw-him-out" expression, "that certain objects—such, for instance, as letters—have spheres of their own, of an extensible nature, which can and do travel on ahead, where, impinging on the sensorium of the person to whom they are written, they produce an impression or image or thought of the writer in the brain of the individual against whom this sphere impinges?"

"That is exactly it,"—and I caught a flying look from the student which telegraphed that he was the one who had paused so as to draw the Professor out and on into the web of his own words, which being in his own style, might the more quickly be accepted by his brain.

"The existence of an aura around objects, and especially those belonging to man, has been proved. Letters not only have it on general principles, but also in a specialized state due to the concentration by the writer upon thought, words, and person. It remains with the epistle somewhat in the way a mass of compressed air travels along with a bullet or a cannon ball. This latter is now well known, for by an instantaneous photograph the cushion of the compressed air and the bullet have been distinctly reproduced on the plate. What obtains in physics obtains also in the realm of actual physics, to coin a term.

"In some cases I have measured the time this forerunner will reach me, and found it often to be one day, which meant in one case a five-hundred-mile distance and in another one thousand miles."

"Then, of course," I said, "each mass of this aura, which must be personal to the writer, carries with it the idea or picture of the friend?"

"Yes, this is so with all our thoughts, and we fix them firmly in the letter during the writing. Then the aura is all permeated with our image, and when the brain receives it that image produces an idea about the writer. In some sensitive persons a partial knowledge of the contents of the coming letter is gained, though in most cases only in the vaguest manner. I think we have cumulative proof of this in telepathy and mind-reading."

Just here, in the most annoying way, the door-bell began to ring, announcing visitors not in the charmed circle, and both the Professor and the Student pleaded engagements—with each other, I suppose, to continue the conversation as they walked along.

—October, 1892

The editor let me see the sketch of Dr. Anderson,* and in that the incident of his having never learned spelling is noteworthy. He gave this in detail to the editor, who tells me. He was but four years of age and had not up to that time studied anything, and his parents were thinking of how to go about his education. They found him reading, and he himself could never explain how it had come to him except that he just knew. This is a very interesting fact, and one of many of the same sort which could be gathered if we only looked for them. I told the story at the table, and the Student said he had had a similar experience in the same line. He said,

"I was not a precocious boy nor a dull one; simply ordinary. Sent to school very early, the spelling book was a terror to me and occupied most of my thoughts. I could not get on and was low in the class. One day I was especially annoyed by this, and after thinking of it all day went to bed full of grief and trouble on the matter. A very sound sleep came and I waked in the morning with the first and prominent thought, 'Oh I can spell now and will not look in the miserable book again.' I was then about seven. Without taking the book I went to school and rose through the class. Never again did I study the speller, and am now able to spell all words except the very rare and peculiar."

---

* The "Faces of Friends," in the same issue of the *Path*.—Eds.

"What was that?" said the widow. "Was it your astral, or the mayavi-rupa, or what?"

The Student smiled at her utter disregard of terms, and said that he had not the slightest doubt about its being the taking up of old knowledge from another life, for he declared it had always been a most distinct experience and one he could not forget nor be in the least confused about. Such incidents had happened to him before. In one case he was given as a small boy a missionary book that depicted the Hindus as a lot of miserable black men who were very near savages. This he took home, looked over, and then growing suddenly angry threw it on the floor saying it was a lie. He found in after life he was right, although at the time he had no means of knowing the facts about India or the Hindus, but had to rely on prejudiced tales and interested persons.*

All this while the Professor was looking very grave. The old ridicule was not on his face, and the Student and I were beginning to think some inroads had been made on his skeptical mind. We asked him what he thought of it all.

"Well," said he, "I am bound to accept the evidence offered, and it certainly gives much extraordinary introspective experience. I can hardly put it down to imagination, as there was no basis, and besides, imagination will not confer knowledge. In the Student's case there was a slight beginning, as he had been studying, but in that of the Doctor there was absolutely no basis. Could it be that the cells of the body have a power of transmitting forms of knowledge such as spelling?"

At this all of us, even the widow, had to laugh, for we saw the Professor was, like so many of his brethren, in a very small corner and hardly knew how to get out. The Student came to his relief, to our astonishment, telling us we must not ridicule the Professor, for he had hit on the explanation, provided he went just a little farther. The physical cells have such a power, but it is latent and can never come out until the Ego, the inner man, draws out the latent impression. And this is not possible unless the Ego in the body has been through a similar set of impressions as those tried to be brought out. That is, there must be an interaction and interrelation between the physical collection of atoms and man

* Compare the Prologue to *Gorgo*, by Charles Kelsey Gaines (Lothrop, Lee and Shepard Co., Boston, Mass.: 1903.) Professor Gaines had read Mr. Judge's *Ocean of Theosophy*, published in that same year, and may also have seen this passage in the *Path*.—Eds.

inside. If the inner man has been, say, a speller of English, and the mass of atoms composing the body has been also used by those who have been good spellers, then it will be possible for the person to pick up old knowledge. But this goes to show that it is in any case the remembering of what we once learned, and that always depending on the physical instrument we are using at the time. The Professor looked relieved, as we were all so interested in the solution of the matter that we forgot the person who brought it out.

The very cases that seem against this are really supports to it. Take that of the family of the great musician Bach. His descendants were, indeed, good musicians but not such as he, and little by little his great abilities faded from the family. At first this seems to negative the idea, but if you will remember that the Ego must have the power in itself you will see that though Bach may have left atoms with musical impression the new Egos coming to the family line were not able to draw out the power of the instrument, and so it sounded no more. This is a great lesson in karma and universal brotherhood if looked at in the right way. It was the karma of that family to draw Egos to it of indifferent capacity, and those using the atoms of the family gave them new and other impressions and tendencies until at last Ego after Ego was attracted to the family devoid of talent. The same may and does happen in respect to virtue. Hence as we act and live we raise up or pull down the general standard. This is also beyond doubt the real reason for the ancient insistence on the purity of the family line; it is at the same time the cause for the amalgamation of many races to produce a new one, as we see here in our own land.

—April, 1893

The Professor sat, cigar in hand, watching the upward curl of its blue smoke-filament, his eyes darkened by the intensity of his thought. I knew he had just seen X, an "advanced" theosophist of the occult wing, and I lay in wait for any information which might percolate through upon my humble self. Presently the Professor remarked, dreamily, and as if speaking from cloudland:

"We had many a crisis, but assuredly this was the greatest."

"To what do you refer, Professor?"

"To the departure of H. P. B. from her physical body. It might have been supposed, in advance, that this sudden taking-off would result to our disadvantage. But the fact is, disasters work upon the T. S. in inverse proportion. The greater the (apparent) disaster, the greater the resultant good. The stronger the blow, too, the stronger our reaction. All attacks, all so-called exposures and losses have merely cleared away the impediments of weak and uncertain followers. The apparent loss of our leader did not, for one instant even, paralyze the activities of the working staff in India, England, or America. Now, day by day, we have evidence of growth in every direction. The Press is opening its jealously-guarded doors. The Practical Work of the Theosophic League has won public sympathy for us. Everywhere there is a sudden outburst of energy and new life. X spoke of it today."

"What had he to say of it?"

"We were talking about H. P. B., and he said that, so far as he understood, she (the Adept) expended an immense amount of energy—*vis viva,* you know—in holding together a body whose every molecule tended to disruption. In effect, just think of the cohesive force thus employed!—of the immense friction in brain-centers already worn by disease. X says they were so impaired that senility must soon have resulted, so that it seemed to *her* (?) better to let that body go to pieces as soon as a good opportunity should occur."

"That last phrase is very suggestive."

"It is. And we believe that H. P. B. will be for some time occupied in training a new instrument, and one not so young as to be useless at the present cyclic crisis. He does not pretend to speak with authority, but certain sayings of hers—and perhaps what I might call *post-mortem facts*—bear him out. Certainly she left everything in order. All things were planned out, and evidence was abundantly had to the effect that she knew her departure was near. Moreover, X said that looking upon her as an Adept, whose chief work was done outside of the objective body, it was reasonable to suppose that she is now enabled to use, upon higher (or inner) planes of being, the power previously expended in the maintenance of that body."

"Did he think that the present theosophic increase should be attributed to that fact?"

"Only in part. You see, he believes her attentions to be largely engaged with the new instrument. But, from his point of view, her co-adjutors and associates would naturally lend a helping hand in her absence, especially if the T.S., as a body, called down their help."

"What do you mean by calling down help?"

"I mean that the united impulse of a large body of truth seekers —more especially if they work for Humanity—attracts the help needed for its spiritual efforts. Imagine it as a great stream of energy going out into space and returning freighted with all that it had attracted to itself—all similars—on its passage. That in itself would be a source of power. Again, the increase is largely due to what H.P.B. foresaw. Theosophists are now able to stand alone, are all the gainers by being left to do so. (Take the words *'alone'* and *'left'* in a relative sense, please.) In the same way an infant is benefited when left to learn to walk, even at the cost of its tumbles; it is the course of normal, healthy growth in every department of Nature."

"All that sounds rational enough."

"My dear Sir! Nothing is more rational, more sane than Theosophy. It is like the fairy wand which was used upon the ten billion feathers of ten thousand different kinds; all the facts of life fly out into well ordered heaps."

"Just fancy how the public would receive that statement!"

"The public is well described by Carlyle's estimate of population: so many *'millions—mostly fools.'* Yet tell me what truth, what invention, has not been rejected by their scorn. Let us not be trite. All the truths of Theosophy, all the axioms of occultism are, if I may so put it, the apotheosis of common sense. When you see a lack of that—beware! You may be sure that their knowledge is defective, erratic, ill-digested; every psychic, every seer, every hearer to the contrary. What are their gifts if not supplemented by an understanding of the thing heard or seen? 'My son, get knowledge; but, above all, get understanding.' That power to interpret must be supplied. How?"

"I cannot possibly say. Did you not ask X?"

"I did. His answer was: *'By study of the Ethics.* The Bhagavad Gita shows the way.' In this science, he declared, spirit and nature, or the pure and the true, or ethics and law, are one and the same thing. The inner man may be looked upon as a congeries of powers. Every power is 'the opener of the Door' to the plane from which it springs in Nature. A power of the lower astral, or psycho-physiological, plane opens the door to that plane alone. It does so partly through action and interaction in the cells and molecules of the body. It acts upon its corresponding principle in every cell."

"Can't you enlarge upon that, Professor?"

"Suppose I were able to induce in the optic nerve that vibratory ratio which enables it to perceive the yellow color. How do I do it? I act as Nature does. She presents a given numerical vibration to the nerves, and forthwith they telegraph to the brain the sense impression of yellow. Which do you call the real thing in itself; the sense impression? or the vibratory ratio? I induce (if I can!) that same ratio in the nervous fluid, and the brain again registers yellow. Soon, if I were to continue this action, that nerve aura of the inner man would be in synchronous action and interaction with a whole plane of being—call it the lower plane of the yellow ray, and all the things of that plane which are related to that vibration are perceived. Those parts of specific things which are not in relation to the vibration are not seen, and thus partial knowledge arises. It is literally true that you see that which you are."

"I begin to understand."

"Again, note that every plane has its active and its passive aspects; its principles; its sub-divisions and theirs. It is only the higher plane forces that open the upper doors. What determines this difference in power?"

"Ah! That must be the *crux.*"

"Thought determines it. Motive determines it, for motive determines the quality of Thought. Through motive, Thought becomes contractive or expansive. It is well known that Thought affects the assimilative processes of the body. It has always been a recognized factor in therapeutics. The introduction of the higher, more spiritualized vibrations into the *secret* brain centers not only opens them to the influence of higher spheres, but also it influences the selective action of the whole sphere. As the body exhales and inhales air, so the inner nervous body dilates and contracts with the motion of the etheric or astral Medium. Its vibration is quickened by the action of Thought, and this more rapid vibration prevents the entrance of the grosser particles of etheric substance, causing also a draught upon the infinitely finer currents of that World Soul. In this way the higher intelligence of every atom is opened, 'wooed from out the bud like leaves upon the branch.' Keely gives us a hint of one method in which this is done."

"You mean by his discovery that the production of the chord of any given mass ruptures the molecular association of that mass and liberates finer energies, which energies are infinitely more dynamic?"

"Precisely so. The lesson can be carried still further. You say he produces the chord of any given mass, a chord which represents the vibratory total of that mass. So, too, we must use that force which is harmonious to the plane which we desire to enter. It is easy to talk about it, but who amongst us can do it? And when the psychic does it fortuitously, he sees only partial results, only that which he is fitted to see, and no more. This is why it is so often said: 'A man must live what he knows.' Until he has lived it, he cannot know it; he must *be* that higher vibration; he himself must become that 'lost Word.' By long training in the production of forces within himself—forces which must be absolutely pure if they are to reveal the pure—the student may approximate an understanding of what he sees. Otherwise, psychic experiences are a great disadvantage. They pre-empt thought; they detain the mind, as thorns upon the bushes detain the sheep. This is why the *Voice of the Silence* advises the student to flee from that 'Hall of Learning' where, under every flower, the astral serpent coils."

"Then it is well to be able to show these things by the light of common sense."

"Certainly, if you wish to benefit the sensible. I always go to Nature for an explanation of occultism."

"In that case, drawing a parallel, we may say that the so-called death of Madame Blavatsky brought the theosophic minds to a common focus; that was, the determination to continue her work. This unity of effort on higher lines induced a great volume of energy, all pouring into and from a common center."

"Yes—and results of this action are now seen in a two-fold manner. Firstly, in the increased activity we spoke of; secondly, in the partial unclosing of the doors into higher planes."

"How do you infer that?"

"From what X went on to tell me. It appears that the Leaders of the Society have made themselves objectively felt. Say, for example, in the way of letters. It is affirmed that some such have been received, and that their burden is '*Work.*' In one, a laborer is told to *'not ask for detailed commands,* for H. P. B. *has the* PATH *hewed out.* FOLLOW *in* WORK *and leave us to manage results.'* Again, work is referred to thus:— 'You go on with other work in a field as wide as humanity.' The worker here referred to had been previously working in purely ethical ways. Another student is told: *'Be careful, then, so to act that your life shall not hurt the Society, now having* so *few.* * * * *Make no profession a lie. Remember your responsibility and your oath.'* The burden of all such letters is devotion to and work for the present organization, as a duly-created center through which work is to be done."

"It must be very encouraging to receive such letters."

"Precisely my remark to X, who gave me one of his sudden shrewd looks, and then said quickly, 'My dear boy, when a plant is mildewed, devoured, broken, growing awry, the head gardener or some one of his authorized assistants comes to its aid, or some few especial plants, doing especial service in the garden, may receive especial stimulus, such as would injure others. But when a plant is following all the natural laws of growth, it requires no re-adjustment; it does not hear from the gardener, who knows it is doing well. In the East, the Guru or Teacher is called the Re-adjuster. And He may communicate with some sub-center already established, which sub-center is to give out the help thus extended to those working in the same line'."

"Then those workers who do not hear in some specific manner may still feel that they are seen and are doing well?"

"That is what X said; also that with closer relations to The Lodge comes also a greater, a terrible responsibility."

"It often seems to me hard to know just how to work."

"That is so. The best advice I ever found was: 1st, Use your predominant gifts to the best advantage. 2nd, Do not impede your fellow in so using his. 3rd, Follow the methods of Nature. Find a current or a nucleus, and work in it. No matter whether it seems perfect to you or not. Leave results to the Law. But if no nucleus is found, become yourself a center. The Divine will enter and work through you." . . .

—September, 1891

GLEANINGS FROM THE "PATH"

In the great struggle of Humanity nothing is lost. No labor, no love is in vain. We live over again our own trials in those we desire to assist. We are drawn upward and outward by those who are trying to assist us.

—May, 1890

Books will do you little good. They will serve to confirm after you already know. They cannot give anything new, for it is the old which they strive to teach and we to find. Keep your motive pure, your will to rise higher strong, and you will pass on. * * * Shut up your books and *think*.

Do not rely upon books to guide you or teach you. They are good to give men earthly knowledge, they are good to start men thinking. They will not give men heavenly wisdom or the True. You can obtain good from all things, books included. You cannot know yourself through books.

—April, 1890

Look for the real beneath the unreal; look for the substance behind the shadow; and in the midst of confusion look for the silent centre where the Lodge is ever at work.

—December, 1895

The remarks of our President* last Tuesday [were] upon the multiplied force of concerted action, in showing that, side by side with what we are *doing*, runs the hidden current of our *being*, slow-moving, perhaps, but nevertheless sweeping on with a resistless force, none the less great for being unsuspected.

—August, 1889

NOTE.—Bracketed passages are those of the writer (usually "Jasper" or "Julius") who is quoting Mr. Judge.—Eds.

* Mr. Judge, president of the Aryan T.S., the Parent (New York) Branch. —Eds.

[An adept writes:]

Before you can become an occultist you have to give up every prejudice, every earthly liking, every feeling of preference for one thing over another. It is easy to fall into Black Magic. The natural tendency is to Black Magic, and that is why several years' training is necessary to cut away every source of prejudice before power can be intrusted to you. An Adept must entirely separate himself from his personality; he must say, "I am a power." A Black magician prepares to do mischief without giving a thought to whether it will harm others. A deed of kindness done with partiality may become evil, *e. g.*, by stirring up animosity in the mind of others. It is necessary, when acting, to lose all sense of identity and to become an abstract power. Justice is the opposite of Partiality. There is good and evil in every point of the universe, and if one works, however indirectly, for one's own partiality, one becomes, *to that extent*, a Black magician. Occultism demands perfect justice, absolute impartiality. When a man uses the powers of nature indiscriminately with partiality and no regard to justice, it is Black magic. Like a blackleg, a Black magician acts on certain knowledge. Magic is power over the forces of nature, *e. g.*, the Salvation Army, by hypnotizing people and making them psychically drunk with excitement, uses Black magic. The first exercise of Black Magic is to psychologize people. To help a sick person is not black magic, *but* no personal preference must guide you.

When the 6th race reaches its close there will be no more Dugpas (Black magicians). A Dugpa may become converted during life at the expense of terrible sufferings and trials. On the astral and psychic planes the Masters are always stronger than the Dugpas, because there good is stronger than evil. But on our material plane evil is stronger than good, and the Masters, having to exercise cunning if acting on this plane, which is contrary to Their natures, encounter great difficulties and can only palliate evil effects. In powers *not* good there is absence of good but not presence of evil, and the higher we go, the more does evil become the absence of good. Only by following the absolute sexless *unity* can the white path be trodden.

—August, 1890

[Some MSS. remarks by an Adept:]

All illnesses, diseases, and abnormalities of the body come from astral planes. The physical cannot infect the astral. The occult and and the physical must never be mixed up. It is absolutely necessary to concentrate on one or on the other.

—August, 1889

How much I wish you could keep quiet; I mean, quiet inside. You are allowing yourself to chafe and rage inside. Outside quiet does not amount to anything unless all inside is quiet too. This has to be learned, and, good boy as you are, you have not yet learned it. Can't you? I have learned that, or else I should have gone mad, as much from myself as from others.

What is to learn, is to be content, or, rather, resigned to ourselves and our limitations even while striving to get above them; and when a bold and loyal nature like yours achieves that knowledge, a great advance is made. You need never excuse yourself at all in the forum of your own judgment, but when you have passed your judgment, bow your head. We cannot all at once live up to these high ideals as some others live up to theirs. Some are pleased with themselves because their rules allow it, and they are thus quiet, but it is not that quiet I refer to. Your soul may be quiet even while the body rages. (See *Voice of the Silence.*) I am never, nor you, satisfied with ourselves, but we must be resigned to the limitations of our character as they appear to us. The greatest error in occultism is to doubt one's self, for it leads to all doubt. The doubts of others, which we have, always spring from the inward doubt of self. Do not doubt, then, even so much as you admit, in yourself.

—April, 1890

The processes of preparation go silently on till the individual, all unconscious, reaches the moment when the one needed force touches him, and then every prepared constituent falls instantly into place and the being is—as it were—reconstructed at once. Conceptions, relations, aims are revolutionized.

—May, 1888

[One versed in holy mysteries said recently when consulted about an aspirant for chelaship:]

Having the right *motive* he is all right. His *views* are of no use to him. * * * He had better be ready to alter them as he passes on.

—September, 1887

I want you to stop as much as possible any wish to progress. The intense desire to know and to become, and to reach the light, is different from the thought: I am not progressing; I know nothing. The latter is looking for results. The right position to take is the wish *to Be*. For then we know. *The wish to know is almost solely intellectual, and the desire to Be is of the heart.* For instance, when you succeed in seeing a distant friend, that is not knowledge: that is the fact of *Being* in the condition or vibration that *is* that friend at the time. The translation of it into a mental reckoning or explanation, is what is called knowledge. To see an elemental on the astral plane, is for the time *to be,* in some part of our nature, in that state or condition. Of course there are vast fields of Being we cannot hope to reach yet. But while we strive to become divine and set our final hopes no lower than that supreme condition, we can wholly and entirely learn *to be* that plane which is presented to us now.

—January, 1888

Unlike those who grumble at not being "helped," I think there is more danger of our being "helped" too much than too little. Machines break from over-speeding, not from being run too slowly —save in exceptional cases.

—April, 1891

[One who had won the right and the sacred duty of teacher, once said:]

That law is immutably fixed which declares that he who has received spiritual benefit, no matter how little, must not willingly die, unless he has communicated that which he has received to at least one other person. And therein it is also stated that by *communicating* is meant, not merely verbal delivery, but patient care until that other person fully understands. Having once turned thy mind to the light of that True Sun, thou hath cast thyself upon that great stream of divine energy which flows to and from that Sun; and nevermore canst thou claim back for thyself that life; live, then, so that the duty may be well performed.

—January, 1888

[A comrade writes:]

This battle does not seem like the real one. That will come when, for purposes of testing the staying force of her supporters and the influence on them of theosophy, H. P. B. will *seem* to give herself away.

—July, 1889

The image of the Master is the best protection against lower influences; think of the Master as a living man within you.

—September, 1890

I faint with the desire to find those who will unselfishly accept me and work for the rest. I give myself in all things for your benefit and would be glad if by my death or by my loss you could reach enlightenment. I would transfer, could I do so, all my experience to your soul and give it away to you. For what? For nothing at all save your acceptance. You know very well we can do no more than offer these goods. We set up the wooden image before the eyes of men and not one taking the sword cuts it in two, to find the jewels within. Then we sadly go on again.

—June, 1887

[The following extract from a letter of X. shows the attitude of the clear-sighted seeker:]

Like you, I merely want to work. I seek no powers; *nothing.* I have made in my heart the martyr's vow. I am devoted as far as my lights in each life will permit to the service in the altruist army. Just now I only find T.S. to work in here. Next time, some other way—or the same. I am ready "to step out of the sunshine into the shade so as to make room for others," and I seek no

Nirvana. This is your way, too; so be troubled not by words, titles or confusions.

—December, 1889

[Some are being wounded in the fray, and to one of such this letter was lately written by a friend.]

Hearing that you are not well in health and have as well another grief to bear, I make bold to write to you and say that I am sorry. It is not consolation that I have to offer, for I think that is too often a mere mockery of sorrow. Yet I would tell you that you are not quite alone. A friend who is dealing blows to right and left, and would fain make of herself an enemy, has not spared you in that respect. But I think we have only to remember what we have already learned for ourselves—that it is all from delusion—and then we shall not mind and shall be prepared to wait until great Time brings its magic changes. We can wait: "those also serve who only stand and wait." And that, too, has to be learned—no doubt like other things—through pain. But let us not forget that it is we who make our own pain. I have found that grief and sorrow spring only from wrong thinking. Not wrong in the sense of wicked, but in the sense of something out of harmony with the scheme of Nature; something *unscientific* and therefore contrary to the highest ethics. If we confined our thoughts as well as acts to our own clear duty, leaving results and the morrow to the Law, what room would there be for sorrow?

So, let us lean back and smile at the show and seeming of things, knowing that even if we are tied by hands and feet for a spell of days or years the heart of the world will throb on quite well without us. Therefore, do not let us get mentally involved in this or any other matter, but stand aside—spectators, though doing with power all that comes to us to do and ready to do nothing if that be needed. Then, Brother, let us be glad at whatever comes and at all that is said and whispered, for though to-day may seem dark, these things work out in the end for good. The more violent the storm, the sooner shall we see the face of the sun which shines behind the clouds that hide it for only a very little while. You are quite happy and serene, ready for all and indifferent to each, at rest in the silent place of your own abode. But, like all of us, you are not known to every man, for the soul alone knows the soul. That is why there is little need to hide in Kali Yuga! You may tell all, and they are not one jot the wiser. These people who imagine that they know the heart, the mind, and the soul of either you or me are not wise at all. They do not understand. They do not believe in their teaching, but merely hold it in their heads. So let it turn there, and perchance in the course of ages a flower will bloom in the heart of each, and then we will rejoice. If man could be strong in himself as a part of the whole, the noise of the world would not so much as reach his ears. My love to you.

—April, 1895

FROM UNPUBLISHED LETTERS

There are no authorities in Theosophy except such as every one chooses to accept for himself.

No effort, even the smallest, is ever in vain; and knowing this, each one can "try, ever keep trying."

It is unwise to consider phenomena or try to understand them, until one has thoroughly grasped the philosophy of nature and man found in Theosophy.

Phenomena are wholly illusionary, and if considered lead away from the reality of life and truth.

The accounts of other incarnations are not useful nor reliable; they will do no good in the end, but may lead to vanity and gloom; and therefore, they are to be avoided. I never knew a case yet where such were followed or relied on that had not bad consequences. And the only Adepts I ever knew refuse to tell of one's past life: it is a rule of occultism that relations of past lives shall not be indulged in, similar to the rule against relating your progress in the higher life *in this life.* A study of spiritual philosophy as found in *Bhagavad Gita* will shed light on all possible events, which are mere motions and unreal apparitions, hiding the truth from our perception.

As to yourself, of course those powers that come naturally are good, and may be used naturally, and the caution I would give (that to you may not be necessary) is that the less people to whom

NOTE.—These fragments were originally published in *The English Theosophist,* October, 1898; April, 1899; and January-March, 1900.—Eds.

you actually reveal yourself, the better for your progress, and for them, too. The way to do good with those powers is never by the exhibition of them, but by the influence they may silently exert on others, and by the cues, clues, and points they may give to their possessor if rightly used; in that way, they may become of use, but not by talking of them, nor by any show. This is a great point in all true schools of Occultism.

Do not be discouraged; there is no cause; nothing that is done with ease is really very good or lasting; there must be annoyances and strains here and there.

Do not harbour the idea that ——— and others do not attend for "caste reasons" and the like. Better to assume that they have other reasons; better to hope for the best and the best will come; . . . besides, I do not think it is the fact. Gossip gets up these ideas.

The circumstances we are in *are* the best for us if we will only so regard them. Try to do this, and thus get the best out of them, and escape them in another life.

Try to get people to practise true theosophy and brotherhood.

As to the matter of ———, the best way is to wait with moderation, to do the best possible, to refuse to listen to calumny and see what will happen. . . . We are not always to be reforming others, while at the same time we can refuse to let the others damage the work. . . .

Stand firm, avoid controversy, and continue work.

Try to progress in harmony; the other kind of progress will then follow in due course. Be a centre of harmony yourself and others will help you in spreading that feeling throughout.

Let us all draw closer together in mind and heart, soul and act, and try thus to make that true brotherhood through which alone our universal and particular progress can come.

I think you and ——— ought to change your attitude of mind in this one point: it seems to me—though I may be wrong, and, if so, excuse me—that in wishing to have harmony you try, either in thought or act, to make harmony. Now, I do not think harmony can be made, but is the result of either action or thought. Consequently, you and ———, being persons who do their duty, should rest on that and let results go. If you do right, and do not think about whether harmony is the result or not, harmony must result if your actions are harmonious. This attitude will prevent nervous troubles, for very often we are nervous about a thing because we are thinking of the results. Now, if you do your best, and harmony does not result, it cannot be your fault; consequently, you should not think about it; the less you think about it, the sooner harmony will come.

The Society seems to be entirely different from all other organizations in this: that in others plenty of money is furnished by members—clubs and churches can raise large sums of money because they offer definite creeds. I suppose that human nature comes in its real colour before us in the Society, where we offer nothing of that kind, but demand real altruistic work.

And now as to the Branch. A rush of members is not good for it unless those in are able to cope with the rush. Hence it is of high importance that the branch should educate and strengthen itself, or it may grow too rapidly, like a child, and get weak, and thus retard itself. If, on the other hand, a large number of its members become each one a centre and a power from having good knowledge of the subject, then you would see the branch go on with undoubted power and force. If you had lecture after lecture, and merely new members and no building up of the old members, your branch would die the moment the supply of lecturing was cut off. Try and impress this on whatever of the members are willing to listen.

I regret to hear that you are not reconciled to your son's departure from this physical plane. It is hard to part with those we love, but death is only a parting on the lower planes; it is not a "loss" on the higher. But the true union on the inner planes, which always exists though we may be unconscious of it, cannot be *consciously* felt so long as there is any feeling of "disappointment." Try to think within yourself what would be the real desire of your son, and what is your own real inner desire, though you may not know it, in regard to your attitude. It would be, and *is,* on the inner planes, that you should not sorrow or grieve, but "rejoice"—yes, rejoice in the position in which you now are, because there is your great opportunity, because the Law and Nature always provide the greatest opportunity and bestow on us the greatest *blessings* we are capable of receiving. From the standpoint of the soul it is all we *ourselves* (the "souls") would have it.

If you find friction between yourself and another or others, never stop to think where they are wrong. Everybody is always wrong somewhere; and, apart from that, it would be easy enough to find their errors in your own imagination. Their errors, real or imaginary, are no concern of yours, are not your duty, and need not and should not be considered by you. For you to do so would be to make an occult "break." What concerns you and what is your duty is to discover wherein you have been at fault. If, on finding friction of any sort, you will look back over your past thoughts and words and deeds, you will surely find you have erred, either directly or indirectly, by leaving something undone or unsaid. By living that way you will learn a good deal about yourself, while by looking for and noting the possible faults of others—no matter how greatly they have sinned, in your opinion—you will learn nothing and will merely prove yourself an ass.

Difficulties and friction are the accompaniments of existence, and if everything was smooth and all right all the time we would have nothing to do. Our movement is a reform one, dealing with the very character of the race, and therefore neither we nor the other members of the race are perfect. Did you ever reflect on the question: "What would you do if all our ideals for man were accomplished, if altruism were universal?" We would have to emigrate to some worse planet to have scope for our feelings. Hence we should accept all the difficulties as part of the day's work, and try to get as many people, including ourselves, arranged for help as we can.

Do not think you do nothing for the Cause which is so dear to you, for indeed the truest work is done on the inner planes, and without this there could be no work done on the outer planes. So, remember that you *can* work and are doing real work to help the cause by being strong in heart, in trust, and in devotion. In this way, you help to keep the centre of the whole movement strong, and others, who can work on the outer plane, will be helped to do their work because the centre is strong, and they themselves get help from it. This is what you can do and you should think of it often.

We are now to be like the Freemasons, who are one and all, in every part of the world, Freemasons. Yet each Grand Lodge is independent, autonomous. That is the way to look at it. In the U. S. there are about forty independent States; in each a Masonic Grand Lodge for the state, every one autonomous, and yet every member a Freemason and travelling into every Lodge if he follows the rule.

It was quite right that Autonomy was agreed on as the method. There would be very great clumsiness and friction in being part of the American T. S. Each great territory, like an individual, stands on its own feet, while all are united in aim. . . . After everything is arranged it is to be hoped that you may be able to reach many more minds than before. If we keep in mind that what we ought to work for is to bring the truths of Theosophy before the greatest number of persons and not that we seek office or honour, then our best efforts must have good results. I congratulate all, and hope for the very best.

I have your letter, and reply as best I can. In the first place, I am neither wise enough nor good enough to be the guide for anyone, but am willing to help all I can to the best of my ability, always premising that we are on quite an equal footing. So much, then, to begin.

I am glad you have such an earnest desire to help in the T. S. cause, and to try and spread truth as you understand it. This attitude, being persisted in, will lead to the right end. It is the only one you need assume, and if you listen to the voice of your own soul, it will guide you aright and better than I could.

You are now in the flush of a new thing. This flush will wear off to some extent, to be succeeded by a deeper knowledge, and hence a greater strength. So, then, all you have to do is to continue doing all you can for others, and at the same time keep up the process of purifying the mind of old notions and of getting the new ideas well fixed, well grounded and well arranged. Then you will be all the better able, each day more and more, to help all with whom you may be thrown.

But I would not advise you to use your strength in curing people of ills, save now and then, for the reason that each one has just so much power, and, if used, it is gone. The Masters have more power than you or I, yet they are not found curing diseases now, but are at work all the time at the souls of men and at their minds. For the deep darkness of the soul and the mind of the race are more important than their outer miseries, as the latter will all soon be ended by death. Thus, we are not justified in using all our strength to help the very few that one person might reach in a lifetime. Use your power that way, and you die having helped in body a few. But use your power for the souls and minds of men and you will have cured many, for many lives to come, even in this present short life.

Later it will be time for you to look into the other and higher flights of Theosophy. At present your test and your trial are in the great enthusiasm you have with but little vent. By standing this, it will do you good; but, using all opportunity for others in your present circumstances, you will take all that nature offers and she will, later on, offer you more and better chances if you are fit—not otherwise.

In regard to the movement, you may be sure that it will be taken care of if the members do their part. H. P. B. laid down the lines of work and if we follow these we may safely leave the results in the hands of the Master and the Law of Karma.

I shall use the story of your little girl's conversation in the *Path* without giving any names or places so as not to involve you.* It will be useful and interesting for the readers. It is very instructive and more like it would be if people did not repress the children. In the past I published a good many such in the *Path*. ***

As to the child. It is true, of course, we are not perfect, but, while we are not so, it is not true that we cannot give the children as nearly perfect teaching as possible; they may be more perfect and make better use of it when we give it to them. Hence I would tell her all of reincarnation, and not make the mistake of letting her explain away a truth, as she did by a mere mechanical and mental reply—like her saying it was a picture in the mind. Why not say, "Why, that is a fact, you lived before and many times, and it is likely you saw with your real memory the picture of another mother who may have been myself when I lived with you." Then tell her the simple truth of the soul and its unity, and of the great Soul of all and of the actual immortality now and not after, and that eternity is now; and also of Karma. She will understand perhaps better than yourself, for her mind is not filled with nonsense. How much could be avoided for the children if they were not left to the fight we have had, and is it not your duty to save her from such a long struggle to get over bad education? What you find good for your own mature mind should not be kept from your child, and she can understand very well and will not forget.

I should advise you not to talk *much* to the child of her other lives. Let the fact of those be a tacitly understood thing. Teach her all you like of law and ethics and duty, and what not, but you will do well to avoid now particularizing old events. In time, living in an atmosphere where the real truth of things is taught and believed, her soul will expand and she herself will know when to speak of those former events and when not.

When you feel lonely, remember that on the higher planes we are never alone, but that those who are striving to follow the right path are linked together by bonds of sympathy and true brotherhood, and remember, too, that the greatest work is not done on outer physical planes but on the thought plane. Here is something, then, for you to do:—to think strong helpful thoughts for all the members of the T. S. and for your friends, and then for the whole of humanity. It may be that when a bright

* This correspondence is published in the *Path*, March, 1894. —Eds.

helpful thought comes into your own life, it has been sent forth from some other, who is trying to lighten the load of the world's suffering, and all the loving helpful thoughts that you can send out will help to lighten someone's sadness, and bring a ray of hope into someone's life. Each thought is a seed, and will bear fruit in due season.

Around the word Spiritualism in your letter, is the bad influence that is against you. My advice to you is to keep that whole influence off as much as you can, try to work for others, and rely on your Higher Self.

I am glad to hear of your work in F——— and trust that you will be able to get together a strong Centre; remember, however, that you yourself can be and are a centre to the extent that you make Theosophy a living power in your life.

Sexual intercourse is a right and proper thing when used for its right object as intended by nature, *i. e.,* the propagation of children. But, if indulged in simply for personal and sensual gratification, it becomes like any other passion, and as regards this you can decide for yourself.

The arguments *pro* and *con* on this point will not help you much. Better get them out of your mind, and depend on the leading of the spirit and the voice of conscience.

Endeavour to do that which is right from the standpoint of your inner consciousness, and you will be led in the right way.

Instead of being annoyed, I am glad to get your letter, for it shows *you* see. It is a twenty years' experience with me to know what you see and not be able to destroy the mask born with another and now mine. But it has been useful. Did I know how to destroy it perhaps it would be better, perhaps not—it might mean death.

If you look at its hand you would find death shown fifteen years ago and now—yet it lives. Too much effort might kill it now—I do not know. But so many thinking as you do may have effect in time unconsciously, so to say. The whole thing comes from the peculiar fact of a person living in a house he did not build, and having two astrals at work.

No, your friends do not and will not forget you, but remember that the greatest and truest friend is the Higher Self. He who has the Higher Self as his friend possesses all things and lacks nothing, and the Higher Self is your friend if you will but receive that friendship.

Take courage and be patient: the light is shining in your heart, and, if you will but go on, you will find it there, and it will be brighter far than you can now imagine.

It is true that too often when we begin to meditate on some elevating thought, dark thoughts come in, and this is not easy to overcome; but if we remember that the very essence of our being, the inmost sanctuary of the Soul, is divine, we can enter into it and shut out the evil. The tendency of the mind is to wander from subject to subject, and so we should try to follow the advice of the *Bhagavad Gita*: "To whatsoever object the inconstant mind goeth out, he should subdue it, bring it back and place it upon the Spirit." "There is no purifier in this world to be compared to spiritual knowledge, and he who is perfected in devotion findeth Spiritual knowledge springing up spontaneously in himself in the progress of time."

Although so far away, yet through ——— I hear something of all that you and your co-workers are doing. It interests me very much, it must be of great effect and value, both now and in later days. As I understand it, your work is with those who are called in England "common people." In this country we are all common people, and such work strictly is hardly possible here. It is therefore very interesting, because from the better (so-called) classes no great improvement will come. If you can sensibly alter those "common people," you will have done a great work for the world. The cultured classes do not give us any hope for theosophy —they are too selfish and too superficial.

I feel sure you do not hold that erroneous opinion that theosophy can only be understood by the highly educated. Any man can understand it and make it a part of his life. In fact, I think that its essential truths are easier for the humble than for the polished. For a lot of education and a smattering of different notions in the heads of the better educated make it difficult for them to come to any conclusions in any such matters.

I trust you will go on unfalteringly. Do not be depressed by anything. It is of no use. Besides, it may be avoided if you will avoid setting down, to be achieved, any certain results as to persons, numbers, times or otherwise. We must be satisfied with what the time and Karma give us after we have done our duty and the best.

Let us simplify our teachings, avoiding long and strange words. "Merit" and "Demerit" express part of Karma and are words well known to Catholics. And so on, in all directions, we should try to avoid all pedantry and the making of a new language.

Let us not judge others too much, for they also may be acting up to the best light they have. Besides, Karma ever works, and ever the T. S. must feel it even more than other bodies. The effect of the fuss—for it is but that—must be for the best, for, if it kills the T. S., that proves a deserved death; if not, then T. S. is stronger than ever. The latter is what I see as the final end, however far off. . . .

Our duty, these days of trial and transition, is to engage in propaganda, so as to place Theosophy before as many of the race as possible. To do that, the most common-sense, simple presentation of theosophy, free from vagueness and big words, is the best.

The very best I can say to you is that, as you know, all our troubles in life arise from ourselves, no matter how much they may seem to come from the outside; we are all parts of the one great whole, and if you try to centre your mind upon that fact, and to remember that those things that seem to trouble you are really due to your own way of looking at the world and life, you will probably grow more contented in mind. It is your own mind you should watch, and not the circumstances in which you are placed. Others have been in worse circumstances than what you think surround you, and have not been disturbed as you seem to be. It must be, therefore, that it is the way you yourself look at this thing; stop looking at it, then, in that way and look at everything in a contented spirit, feeling sure that they are all more or less illusionary, and you will do better.

A teacher, and that is your present status no matter how or why, has to have not only a pleasant manner on the outside but must have a purely pleasant and sweet feeling inside; for if the inside does not, in fact, coincide with the outside, then there is trouble. When the outside is pleasant but the inside is false, then it is a hollow shell and all the good magnetism is cut off. When the outside is rough but the inside wishes to be right, there is sincerity; then the magnetism is not cut off, but a current in opposition is often raised which engenders error and misconception and makes a big obstacle, though many friends arise who overlook it.

But it is not to be so left. The inner attitude must be made entirely suave, and the outer will soon be made to correspond. Surety of conviction is not best conveyed by force, but by the great onward quiet movement of the glacier, the best example of this. To the quiet motion of the glacier add the steady fire of the genial Sun, and nothing can resist. This is the way, and, if it is comprehended, there will be more and better work done and more help given.

When one stops to think, to weigh, and to consider what is one's duty, or which of many duties should be performed first, it is indeed perplexing and difficult to know *what* to do. But if you will do just what lies before you without thinking about all the other things, and without troubling your mind about all the things you can't do, then it will all be different and everything will grow brighter for you. Do what you have to do now, and don't trouble about other things, they will be looked after in due time; but what will help you in all these matters is to be content, to do what you can, and to let the rest go; act with a high motive; have kindly feelings towards all; do some little act of kindness every day and try to realize that the end of all this will be happiness and peace for all humanity. Then, a foretaste of that peace will enter your own heart. There is a bright side to life, and what makes the brightness is the love which each of us may have for humanity.

Generally speaking, the habit of drinking intoxicants is due to a desire to get rid of what might be called the present personal consciousness. When people drink to try and drown sorrow, pain, worry, they clearly do it with that motive in view. But others drink without any such ostensible motive, though still with the same actual motive, for they long to get rid of what is to them an intolerable sense of identity, of monotony, of sameness. It is an effort to produce by extraneous aids what can only be done properly and lastingly by interior development. People read trashy novels, gamble and so forth with the same motive, that is to say, with the intention of getting rid of their personal identity for the time being. Ultimately, the race will come to realize that this can only be achieved by identification of the ego with the higher instead of the lower nature. Meanwhile, and for the ordinary person, healthy and interesting occupation is the best cure for such a habit. If possible, he should be made to understand that the desire for drink is now a habit in certain lives in his body whose very existence depends upon their being fed with alcohol. The desire is not in himself unless he is foolish enough to identify himself with the desire. Once he ceases to so identify himself, the desire will lose more than half its power over him.

FROM "THE IRISH THEOSOPHIST"

Mr. Judge, during a few remarks at the close of the meeting, explained the method of study adopted in America.

Each Branch, he said, formed itself into sections for the purpose of studying a certain subject, such, for instance, as the *Bhagavad Gita*. When the study was completed the sections compared notes, and produced, subsequently, a general statement of decisions upon which they could all agree. Without such a system as this the movement could not have solidarity. Moreover, it was the system adopted by groups of Chelas under the direct supervision of the Masters.

When he first heard of the Dublin Lodge he felt that it "rang" in his ears. When one heard of some Branches (and he was glad to think that they were few) the sound seemed to fall dully. In this case he felt that it was real. He hoped that it would become a living power in Ireland. He knew of no European race that was more naturally occult, especially the western Irish.

In conclusion, he said that he would counsel the Lodge to aspire to the principles of the Masters.

—February, 1895

Say, my friend, remember that title: The Cause of Sublime Perfection. That is the name of Theosophy. Opposed to the idea of inherent sinfulness, it may work a change. Use the title now and then. So will I. Those three—(*a*) Perfectibility of Humanity, (*b*) Cause of Sublime Perfection, (*c*) Masters are living facts, and not cold abstractions—should be well spread abroad. They pulverize the awful wrong of inherent sin, they raise a hope in every man above a sot, they illuminate the sky of the future. We work for the future—oh, the glorious future!

—February, 1897

FROM "THE PACIFIC THEOSOPHIST"

[Experience proves that Theosophy can be most acceptably presented to the laboring classes. Especially can karma and reincarnation be explained as enforcing Brotherhood. Persons wishing to study and work along these lines are referred to pp. 37-39 of the *Key to Theosophy,** for practical hints. Also pages 197-249 of the same work, will be found to present many valuable points to use at such meetings. No leading-up policy is required. Plain, straight Theosophy—karma and reincarnation—is what is needed. These, and these alone, meet the wants and solve the problems of laboring men. These are extracts from letters from William Q. Judge, in regard to this matter:]

Strive to get a clear, comprehensive and common-sense view of Theosophy, and to the world give only that view, and the world will appreciate. Never consider yourself as the actor, and think of the real Self.

Never consider that you have done better than another; always strive to improve.

Do not soar to ridiculous heights where no one can follow you, and where you will not be at home yourself.

And karma, reincarnation and the seven-fold constitution of man are the important doctrines, and can be presented in every manner.

Do your best and you will have all the opportunities you can manage, and all the experience you require.

—October, 1895

* These references are to the original edition. (See photographic reprint by The Theosophy Company.)—Eds.

FROM "THE INTERNATIONALIST"

You must find yourself out. And you had better do something concretely practical for some other needy person rather than aim at "ideal thoughts," soaring in clouds and other useless things. Envy no one. You express envy for ———. They need aid as much as you. Their conditions and capacities are not yours: better find and measure your own. As you say, your brain wavers, then give it a long rest and do simple constant acts of kindness for others. . . . There are all too many members who too hastily aspire to be great writers, orators, leaders. . . . The tortoise and not the hare won the race. The purely practical part of the movement needs workers. There are too many dreamers.

—October, 1897

FROM "THE SCREEN OF TIME"

Once a vision was seen. The seer is known to the writer by letter only, though well known. He was in Paris. Passing up from the Luxembourg Gardens, along narrow streets that seem to be a centre of equal attraction for priests, restaurants and funerals—though hiding perhaps beneath this safe disguise an inner life of different and loftier order—he came out upon the *Quai* directly opposite the site of the Tuileries. Leaning over the parapet, gazing at the muddy waters of the Seine, his thoughts were in no way enticed by the miles of second-hand bookstalls that extend along the south side of the river. Their volumes in every language and on every subject (a battered *Key* among the rest!), rare and curious, cheap and very nasty, no more occupied his mind than the tragedy of the fallen Empire which had played its last stake within two hundred yards of where he stood. Paris, once the temple of Pleasure and still the *rendezvous* of pleasure-seekers, was all in holiday attire. Laughter was in the air—but what are surroundings to a man whose mind is occupied with thoughts that are worth the thinking? Nothing. Truly it is the mind which makes the surroundings, and Archimedes was neither the first nor the last thinker who has remained faithful to a thought during the sacking of his city.

NOTE.—This concluding portion of an article by "Julius" (*Path*, August, 1895) evidently renders an experience of Mr. Judge's—Eds.

My friend soon found realistically the truth of this oft-repeated adage. He had been pondering over the history of a life, a friend's life; studying it, not unkindly, but in relation to universal principles and with fraternal sympathy. He came down along the record of events until he reached the present. Looking out across the river, gazing without sight at what had once been the palace of a tinsel Caesar, there suddenly appeared to him a gray figure, stooping, meditative. Then it waxed clearer and he saw that the head of the figure was bent over some object held in the hand. It seemed that the whole being—the mind, heart and soul of this silent spectre—were riveted on this one object. My friend looked more closely to discover what this was: only a worm, a poor, struggling worm transfixed on a pin, writhing in agony. A feeling of disgust at the cruelty of it came over him, and he turned to reproach the torturer, who had not seen him, who had eyes for nothing but the sufferings of the captive worm, regarding it with interested pity and yet with satisfaction. "Why not take it off—?" my friend began, but as he turned to speak he started back in momentary horror. The figure was that of the person whose life-history he had been pondering, and the worm, as he now saw, bore a similar likeness—the picture of a mind gloating over its own self-inflicted sufferings.

Then all vanished. A company of French infantry passed by him with strident bugling that could be heard for miles. It sounded miles away. The picture still fascinated him. The pity of it! For it was true: This had been the symbol of that life. The Worship of Pain; a sublimated form of selfishness that longed for a martyr's crown, but which would welcome the martyrdom for its own sake, even without the crown. A selfishness that in its grosser form would be but hypocrisy and conceit. A passion for pain which made it seem that to inflict it on others was to confer a benefit rather than a wrong. How could they grow without pain? See how I have grown through pain! A disease, my brothers, a disease of the mind. "Think not that breaking bone, that rending flesh and muscle, unites thee to thy 'silent Self'." And remember that "these vices of the ordinary man pass through a subtle transformation, and reappear with changed aspect in the heart of the disciple." The St. Dominic of yesterday may well continue to try to purify the souls of others and his own, by the pain he thinks it right to inflict, though now perhaps he uses some mental torture. The St. Simeon Stylites of one life may pass from racking his body for "the greater glory of God," to racking his mind, and with the same motive. He may now cry as then, though in different form:

> O my sons, my sons . . . mortify
> Your flesh, like me, with scourges and with thorns;
> Smite, shrink not, spare not . . . .

* * * * *

> O Jesus, if thou wilt not save my soul,
> Who may be saved? Who is it may be saved?
> Who may be made a saint, if I fail here?
> Show me the man hath suffer'd more than I."

But that is not Theosophy: nor is it Occultism. It is far removed from either. Once more we see that growth does not depend upon the amount of pain or pleasure that is endured, but upon our attitude of mind towards all that may meet us on life's journey. "It is not *what* is done, but the spirit in which the least thing is done that is counted." JULIUS

FROM MS. LETTERS

New York, July 25, 1893

Dear Brother:

I have but little time to reply to yours, as my recent trip to London has made a lot of business grow, and the Congress at Chicago of the T S has added more still to the load.

I asked ——— to write you about the Sunday School as we have run it here, and he has done so. That might be done at any place by sincere members if they like to try. It is a success here. I hope it will be the same with you.

As to the other matter, let me tell you what has guided me all my life and may guide you. When an idea of work for the T S comes into my head, I go at it even if I do not see just how, and always the help and the right line comes to me, for I have a supreme faith that the great Lodge will foster all such, even if we do not hear from the Lodge. So if you have the idea of a regular and systematic gathering, go ahead, and your faith and sincerity will carry you through. But make it fully theosophical. This means not sectarian. And that will enable you to give out what you believe to be right, if you always say and let it be constantly known that no man is forced to believe.

Let it be a large T S if you like, with its creed universal brotherhood, and if some might object to being an actual part of the T S, then let the formal branch part of it be for those who are willing—the others getting the benefit by their attendance. There is nothing to prevent one having music at such gatherings if such is the desire. All that is wanted is a clear head and a strong hand at the top, to see that no creed as such is indulged in. It might be a success. I know there are many who want to attend such meetings and who like a little music. But in that case I would either (*a*) eliminate all references in the hymns to Jesus and the religion of the day, or (*b*) insert references to every religion and make the one as prominent as the other.

Maybe this idea of yours is the beginning of a great and new success, for while many ministers really steal and preach our ideas without credit, none are bold enough to say "I am a theosophist

---

NOTE.—These letters, all (except the last one) to the same person, are in the archives of the United Lodge of Theosophists.—Eds.

and preach it, not compelling you to believe." If you did so you would compel respect, and at the same time gain perhaps a great hearing. I have wondered some did not do this, but I see that vanity and personality and fear have prevented it. If you did it, it would be the first distinctive effort of the kind, and at the same time it might be carried on in full sympathy with the T S and its administration.

Let me know what you think of all this, and may you have luck and also confidence, hope and a good inspiration.

Sincerely yours,

William Q. Judge

New York, November 8, 1893

Dear Bro. ———:

I wrote you a long letter in August, in reply to yours of the 13th of July enclosing the catechism, and expected, rather, an answer to that from you. As immediately thereafter I was plunged into the work of the Chicago Congress, which is not yet quite done, I have been too busy to take the catechism up again particularly, and, as I said, have been waiting rather to hear from you. I will endeavor soon to get the time to look over it again and send it to you. It is a very difficult matter to do, as the making of a catechism tends in the direction of dogmatism which we ought to avoid. Although I have very definite beliefs of my own, still I hesitate to put them in a dogmatic form for the use of others, such as a catechism would involve. One great difficulty that we have to encounter is that although children are easily taught and quickly understand, the adults who take up theosophy do not themselves understand it because they have so many old notions to get rid of.

Sincerely yours,

William Q. Judge

That catechism was a mistake I know well. [Pencil notation at bottom of letter, by recipient.—Eds.]

New York, May 3, 1894

Dear Brother ———,

On return from an 8,000 mile tour I have yours of 23.3.94. Well, so you are out. Perhaps it is a good thing to be well quit of the incubus of a cult you don't believe. All success to you. Am glad you are encouraged by the start of your new venture.

The matter of ——— is still pending, and as I am soon off to London to attend that blessed Jud'l Com'te, I cannot do much about him.

What your clairvoyant saw about the Church is true, only it will take over 100 years perhaps. It is now tottering on its rotten creeds.

I thank you for all your news. Write me again. And have patience with me for such short letters, as I am overworked and banked up high with unanswered letters on all sides, together with Path work for 2 advance months—all to be done in 3 weeks.

Goodbye and good luck,

William Q. Judge

[Cincinnati] May 20, 1895

Dear Bro. ———

I am away from home for my health [which is] much hurt by others' hate. * * *

Besant has had what ought to be her last say, and I read to the delegates at our Conv'n my explan'n of the charges—my last word. It will soon be published.

I wish we could all ignore Mrs. B once and for all. She lives by fighting or flattery now. But what blasphemy to say that, even be I guilty, the Master would stoop so low as to bid her hound me over the world trying to murder my character. *I pity her in her next life.* It will not be I who will then annoy her but the hundreds who have been insulted and outraged by her acts and words ag'st me. Instead of one she will then have hundreds of enemies and obstructions.

Well, goodby and best wishes. . . .

Yours,

William Q. Judge

3 Oct 1895

Dear Bro. ———

* * * As regards T. S. organization in N. Z. & Australia I cannot express any opinion. You must do what you as a body consider the best thing to be done, and if people won't work without having office, why, let them have it—it is work we want. But think the matter over carefully and consult together, so that you may do what on the whole you consider best for the Movement.

I hope you will be able to form a strong centre. . . .

Fraternally yours,

William Q. Judge

New York City, November 18, 1895

Dear Brother ———,

I thank you again for your very kind invitation to visit New Zealand and Australia, but I certainly cannot come now for my health would not permit of the journey, nor could I at the present time and in the present state of affairs go so far away from the center of the Work in America. The matter must therefore be held over indefinitely, but I ask you to please express my thanks and good wishes to all who joined with you in inviting me to visit you.

I am glad to hear that "your people" will listen to your Theosophical talks on Sundays—much good seed can be sown in this way. As for the other Branches and Centers in N. Z. they have to be let follow what course they consider right. ——— writes me that here and there are members who are at least not unfriendly. This is good; and steady quiet work on your part will not fail to have its effect. . . .

You had not before told me about the notes taken of A. B.'s talks in Auckland. As a general rule it is better to let such matters drop, and turn your energies in other directions. But always use your own judgment, and if in a particular instance, should opportunity offer, you think it well to bring up the matter it would be all right for you to do so. But I believe A B did speak that way of the "old Tibetan woman" as that was constantly said at

Av[enue] Rd. by her and others who all knew nothing of it. Mrs. B has the habit of "forgetting"—we call it a very "bad forgettery."

Many thanks for the kind wishes. . . .

Fraternally yours,

William Q. Judge

May 26, 1888

Dear ———,

I have your letter. Am glad you like the Bhag. Gita. The reason for these similarities and coincident times is that *we all move together*. You will notice that the June Bhag. G. article* in type and in MS. long ago agrees precisely with Lucifer just at hand in *its* first article.† The latter should be studied by all, especially by those aspiring beings who would pull down the moon without a step ladder while their ordinary duties are ignored.

The last of Idylls‡ is already set up. My great pressure and hurry prevented me sending proof. And here I will say that in any future articles for Path I am obliged to cut out so much poetry. It is wasteful of space and does not suit so many as prose does. Part 2 of yours takes 8 pages and has thus crowded out matter equally valuable.

Baxter is back and I am glad. He must have been missed by Malden T. S.

The old obligation has not been altered. It relates solely to signs and passwords. I have sent you some.

Fraternally,

William Q. Judge

Staying out of Devachan is for those who are really pledged and accepted and not merely for those who aspire. Besides Devachan *may* be enjoyed while you are yet alive. J.

NOTE.—The last letter is reproduced, pp. 188-9.—Eds.

* The fourth paper on the second chapter. (See *Notes on the Bhagavad-Gita*, p. 69.)—Eds.

† "Occultism *versus* the Occult Arts," in the May *Lucifer* (reprinted in *Theosophy*, XXXI, 149).—Eds.

‡ "Theosophy in Tennyson's 'Idylls of the King'," *Path*, May and June, 1888.—Eds.

May 26, 1888.

Dear Collins

I have your letter. Am glad you like the Bhag. Gita. The reason for these similarities & coincident times is that <u>we all move together</u>. You will notice that the June Bhag. G. art. in type and in MS. long ago agrees precisely with Lucifer just at hand in <u>its</u> first article. The latter should be studied by all especially by those aspiring beings who would pull down the moon without a step ladder while their ordinary duties are ignored.

The last of Idylls is already set up. My great pressure and hurry prevented me sending proof. And here I will say that in any future articles for Path I am obliged to cut out so much poetry. It is wasteful of space and does not suit so many as prose does. Part 2 of yours takes 8 pages and has then crowded out matter equally valuable.

Buxton is back and I am glad. He must have been moved by Madras T.S.

The old obligation has not been altered. It relates solely to signs & passwords. I have sent you some.

Fraternally

William Q. Judge

Skipping out of Devachan is for those who are really pledged & accepted & not merely for those who aspire. Besides Devachan _may_ be enjoyed while you are yet alive. J

LONDON AND PARIS LETTERS

[On his way to India, in 1884, Mr. Judge had to spend some weeks in London, waiting for the coming of H. P. B. and Col. Olcott from India. During those days he wrote letters to a "long-time friend," Mrs. Laura Langford (formerly Mrs. Holloway, co-author of *Man—Fragments of Forgotten History*). For another phase of his London experiences, see "A Weird Tale."—Eds.]

This is the end of this chapter. This sheet of extracts I enclose to you I took last night from the letters in S.'s possession.* Of course, that is not one twentieth part of what he had, but I thought those would be of use to you and the other two disciples.† . . . A letter came from H. S. O. yesterday to S., posted at Marseilles, saying they, H. S. O., H. P. B., Mohini ‡ and one other chela, would be in Paris perhaps one week, and then would be here, except H. P. B., who is furious at treatment of the ∴ by the London Branch, and who says she will not, but will stop in Boulogne, in France, or other place, to go on with the new *Isis*.

Today forenoon I have had an awful time, such as I never had. It was at 5 A. M., your time, but 10 here, onward and up to now. Awful. Such an outside pressure on me to go back to the U. S. and to any other fancy you can imagine—suicide, anything. There is no cause for it in me. Went to bed early last night. Maybe the influence in ______ is bad, or that in my hotel. But whatever it was and is, it began in the street suddenly without preparation, and instead of growing up to strength it rushed upon me just as if you had made the determination to force me out of my path.

Ah, my friend, the path is dark, and now as I write, I am in the valley of the shadow, which is so horrible because I know it is not caused by my wrong doing. My time has been spent in the day in going about to see this place instead of in writing, and in the evening at S.'s except last eve when I was home at 9:15, read the *Theosophist* till 11 and then to bed. Nor have I had bad thoughts. They have dwelt upon the Masters, upon you, upon the situation.

NOTE.—Originally published in *The Word*, March and April, 1912.—Eds.

* A.P.Sinnett, Vice-President of the London Lodge.—Eds.

† Mrs. Hollis-Billings and Emma Hardinge Britten, the △ later referred to.—Eds.

‡ The other author of *Man*.—Eds.

I shall telegraph Olcott today and then when I get reply—what? Such is the state of my mind. I have lost my steadiness, and after all these years. Dear friend, help me. Of course, when you get this, I may be out of all annoyance, but there is a comfort in addressing you in this letter. You are now either up or awake, as it is 11:30 A. M. here. . . . Goodby, Love to the whole △ and may we soon be able to see clearly what the whole affair is to be.

Just before dinner I went up to the Dome of St. Paul's and into the great bell placed on top from where a grand view might be had. But the eternal fog prevented, although this is an exceptionally fine day indeed.

The stairway is inside between the two sides of the dome, and the ascent to the bell is difficult. Don't know how you could do it. It is a cylinder with heavy iron bars on each side and a perpendicular wooden ladder. You brace up against the sides, and ascend the ladder, holding on by the heavy bars—only one at a time can get up, and up there it is open, but not enough to fall through. So I have done nearly all there is. Today I am going with Thomas,* a friend, to the Parliament Houses.

My depression must not affect you, as it is quite likely to go away soon.

I must close again. 1st, An engagement. 2nd, The Mail closes. 3rd, There is a snuffling man in this room, whose continuous snuffle drives me mad. Goodbye again.

Your Brother, W.

Grass from St. Paul's Church yard.

Last eve I went to dinner to Miss Arundale's, . . . West. Keep that address. She is a very charming woman and so in earnest. She lives there with her old mother who, although aged, is as fresh and intense in Theosophical pursuits as a young man. Today I went to S.'s. He was very glad to see me, and showed me his treasures. I will copy M. picture for you—a side view—and send it in my next. He has three heads of K. H., a very beautiful man. One is finished very highly, and the next are merely outlines surrounded with blue. But he says all are genuine. He has also some pictures of two or three chelas in Madras. He has

* Probably Thomas Green, co-editor of Book II. (See also p. 297.)—Eds.

another photo of a man lying on his side, with long hair—and such eyes! The face has strangely affected me ever since. This is his position. He is leaning on his left arm with two fingers under his mustache, which is large and black. His nose is very large and straight, and the eyes are enormous and have a similar expression to those in that of your Master. The face is youthful and strangely old. Do you know who it was?

The dinner at S.'s was of vegetables, and I stayed there until 11:30 P. M. coming home to hotel on the underground railway. I was therefore at S.'s and I thought much of you—from 3 to 7 P. M. your time. Zeno was there in full force, rushing about the room after dinner, and I was wondering why, when there arrived an Indian mail containing a letter from Olcott from Adyar in S.'s care. Olcott and H. P. B., if she comes, will stop with S. What you saw of her prostration was right. S. says she is very sick, and oh, how tired. There is a late picture of her there, showing her the image of fatigue.

I read them some of Damodar's letters, and they were very much interested. But, notwithstanding their large opportunities, I do not think they are as advanced as you and, of course, they have not got your powers.

I am rather at sea, not finding anything from India, and until I heard Olcott and H. P. B. were coming so soon, was tempted to go on the next steamer to Madras. I think I will await their arrival, as Mohini will be able to communicate with ———. Mohini is coming for the purpose of instructing these Londoners. . . .

Well, another week has passed by, and I am really further back than I ever was. The magnetic atmosphere of London is horrible. There is a place on the Strand on my way up here which I located this morning, where a wave of despair just overwhelms me, and I keep it after that nearly all day, and there is no other way of getting here. And then my dreams are bad. Last night I was watching the sea as it rolled in fiercely upon the shore, and although I was safe, yet I do not like it. Then I was among rivers that had dried up almost, leaving poor fishes gasping. The only redeeming feature was that I had a lot of birds. Then I slept again and met my sister A. and asked her what those dreams meant. She said, "They mean well, or that you will spoil your business, or your aims by your own acts." Curious, wasn't it?

Sunday in London is dull. Such is the respect for the day that by law all the public houses are shut during church hours, and all the underground trains stopped. Then, with church over, all the gin palaces are wide open again, and everything goes on in full vigor. What hypocrisy is this! I suppose that they are afraid that the working classes may disturb their worship of the most High God, if the public houses were allowed to be open. After that worship is over, and all the silk and broadcloth has gone home, the poor people may revel and drink as they like, and then go to the abbey for the evening service.

I went there last night at 7 and was soon flanked by an old habitué of gin shops, whose liquor-laden breath mingled with the strains of the music and the voice of the preacher, so that I began to fancy I was in a cell with a roystering keeper, while the priests and boys passed my cell-window chanting.

Such are the softening influences of English civilization and municipal regulations. Here was this drinking man actually listening in the sacred Abbey to the platitudes of Rev. Canon Maurice Spence, who was dilating upon the necessity of the well-to-do making sacrifices for the poor, while he, the Rev. Canon, no doubt went home every evening to his chops and ale.

What, a Canon drink ale? Why, of course. Everyone here drinks ale or beer and eats chops eternally. The English phrase is either "Let us go and kill something," or "Let us have a chop and some bitters." For my part, considering this love for beer, I cannot understand why the English and Germans have not long ago consolidated with beer for a basis. I presume the reason is the difficulty of drinking beer and talking German at the same time.

I went over to see M——y* at 11:30. . . . M——y is now well off, his father having died leaving him means. He has given up the law and studies philosophy. He has known H. P. B. and occultism as long as I have and hesitates about India. I asked him why, today, and he says there are so many dubious things about it for him. He knows the voyage is not much, but is afraid after getting there he would find out nothing whatever, they seem to dislike English and Americans so much. His trip to America in 1875 was taken solely from reading Olcott's *People from the Other World*, and in order to see the Eddies. It was then that he met H. P. B.

* C. C. Massey, a Spiritualist, one of the original members of the T.S., and first President of the British Theosophical Society, established in 1876.—Eds.

No news yet from Olcott or the native. I walked over to M——y's from the hotel and it took me forty minutes. I went along the Thames embankment, across by the Abbey and Parliament House and down Victoria street. The way was fine and the walk delightful. All along I was thinking of you and wishing you were with me.

This letter goes tomorrow, Thursday—so I will drop it now as I am going out with Thomas.

This paper I am writing upon is the last of my acquisitions through my South American speculations. Behold, then, the result of much weariness of spirit and much investment of money.

Yesterday I went to the British Museum, and found that the building, like nearly every other one in London, is hidden from view as you approach it.

It is a fine building, standing in front of Russell Street, and you could walk within two blocks of it, as I have done several times, and not know it was there. I assure you that had I been aware it was there, I should have visited it several times. As it is not furnished with a dome as St. Paul's, it is not caught by the eye from a distance. The street coming up in front of it is Museum St., and is very narrow indeed, so that as you come along all that you see is a small part of the vestibule. Museum Street leads into old Drury Lane, one of the most tortuous, narrow, old streets that I know of.

Outside on the steps are placed two New Zealand stone gods presented by Queen Victoria. Inside the door you have to leave cane and umbrella, and can buy, if you wish, the general catalogue—of which I send by this mail a copy to you—or any number of special ones.

You pass up the flight of stairs on the left, along which are placed a lot of East India bas reliefs from the Buddhist Temple of Amravati. This interested me very much, and I spent a good deal of time I knew I could spare from the Greek Gallery, in examining the figures and their attitudes. The collection of Indian articles is not large, but the Assyrian and Egyptian collections are very large and splendid. There are some corriders filled with these objects, such as statues, coffins, etc., and the impression made upon the mind is very solemn indeed. These enormous stone sarcophagi and colossal statues fill one with awe as well as admiration for the people who made them. I felt more at home there than I did in any other part of it. There was one enormous reddish stone arm and hand 16 feet from the shoulder to the fist. Just think of the whole of which it was but the arm! As one looked at the colossal black granite figure of the guardian of one of the gates of the lower world, the imagination ran back to the glorious past of Egypt, when that statue sat silent and motionless in the hall of the temple, while the processions of priests went by, or while their incantations evoked to view the elemental shapes of which the statue was but a copy. Oh, how I longed to have you there with me that you might relate what dim shapes you would see flitting about, harmless, sad, wondering where the past had gone; questioning why the rites of the ancient days proceeded no more, and looking with still greater wonder upon us, the modern barbarians.

There were no dire or evil influences there, and my sleep was not as much disturbed afterward as it often is by the things I succeed in taking over from the Theosophical Fellows.

I want very much to learn what is the connection between me and you and Egypt's past.

I felt quite at home also in another gallery or stairs, where the Egyptian Book of the Dead is, and where I could see the same figures as you find on that little panel I painted you.

The mummy room was also intensely interesting. What thoughts crowd upon one in such a place! How you realize the vanity of human life and the constant turning of the great wheel of the universe, in the rapid and rushing river of Time. There on a shelf is the arm and hand of some being who lived so many centuries ago.

After dinner I stopped in to a tailor's on Ludgate Hill and ordered a pair of trousers costing $4. They would be $10 in N. Y. You don't care about that, but it is an item of news!

Went over to S.'s last eve in response to the enclosed letter which I send you. Found there himself, his wife and Madam Gebhard. He had another letter from Olcott saying they had sent ahead of them to London Sorabjé Padshah, a native and chela whom he asked him to meet. S.'s object in sending for me was to ask me to take the young man with me, which I will do gladly. S. said of course he would meet him, but he couldn't imagine why they sent him, nor what they expected him to do. Now my idea (which I carefully concealed) is that they are sending him so as to try S., and already S., in advance, does not do the hospitable thing.

The idea of a Londoner leaving a stranger the task of selecting a place for a Hindu, who, of course, is a strict vegetarian. He cannot get on as I can, and it is ridiculous to propose putting him in my hotel. I suggested a room for him near S.'s house, and he replied that that was a vague thing. Well, it is vague in that he would have to select it.

He used up a good part of the evening in a discourse as to what name the grandsons of the Duke of Edinburgh would be able to bear. Of course that is all right, but it seems to me there is but little time to spare for such discussions.

I did not go to S.'s dinner last night and refused an invitation to dine there tonight on plea of previous engagement. I asked him about his sight of K. H. and he related this: "He was lying in his bed in India one night, when suddenly awakening, he found K. H. standing by his bed. He rose half up, when K. H. put his hand on his head, causing him to fall at once back on the pillow. He then, he says, found himself out of his body, and in the next room, talking to another adept whom he describes as an English or European, with light hair, fair, and of great beauty. This is the one Olcott described to me in 1876 and called by name ———. Please erase that when read. I think it is also the one you have seen and called English, with light hair. S. says he is very high. He described K. H. as looking then not exactly like the picture now in his possession, but with some resemblance to it. . . .

Now am I not —— a good correspondent? Since February 27th have not met a congenial soul save Thomas, and he does not reach up to your elbow in sympathy with me. Surely I will never meet again three souls so kind to me as you three, and never again one like yours, until I meet myself. Good-night.

March 20th. Good morning. No further news from Olcott or the rest. Give my love to the other two sides of the triangle. I will consign this as it is to the mails, and write you again Saturday. And I ever remain,

Your Brother, WILL

Yesterday I spent a few hours in Hyde Park walking along Rotten Row, and looking at the blood roll by. It was very common in appearance. The best people are away, they say, but I saw enough to show what the average of beauty is here.

The Albert Memorial is here with those groups at the corner that have been so much photographed and distributed over America. It is very homely on the whole: too much gilt and colors. Prince Albert is seated, colossal in size, all gold from head to foot, in a gold chair inside of a little temple. However, as a memorial, it is a magnificent thing. The next thing for her Imper. Majesty to do now is to put up a memorial to John Brown.

Telegraphed Olcott to Nice yesterday and just got reply. It is now 11 A. M. He says to meet him in Paris on the 27th and that a letter follows the telegram. Well, this is some encouragement for a weary pilgrim, especially as said pilgrim is getting blue. . . . You can easily see how blue I was getting with the surroundings here. . . .

Oh, how I wish I was out of this. London is horrid. Too much beef and beer. I walk about in a mental cloak, and do not care either to see or hear.

There is no more for me in London, so my next epistle will be from Paris.

W. Q. J.

[At the end of March, 1884, Madame Blavatsky, Col. Olcott, and the young Hindu, Mohini Chatterjee, arrived in Paris from India. The fourth member of the party was Babula, a young Hindu, who was the special attendant of Madame Blavatsky. Mr. Judge was at the station to greet them on their arrival, and he remained several months in the house with them, working on the the revised edition of *Isis Unveiled* which became the *Secret Doctrine,* then being prepared for publication.—Eds.]

I have been here now since the 25th (March), and H. P. B. arrived on the 28th. Crowds of people have been here constantly, and, therefore, I have not been able to have any long private conversations with her. I have had some talks with her and can tell you now that I have confirmation of much that has occurred. She told me independently and voluntarily that the Master had told her in India, that he was doing, or "about to do something with and for me."

* * * * *

I am happy to be able to send you the first confirmation of the truth of the experience and messages had in ———, and I expect to send you the picture of the young Hindu who came there—also that there is an English Adept or European with rather light hair, who is very high. This first young man is a friend of Mohini, and has been studying for many years. I described him hypothetically to Mohini, who rushed for his bag and got me a picture and said that was the one.

I feel quite strongly that I will stay here quite a while, and probably go back to London.

Although I wrote you yesterday, I cannot resist the temptation to write again today because I am sending off so many letters to the U. S. in today's mail. For several days, until yesterday, I have had the most awful blues that ever were. So bad indeed that H. P. B. was very much worried. It seemed impossible to stave them off, and as they were accompanied with an uncontrollable desire to weep, I was in a bad way. She said I had got into my past current, and also that in going about I had absorbed some old elementaries which she saw about me. She gave me to wear all day her talisman ring, which is of great value and strength. It has a double triangle and the Sanscrit for "life" on it. This helped me, but all the while I felt that something was to be done by me.

It is a hard road, and each soul must travel and work to grow strong. This point in my career I feel is a turning point, and I hope to turn it with advantage. I trust you are not the cause of my depression, although if so that is better than any other cause. It has seemed to be from without. Give my love to the beloved ones, and keep me in kind remembrance.

I sent you the other day a rough sketch, being a resemblance to Mahatma M and I inclose to you a photograph of Madame, Subba Row and Dabajeri Nath, or Babaji, as they call him, at headquarters. He is not always at headquarters. S. told me there was something mysterious about him. Mohini told me also that he was far advanced, and can easily leave his body at will.

I telegraphed you yesterday that my address for a month would be American Exchange, Paris, as I am ordered by the Masters to stop here and help Madame in writing the *Secret Doctrine*, which you see advertised in the *Theosophist*.

To resume with coherency. After the first hurry was over here, I said I had to go to India at once. Olcott thought I had better stay with H. P. B., and so did she. But I said that all the orders I had were to go to India, and without further ones I was going, and so she said I was probably right; and then it was decided that I would wait here until O. could get me a steamer in London where he went on the 5th. All was thus arranged definitely. But the next morning, as I was sitting in the bedroom with Mohini, in which he and I slept, and after we had been there about an hour after coffee, Olcott came from his room, which was at the other end of the hall, and called me out, and told me privately that the Master had been then to his room and had told him that I was not to go yet to India, but to stay and help H. P. B. on the *Secret Doctrine*. By the way, my fate is mixed up with *Isis Unveiled*. I helped her on that, and, as she reminded me yesterday, I suggested the use of the word "elemental" to make the distinction clear between them and the "elementaries." As she said, "That was your word, Judge." It shows she is not ungrateful, nor like so many who are unwilling to concede what they are indebted to others for.

Mohini and I had not yet left our rooms and H. P. B. was still in bed. Perfectly convinced after a few minutes that O. was right, especially as the afternoon before I had had an intuition of it in the street, I returned to our room and told Mohini nothing. But after about half an hour he looked up and said, "Judge, I believe your Master has been in the house this morning for some purpose." I then told him of the change of plan, and he said, "it must be right."

So then, here I am for how long or short I do not know, and I am to make suggestions and write upon the work. So, see my fate again linked with the second working up of *Isis*. In this place you will remember her letter of last June that my fate was indissolubly linked with that of theirs (the ∴).

I am now able to give you proofs of the Adepts from these Hindus who know and revere them.

I find, also, that I was right in insisting on the *Bhagavad Gita*. Mohini says he reads it all the time, and does not yet understand it. Those commentaries which he shall make for me I will give to you. But let me again insist upon your trying to realize in yourselves that you are a part of the All. That is the constant subject of meditation, and will bring the best and most rapid progress.

Furthermore, too much must not be expected of the Mahatmas. They cannot interfere with Karma; and so, if a man starts out to them, they say, "Try." If he fails he has done so on his own judgment. It does not follow that they are always helping him because he has made himself a chela. Of course, there are those whose Karma is such that they are helped. But it is not right to suppose, as some do, that because they are chelas they can therefore go into a den of lions and be safe. Of course, if the Master sends one, then he will protect.

Another thing. As I told D. the spleen is the seat of Astral or Vital air or life. It radiates its power in curves the same as those which are made by the magnet upon filings of iron on paper. There are five centers beginning at the spleen and ending at the point on the forehead just above the nose. When you can straighten all these curves out, then you project your double. This is how you can do it. I spoke with him about meditation, and he says we should try to realize first intellectually, and then transmute the knowledge into ourselves, so that it becomes a part of ourselves.

We say we are a part of the All. Well, we must intensely meditate upon that until we begin to realize it, and from then we will receive instruction.

We have had a lot of talk and I cannot now go into all, as I have no time today. But I think he has confirmed me in my old views of the matter, and shown me that where I have erred has been in not being faithful enough to my own convictions, not only as to *what* to believe, but also as to *how* to believe and meditate. He also says that there can be no doubt of the truth of those Maji messages and that he thinks they have the stamp of the Master. Mohini says he is sent here to try to straighten out the difficulties in the societies, but he is left more or less to his own judgment.

If he errs he will hear of it, but not always so if he is right. This is proper, or else the judgment would not be formed, the Brotherhood would become merely the Gods of the Church to us, and we would be like little children who could not walk without assistance.

There is an answer to that question whether the Masters love anyone, which I will tell you.

Mahatma ——— wrote in a letter referring to Mrs. K.,* who is causing the row in London, "that her efforts for the poor animals in regard to vivisection have gained her consideration from the Chohan." The Chohan, as you know, is the Guru of the Adepts. If those are their sentiments, surely they love human beings.

No doubt it will interest you to tell you of a remark Mohini dropped. It was the other night while we were talking of the calumnies circulated by many people respecting fraud. He said, "Well, there is one fortunate thing and that is, that I saw the Master before I ever heard of the Theosophical Society."

I must give you a little hint he gave me about Karma and Devachan, that is not in Sinnett's book, but ought to be. There it is only given that you take your good Karma to Devachan, and the other waits for you. That slightly bothered me and many others. He (Mohini) says you take *both* with you, but the bad has no opportunity there to exercise itself and remains quiescent until you return, when it begins to work. Of course, you must remember the terms used here are indefinite, and that included in "bad Karma" is "good" material Karma. For, in saying "bad Karma," I mean the Karma which works out in physical life whether it be a good or a bad Karma, and in saying "good Karma in Devachan," I mean that good or spiritual Karma which can only be worked out in Devachan.

He tells me, also, that there are many errors in that *Bhagavad Gita* I sent you, and now I see that it is Thompson's and not Hurrychund's translation. Turn to the first chapter, 1st verse, and correct it to read as follows:

"What doeth the lower parts of man's nature which holds thirst for renewed life, and his other or spiritual parts, who are assembled for the purpose of fighting in the body which is acquired by Karma, Sanjaya?

"Oh, Brahma, what is this mystery which takes place every night? When lying on the matting, the eyes closed, the body is

* Dr. Anna Bonus Kingsford.—Eds.

lost sight of, and the soul escapes to enter into conversation with the ancestors (pitris). Watch over it, Brahma, when forsaking the resting body it goes away to hover over the water, to wander in the immensity of heaven and penetrate into the dark and mysterious nooks of the valleys and grand forests of the blessed Himavat (Hymalayas)."

This, it seems to me, is our work just now. Let us deserve and then desire.

It is quite a task, this selecting and collating from the matter of *Isis* so that all may be preserved, and all useless matter expunged. For this work you are peculiarly fitted; and even if you worked at it with the intention of returning to New York, that would be a good Karma for you. I am fitted also for certain portions of the work, and together we would revel in knowledge and advance hand in hand along that path.

N. went away at night and then for about an hour the Masters sent messages through H. P. B. in the parlor, questions to me to try her. Each message made a distinct effect upon my skin before she repeated it.

She says that when I started for Mexico, one of the Masters said: "Why does he go there; I do not like that." But my Master merely looked at me and smiled.

On the fifth Olcott and Mohini left for London, leaving Madame and me here, as she had been ordered not to go to London. We went through the day and in the evening were sitting together in the parlor alone, talking very seriously of old times.

As we sat there I felt the old signal of a message from the Master and saw that she was listening. She said: "Judge, the Master asks me to try and guess what would be the most extraordinary thing he could order now?" I said, "That Mrs. K. should be made the President of the London Lodge." Try again. "That H. P. B. should be ordered to go to London." That was right and he ordered her to take the 7:45 express, giving the exact hours it would arrive at the different stations and in London—all of which was correct, and we had no time table in the house. She disliked the order awfully and I can tell you, knowing her ill health and present unwieldly size, it was an awful journey. But last night I took her to the station and saw her go off in the train with a little hand bag. There is some peculiar object in this, as she might have gone with Olcott. She was ordered to stay in London only 24 hours, and will return here on Wednesday.

All the time she confessed her inability to see why she was ordered, as the Londoners will think it done for effect after her refusal to go then, and Olcott, when he sees her, will certainly feel like swearing. But the London situation is serious, and maybe they intend to work some phenomena there for some good end. So I am left here alone in this house, and am going to work a little on the book.

Let me go back to the change of orders about me. Mind, we had decided I was going to India, and the letters were posted to Damodar and several others to that effect by both Olcott and myself and H. P. B.

I am deep among Counts, Countesses and Duchesses. Called on Countess d'Ademar yesterday, who is a Kentucky girl. Lady Caithness Duchess de Pomar is to be here in a few days, and has requested the infinitude of pleasure to be derived from my company. And so things go.

I will give you a short account of the last week. After Olcott left, Madame left also, as I told you, I remaining here with Babula, Mme.'s servant. He is a Hindu boy she picked up five years ago. She taught him French; he already knew English and Hindustani. He is a genuine servant and a good boy. When she is here he sleeps on the floor outside her door. He now waits on me at meals. There is a French woman to cook and fix up the rooms. She has an easy time. In the morning I have coffee and bread; at 1 o'clock, rice; at 6, dinner of vegetables. The weather has been cold, and I sit here in this east room with a wood fire in this beastly French fireplace, where two-thirds of the heat goes up the chimney. After Mme. left I had one entire day devoted to the most awfully severe attack of neuralgia any poor devil ever had. The other days I have occupied in going over *Isis,* and making notes and suggestions for the "Secret Doctrine." So have led a hermit's life, except when I took an hour's walk, which I did every day.

I have given some time every day to the endeavor to see it———, but I cannot report success. It may not be well for me to go there in spirit, for, not being skilful, I might easily bring back with me influences met there among which could be some very distressing ones. Perhaps this is the explanation of some of my horrible days of distress and despair.

Nothing new as yet. . . . Olcott still in London where they have now two societies, caused by a split in favor of Mrs. K.

These last days (12) have been a trial to me. Quite vividly the question of sticking fast or letting go has come up. I believe that I have been left alone to try me. But I have conquered. I will not give up; and no matter what the annoyance or bitterness, I will stand. Last night I opened the *Theosophist* that Mme. has here, and almost at once came across those articles about chelaship, its trials and dangers. It seemed like a confirmation of my thoughts, and while the picture in one sense was rather dismal, yet they strengthened me. Then there was one passage by Damodar in which he hinted that those whom the Masters themselves selected did not fail. Do you not think—that I may call myself one who was selected? But even if I cannot, it will make no difference to me.

Well, then, goodbye, and may you daily realize more and more the indivisibility of the supreme Spirit which is one with us all.

Do you remember what the Master says about motives? I quote the paragraph lest you have forgotten it.

"Motives are vapors, as attenuated as the atmospheric moisture; and, as the latter develops its dynamic energy for man's use only when concentrated and applied as steam or hydraulic power, so the practical value of good motives is best seen when they take the form of deeds."

Now I send this before seeing H. P. B., and will send you just what she says. I have no doubt of all this, nor that Karma has brought us together and will keep us the same.

I never forget
I will never forget
I have never forgotten
White can never be black.

Into the Master's hand I consign you.

MR. JUDGE'S STORIES

MR. JUDGE was never at a loss for a new way to call attention to old truths. Besides the several pseudonyms he employed in the *Path*—Hadji-Erinn, Murdhna Joti, William Brehon ("Brehon" means Judge in Gaelic), Eusebio Urban, Rodriguez Undiano, and a dozen others he created and used but once—he used the ancient device of the historical allegory. Thus, at intervals from 1885 to 1893, he published ten of these strange tales, using (for all but the first, "A Weird Tale," which was published in the *Theosophist*, and which, furthermore, was a recital of *contemporary* happenings) the name "Bryan Kinnavan."

In these stories will be discovered both philosophy and history—teachings on the elementals, on symbols, on "borrowed bodies," and graphic pictures of the Karma of delay, doubt, superstition, and the abandonment of the true religion and practice. Here, also, is an *historical* account of the final submersion of Atlantis, of the establishment in Ireland of the Lodge, and of the Teachers' leaving the island at the close of a certain cycle. "The Magic Screen of Time" and "The Skin of the Earth," in especial, belong with Mr. Judge's wonderful series, "Conversations on Occultism."

Above all, these curious tales are direction, guidance, warning and prophecy for theosophists. Month after month, year after year, in the *Path*, Mr. Judge strove to bring before the minds of his readers the meaning of the Work they were engaged in, the way it must be carried on—each man for himself as to method, but all men together on the principles of Theosophy. He pointed to pitfalls, described dangers, and gave the formula for surmounting all difficulties: Devotion, Study, Work. Then, from ancient history, he selects the materials for telling the story again.

The "Occult Novel" (or the notes therefor), which follows the stories, is another series of invaluable hints—on violent death, on reincarnation through cloud, rain and seed and thus to man (compare Mr. Judge's *Ocean of Theosophy*, page 68), on insanity, and, most important and extensive of all, on borrowed bodies. Of the many ideas for stories among these jottings by Mr. Judge, only one was developed and published—"A Curious Tale."

TALES FROM THE "PATH"

A WEIRD TALE

I

THE readers of this magazine* have read in its pages narratives far more curious and taxing to belief than the one I am about to give fragments of. The extraordinary Russian tale of the adept at the rich man's castle when the infant assumed the appearance of an old man will not be forgotten. But the present tale, while not in the writer's opinion containing anything extremely new, differs from many others in that I shall relate some things I myself saw. At this time, too, the relation is not inopportune, and perhaps some things here set down may become, for many, explanations of various curious occurrences during the past five years in India and Europe.

To begin with, this partial story is written in accordance with a direction received from a source which I cannot disobey and in that alone must possess interest, because we are led to speculate why it is needed now.

Nearly all of my friends in India and Europe are aware that I have travelled often to the northern part of the South American continent and also to Mexico. That fact has been indeed noticed in this magazine. One very warm day in July, 1881, I was standing at the vestibule of the Church of St. Theresa in the City of Carácas, Venezuela. This town was settled by the Spaniards who invaded Peru and Mexico and contains a Spanish-speaking people. A great crowd of people were at the door, and just then a procession emerged, with a small boy running ahead and clapping a loud clapper to frighten away the devil. As I noticed this, a voice in English said to me, "Curious that they have preserved that singular ancient custom." Turning, I saw a remarkable-looking old man who smiled peculiarly and said, "Come with me and have a talk." I complied, and he soon led me to a house which I had often noticed, over the door being a curious old Spanish tablet devoting the place to the patronage of St. Joseph and Mary. On

* This tale was first published in the *Theosophist*, in July and December, 1885.—Eds.

his invitation I entered and at once saw that here was not an ordinary Carácas house. Instead of lazy, dirty Venezuelan servants, there were only clean Hindoos such as I had often seen in the neighboring English Island of Trinidad; in the place of the disagreeable fumes of garlic and other things usual in the town, there hung in the air the delightful perfumes known only to the Easterns. So I at once concluded that I had come across a delightful adventure.

Seating ourselves in a room hung with tapestry and cooled by waving punkahs that had evidently not been long put up, we engaged in conversation. I tried to find out who this man was, but he evaded me. Although he would not admit or deny knowledge of the Theosophical Society or of Madame Blavatsky or of the Mahatmas, he constantly made such references that I was sure he knew all about them and had approached me at the church designedly. After quite a long talk, during which I saw he was watching me and felt the influence of his eye, he said that he had liberty to explain a little as we had become sufficiently acquainted. It was not pleasure nor profit that called him there, but duty alone. I referred to the subterranean passages said to exist in Peru full of treasure, and then he said the story was true and his presence there connected with it. Those passages extended up from Peru as far as Carácas where we then were. In Peru they were hidden and obstructed beyond man's power to get them; but in this place the entrances were not as well guarded, although in 1812 an awful earthquake had levelled much of the town. The Venezuelans were rapacious, and these men in India who knew the secret had sent him there to prevent any one finding the entrances. At certain seasons only there were possibilities of discovery; the seasons over he could depart in security, as until the period came again no one could find the openings without the consent and help of the adepts. Just then a curious bell sound broke on the air and he begged me to remain until he returned, as he was called, and then left the room. I waited a long time, filled with speculations, and as it was getting late and past dinner hour, I was about to leave. Just as I did so, a Hindoo servant quickly entered and stood in front of the only door. As he stood there, I heard a voice say as through a long pipe: "Stir not yet." Reseating myself, I saw that on the wall, where I had not before noticed it, hung a curious broad silver plate brightly shining. The hour of the day had come when the sun's light struck this plate and I saw that on it were figures which I could not decipher. Accidentally looking at the opposite wall, I saw that the plate threw a reflection there upon a surface evidently prepared for that purpose and there was reproduced the whole surface of the plate. It was a diagram with compass, sign and curious marks. I went closer to examine, but just at that moment the sun dipped behind the houses and the figures were lost. All I could make out was that the letters looked like exaggerated Tamil or Telugu—perhaps Zend. Another faint bell sounded and the old man returned. He apologized, saying that he had been far away, but that we would meet again. I asked where, and he said "In London." Promising to return, I hurried away. Next day I could not find him at all and discovered that there were two houses devoted to Joseph and Mary, and I could not tell which I had seen him in. But in each I found Spaniards, Spanish servants and Spanish smells.

In 1884 I went to London, and had forgotten the adventure. One day I strolled into an old alley to examine the old Roman wall in the Strand which is said to be 2,000 years old. As I entered and gazed at the work, I perceived a man of foreign aspect there who looked at me as I entered. I felt as if he knew me or that I had met him, but was utterly unable to be sure. His eyes did not seem to belong to his body and his appearance was at once startling and attractive. He spoke to the attendant, but his voice did not help me. Then the attendant went out and he, approaching me, said:

"Have you forgotten the house of Joseph and Mary?"

In a moment I knew the expression that looked out through those windows of the soul, but still this was not the same man. Determined to give him no satisfaction I simply said, "No," and waited.

"Did you succeed in making out the reflection from the silver plate on the wall?" Here was complete identification of place but not of person.

"Well," I said, "I saw your eyes in Carácas but not your body." He then laughed and said, "I forgot that. I am the same man, but I have borrowed this body for the present and must indeed use it for some time, but I find it pretty hard work to control it. It is not quite to my liking. The expression of my eyes of course you knew, but I lost sight of the fact that you looked at the body with ordinary eyes."

Once more I accompanied him to his residence and, when not thinking of his person but only listening with the soul, I forgot the change. Yet it was ever present, and he kindly gave me an account of some things connected with himself, of absorbing interest. He began in this way.

"I was allowing myself to deceive myself, forgetting the Bagavat Gita where it tells us, that a man is his soul's friend and his soul's enemy, in that retreat in Northern India where I had spent many years. But the chance again arose to retrieve the loss incurred by that and I was given the choice of assuming this body."

At this point again I heard the signal bell and he again left me. When he returned, he resumed the story.

If I can soon again get the opportunity, I will describe that scene, but for the present must here take a halt.

II

There are many who cannot believe that I have been prevented from writing the whole of this tale at once, and they have smiled when they read that I would continue it "if allowed." But all who know me well will feel that there is some truth in my statement. It may interest those who can read between the lines to know that I attempted several times to finish the tale so as to send it all in one batch to the magazine, but always found that at the point where the first chapter ends my eyes would blur, or the notes ready for the work became simply nonsense, or some other difficulty intervened, so that I was never until now able to get any further with it than the last instalment. It is quite evident to me that it will not be finished, although I know quite well what it is that I have to say. This part must therefore be the last, as in trying to reach a conclusion much time is wasted in fighting against whatever it is that desires to prevent my going into full details. In order then to be able to get out even so much as this, I am compelled to omit many incidents which would perhaps be interesting to several persons; but I shall try to remember particularly and relate what things of a philosophical nature were repeated to me.

As I sat there waiting for the host to come back, I felt the moral influence of another mind, like a cool breeze blowing from a mountain. It was the mind of one who arrived at least at that point where he desired no other thing than that which Karma may bring, and, even as that influence crept over me, I began to hear a voice speaking as it were through a pipe the end of which was in my head, but which stretched an immense distance into space* making the voice sound faint and far off. It said:

"The man whose passions enter his heart as waters run into the unswelling passive ocean obtaineth happiness; not he who lusteth in his lusts. The man who having abandoned the lusts of the flesh worketh without inordinate desires, unassuming, and free from pride, obtaineth happiness. This is divine dependence. A man being possessed of this confidence in the Supreme goeth not astray: even at the hour of death should he attain it he shall mix with the incorporeal nature of Brahm. He who enjoyeth the *Amreeta* that is left of his offerings obtaineth the eternal spirit of Brahm the Supreme."

The atmosphere of the room seemed to give the memory great retentive power, and when on returning to my room that night I fell upon those sentences in the Bhagavad Gita I knew that they had come to me from a place or person for whom I should have respect.

Occupied with such thoughts I did not notice that my host had returned, and, looking up, was somewhat startled to see him sitting at the other side of the apartment reading a book. The English clothes were gone, and a white Indian dhoti covered him, and I could see that he wore round his body the Brahmanical cord. For some reason or other, he had hanging from a chain around his neck an ornament, which, if it was not Rosicrucian, was certainly ancient.

Then I noticed another change. There seemed to have come in with him, though not by the door, other visitors which were not human. At first I could not see them, though I was aware of their presence, and after a few moments I knew that whatever they were they rushed hither and thither about the room as if without purpose. As yet they had no form. This absorbed me again so that I said nothing, and my host was also silent. In a few more moments these rushing visitors had taken from the atmosphere enough material to enable them to become partly visible. Now and then they made a ripple in the air as if they disturbed the medium in which they moved about, just as the fin of a fish troubles the

* There are some Theosophists who will recognize this. [W.Q.J.]

surface of the water. I began to think of the elemental shapes we read of in Bulwer Lytton's *Zanoni,* and which have been illustrated in Henry Kunrath's curious book on the Cabala of the Hebrews.

"Well," said my strange friend, "do you see them? You need have no fear, as they are harmless. They do not see you, excepting one that appears to know you. I was called out so as to try if it were possible for you to see them, and am glad that you do."

"And the one that knows me," said I. "Can you identify it in any way?"

"Well," said he, "let us call it *he.* He seems to have seen you—been impressed with your image just as a photograph is on a plate—somewhere or other, and I also see that he is connected with you by a name. Yes, it is ——— ."

And then he mentioned the name of an alleged elemental or nature spirit which at one time, some years ago, was heard of in New York.

"He is looking at you now, and seems to be seeking something. What did you have or make once that he knew of?"

I then recollected a certain picture, a copy of an Egyptian papyrus of the Hall of Two Truths, showing the *trial of the Dead,* and so replied, regretting that I had not got it with me to show my friend. But even as I said that, I saw the very picture lying upon the table. Where it came from I do not know, as I had no recollection of bringing it with me. However, I asked no questions and waited, as my host was looking intently at the space above my head.

"Ah, that is what he was looking for, and he seems to be quite pleased," he said, as if I could hear and see just as he did. I knew he referred to the elemental.

In another moment my attention was riveted on the picture. Its surface bobbed up and down as if waves ran over it, and crackling sounds rose from every part. They grew louder and the motion ceased, while from a certain point arose a thin whitish vapor that wavered unsteadily to and fro. Meanwhile the strange visitors I have mentioned seemed to rush about more in the vicinity of the paper, while now and again one of them took what looked like a flying leap from one end of the room to the other with a queer faint boom of a metallic character following his rapid motion.

Here I must draw the veil unwillingly. Let me violate the unities and the frame of this tale by just putting down a few sentences, leaving it to the imagination to draw inferences.

"Those strange delineations of form? Quite easily. They were seen by the seeresses in the temple. It is quite true that elementals have no form as such. . . . But there are undoubtedly types, and [those] Egyptians were not the men to do anything unscientifically. . . . There is an occult reason why, although without form, these particular shapes were assumed. And having been once assumed and seen thus by the seer, they always repeated that form to those persons. So the representative of the astral light, or of wisdom, or of the recording angel, is yellow in color, very tall, with a long bill like a stork. Or the one who takes the weight of the soul is always seen with a jackal's head. No, there is no prohibition against telling the occult reason. It is merely this: were it told, only one in a thousand hearers would see any meaning or reason in it. . . . Let your mind reflect also upon the peculiarity that all the judges sitting above there have heads alike, while in color they differ, each one having a feather, the emblem of truth, on his head. . . . No, it is not Hindu, and yet it is the same. They used to say, and I think you may find it in one of their books, that 'everything is in the Supreme soul, and the Supreme soul in everything.' So the great truth is one, while it can be seen in a thousand different ways. We [Egyptians] took a certain view and made every symbol consistent and of a class consonant with our view. . . . And just as the Hindus are accused of being idolators because they have represented Krishna with eight arms standing on the great elephant, we, who did not picture an eight-armed divinity, are charged with having worshipped jackals, cats and birds. . . .

"Yes, it is a pity, but the sand that buries Egypt has not been able to smother the great voice of that Sphinx, the *esoteric doctrine*. But not through us except in some such manner as this, now and then. In India the light burns, and in a living people still resides the key—."

Just then the bobbing of the picture began again and the same whitish column wavered over it. The faint boom of the airy elementals re-commenced, and again claimed my attention, and then the picture was still.

I may say that the whole of the conversation has not been given. It is not necessary that it should be. My host had maintained perfect silence all the while, and seemed to await my voice, so I said:

---

* *Bhagavad-Gita.*

"What could have induced you to leave those peaceful places where true progress may be gained?"

"Well," he replied, "very likely they were peaceful, and quite truly progress was possible, but you do not appreciate the dangers also. You have read *Zanoni,* and perhaps have an exaggerated idea of the horrible Dweller of the Threshold, making of her a real person or thing. But the reality is much worse. When you get into what you have called 'the peaceful places,' this power becomes tenfold stronger than it is found to be on the plane in which we now live in London."

"Why, I supposed that there, free from the cankering anxieties of modern life, the neophyte sailed happily on through plain seas to the shores of the fortunate isles."

"Far from that. On that plane it is found that, although from the spiritual sun there falls upon us the benign influence of those great sages who, entering paranirvana, throw off their accumulated goodness for our benefit, the evil influence that is focussed by the dark side of the moon falls as well, and with its power undiminished. The little temptations and difficulties of your life are as nothing compared to that struggle, for then it is realized that the self is the enemy of the self, as well as its friend."*

"But," said I, "was the fault committed a great one, that it should condemn you to this task?"

"No, not great as you term it. But quite great enough; and in consequence I had to take my choice. In Carácas you saw me as an illusion of a certain character. There I did what was required, the illusion being perfect except as to the eyes. Now you see another illusion, and yet at the same time a reality such as is connoted by that word when used by modern scientists. It is a body that lives and will die. The Karma is hard perhaps, but I grumble not. But is it not an illusion in every sense, when you know that although this body speaks and thinks, still I, the speaker, am not visible to you?"

These words are not mine. If some of them seem meaningless or queer to many readers, do not blame the writer. There are those who can understand. There are yet others who have latent thoughts that need but these words to call them into life. I cannot give any greater detail than the above as to himself, because

* *Bhagavad-Gita.*

he had reasons for preventing me, although he might perhaps himself tell more to another.

One curious thing of interest he said, which will furnish some with food for thought. It was when I referred to the use of the body he had, so to say, *borrowed,* that he said:

"Don't you know that many experiments are possible in that way, and that some students are taught peculiarly? I have stood aside from this earthly tabernacle many a time to let in those who, notwithstanding that they operated the machine well enough and made quite a respectable use of it, did not know what they did. They were, if you like, dreaming. While here, in this body, they were essentially it, for the time, speaking its words, thinking its thoughts, and not able to control it. Not desiring to in fact, because they were completely identified with it. When they waked up in their own apartments either a singular dream whispered a fragmentary song through their brain, or they retained no remembrances whatever of it. In such a case the body, being really master, might do or say that which I would not—or the occupier, temporarily strong, might say out of real recollection things having relation only to that life of which his hearers would have no knowledge."

Just then some clock struck. The atmosphere seemed to clear itself. A strange and yet not unfamiliar perfume floated through the room, and my host said, "Yes, I will show you a verse some one tells me to show you."

He walked over to the table, took up a queer little book printed in Sanscrit, yellow with age and seeming to have been much used. Opening it he read:

"This supreme Spirit and incorruptible Being, even when it is in the body, neither acteth, nor is it affected, because its nature is without beginning and without quality. As the all-moving Akas, or ether, from the minuteness of its parts, passeth everywhere unaffected, even so the omnipresent spirit remaineth in the body unaffected. As a single sun illumines the whole world, even so doth the spirit enlighten every body. They who, with the eye of wisdom, perceive the body and the spirit to be thus distinct, and that there is a final release from the animal nature, go to the Supreme."*

W. Q. J.

---

* *Bhagavad-Gita,* Sect. XIII, last verse.

A CURIOUS TALE

SOME years ago, I ran down to the Lakes of Killarney, but not for the purpose merely of seeing them as any other traveler. During my boyhood the idea of going there had always been before me, and in dreams I would often find myself on the water or wandering near by. After this had occurred many times, I procured photographs of the scenery and was quite surprised to find that the dreams were accurate enough to seem like recollections. But various vicissitudes took me to other parts of the world, so that I had passed my majority without having visited the place, and, indeed, the decision to go there at last was not made until one day, while looking into a shop window in Dublin, my eye fell upon a picture of Killarney, and in an instant I was filled with a strong desire to see them. So I went on the first train and was very soon there, quartered with an old man who from the first seemed like an old friend.

The next day or two were devoted to wandering about with no purpose nor with very great satisfaction, for the place as a bit of country did not interest me after all my wanderings in many different climes. But on the third day I went off into a field not far from the shores of one of the sheets of water, and sat down near an old well. It was still early in the afternoon, and unusually pleasant. My mind had no particular object before it, and I noticed an inability, quite unusual, to follow long a definite train of thought. As I sat thus, drowsiness came over my senses, the field and the well grew grey but still remained in sight, yet I seemed to be changing into another man, and, as the minutes flew by, I saw the shadowy form or picture of a tall round tower rising, some fifty feet high, just beyond the well. Shaking myself, this disappeared and I thought I had fought off the sleepy feeling, but only for a moment. It returned with new intensity.

The well had disappeared and a building occupied its place, while the tall tower had grown solid; and then all desire to remain myself disappeared. I rose with a mechanical feeling that my duty, somehow or other, called me to the tower, and walked over into the building through which I knew it was necessary to go in order to reach the tower. As I passed inside the wall, there was the old well I had seen upon first coming into the field, but the strange incident did not attract my attention, for I knew the well as an old landmark. Reaching the tower, the steps wound up before me to the top, and as I mounted them a voice quite familiar called my name—a name not the same that I owned to upon sitting down near the well, but that did not attract my attention any more than the old well inside the wall. At last I emerged upon the top of the tower, and there was an old man keeping up a fire. It was the eternal fire never yet known to have gone out, and I, out of all the other young disciples, alone was permitted to help the old man.

As my head rose above the level of the low rim of the tower, I saw a calm and beautiful mountain not far away, and other towers nearer to it than mine.

"You are late," said the old man. I made no reply, as there was none to make; but I approached and showed by my attitude that I was ready to go on watching in his place. As I did this it flashed across me that the sun was nearing the horizon, and for an instant the memory of the old man with whom I had lodged came before me, as well as the express train to be reached by cart, but that faded out as the old watcher looked into my brain with his piercing eyes.

"I fear to leave you in charge," was his first remark. "There is a shadow, dark and silent, near you."

"Do not fear, father," said I; "I will not leave the fire nor permit it to go out."

"If you do, then our doom is sealed and the destiny of Innisfallen delayed."

With those words he turned and left me, and soon I heard his foot-fall no more on the winding stairs that led below.

The fire seemed bewitched. It would hardly burn, and once or twice it almost paralyzed me with fear, so nearly did it expire. When the old man left me, it was burning brightly. At last it seemed that my efforts and prayers were successful; the blaze sprang up and all looked well. Just then a noise on the stairs caused me to turn round, and to my surprise a complete stranger came upon the platform where none but the guardians were allowed.

"Look," said he; "those fires beyond are dying out."

I looked and was filled with fear to see that the smoke from the towers near the mountain had died out, and in my sudden amazement rushed to the parapet to get a nearer view. Satisfied that what the stranger said was true, I turned to resume my watch, and there, O horror! my own fire was just expiring. No lights or tinder were permitted there; the watcher had to renew the fire by means of the fire. In a frenzy of fear I leaped to new fuel and put it on the fire, fanned it, laid my face to it and strove with maddened gasps to blow the flame up, but all my efforts were vain—it was dead.

A sickening dread seized me, succeeded by a paralysis of every nerve except those that aid the hearing. I heard the stranger move toward me, and then I recognized his voice as he spoke. No other noises were about, all was dead and cold, and I seemed to know that the ancient guardian of the fire would return no more, that no one would return, that some calamity had fallen.

"It is the past," the stranger began. "You have just reached a point where you failed to feed the fire ages ago. It is done. Do you want to hear of those things? The old man has gone long ago, and can trouble you no more. Very soon you will be again in the whirl of the nineteenth century."

Speech then returned to me and I said, "Yes, tell me what this is, or has been."

"This is an old tower used by the immediate descendants of the white Magicians who settled on Ireland when England's Isle had not arisen from the sea. When the great Masters had to go away, strict injunctions were left that no fires on these towers were to go out, and the warning was also given that, if the duties of life were neglected, if charity, duty, and virtue were forgotten, the power to keep these fires alive would gradually disappear. The decadence of the virtues would coincide with the failure of the fires, and this, the last tower, guarded by an old and a young man, would be the last to fail, and that even it could save the rest if its watchers were faithful.

"Many years elapsed, and the brilliant gem placed upon the mount of Innisfallen blazed both by day and night until at last it seemed to fade a little. The curious sounding-stones, now found in Ireland, were not so easily blown; only when a pure and faithful servant came down from the White Tower did the long, strange, and moving sounds float over the mountain from the stone placed near the mount on which was the gem. Those stones had been used by the great magicians, and when the largest of them all, lying near the great White Tower, was sounded, the fairies of the lakes appeared; when the stone of the mount was blown together with that at the White Tower, the spirits of the air and the water ranged themselves obediently around.

"But all this altered, and unbelief crept in while the fires were kept up as a form.

"You were relied on with the old man. But vain dreams detained you *one* hour beyond your appointed time on this fatal day, now in the past but shown you by my special favor. You came, but late. The old man was compelled to wait, but still feared to leave you, for he saw with prescient eye the dark finger of fate. He descended the stairs, and at its foot fell down and died. Your curiosity then drew you at the exact fatal moment to look at yonder tower, although you knew the prophecy and believed it. That moment decided all—and, poor boy, you could not hold back the iron hand of destiny.

"The fire had gone out. You returned to the floors below; at the foot of the stairs you saw them carrying off the old man and— * * *"

At this point I saw the shadowy, waving shape of the tower; the building had disappeared, the well was beside me, and I was in the field again. Oh!

BRYAN KINNAVAN

December, 1888

THE SERPENT'S BLOOD

IT WAS an old and magic island. Many centuries before, the great good Adepts had landed on its shores from the West and established for a while the Truth. But even they could not stay the relentless tread of fate, and knew that this was only a halting place, a spot where should be concentrated spiritual power sufficiently strong to remain as a leaven for several cycles, and that should be a base upon which in long ages after ages might be erected again the spiritual temple of truth. These blessed beings remained there for centuries uncounted, and saw arise out of the adjoining seas other lands, first of soft mud that afterwards hardened into rocks and earth. They taught the people and found them apt students, and from their number drew many disciples who were full of zeal as well as patience and faith. Among the least of those I was, and toiled long and earnestly through successive lives upon the Island. And the Island came to be known as the Isle of Destiny, from mysterious future events foretold for it by the greatest of the Adepts and their seers.

Yet I succeeded not in reaching the point where I could hope to pass on from the Island with the teachers, who said that at a certain day they must travel away to other lands, leaving behind them their blessing to those who willingly remained of the disciples; those who rebelled had still to remain, but without the aid and comfort of the benediction of the blessed ones.

At last the day of separation came and the kingly guides departed, leaving well established the true religion and practice. Yet we all knew that even that must have its decay, in which perhaps even some of us might have a hand, but the centre of power was not to depart from the Island until its destiny should be accomplished; the power might be hidden, but it would remain latent until the time arrived.

Many years came and went; still I found myself upon the Island again and again reincarnated. With sorrow I saw the ancient practices overlooked and different views prevailing. It was the power of the serpent.

On one well-known mountain the Masters had placed a gem, and at the mountain's base a tower. These I have spoken of incidentally in a former tale. I knew that mountain well, and saw it every day from the tower at some distance away where my own duties lay. I was present when the wonderful gem was placed upon the mountain, and of all those who saw the grand event, I alone remembered. Since that day many centuries had rolled away, and the other disciples, reincarnated there also, had forgotten the event but knew of the gem. Some of them who in other lives had been my servants in the tower were now my earthly superiors because they had devoted their minds to formal outward power, which is only the weak symbol of the reality that should exist within.

And so the tradition alone remained, but the diamond blazed less brilliantly than in the days when I first knew it. By night its rays shot up into the heavens, and the priests month after month tried ceremonies and prayers in vain, in order to cause it to burst forth in all the glory of its pristine days. They knew that such a blaze was a possibility—indeed an old prophecy—but that was all they could tell, and were ignorant of the remainder of it, which, if they had known, perhaps none of their ceremonies would have been performed. It was that the great and glorious blaze of light from the mountain diamond would only take place after the last drop of the serpent's blood was spilled upon the Island, and that then the diamond itself would never again be found upon the rock where it had rested for so many ages.

I alone of them all knew this; but I knew not where the serpent was to be found. His influence was felt and seen, for in the early days he alone was the sole reptile that eluded pursuit, as his birth was due to the evil thoughts of a wandering black magician who had landed for a week upon the Island—so long before that the priests had no record of it. This serpent had to be killed and his blood spilled upon the ground to remove forever the last trace of the evil done by the magician, and for that event only was the diamond kept upon the mountain through the power of the good Adepts who had put it there. It preserved the germ of truth from the serpent's breath, and would not be needed when he was destroyed. Had the priests known this, no ceremonies for increasing its brilliancy would have been tried, as they would rather suffer the serpent's influence than lose the gem. Indeed, they believed that their tenure of power was in some way connected with the diamond mountain. They were right. I knew the fatal result for them when I succeeded in discovering the place of the serpent.

Day after day and long into the darkness of the night, I meditated and peered into every corner of the Island. At the full moon when the diamond grew a little clearer, I saw the slimy traces of the serpent upon the Island but could never find his lair. At last one night a fellow-student who had passed on before me with those by whom the diamond had been set, and who now and again returned through the air to help his old friend, came to see me, and as he was going away, said, "Look at the foot of the mountain."

So near the sacred diamond I had never thought it possible the foul reptile could be found; and yet it was there where, through the evil nature of the high-priest, he had taken up his secure retreat. I looked and saw him at the foot, breathing venom and black clouds of the soul's despair.

The great day of ceremonies for the diamond was again at hand, and I determined that then should witness the death of the serpent and the last bright shining of the diamond.

The morning broke clear and warm. Great throngs of people crowded about the mountain-temple, expectant of some great result from the ceremonies. It seemed as if these natural psychics felt within them that the diamond would burst forth with its ancient light, and yet every now and then a fear was expressed that in its greatest beauty it would be lost to them forever.

It was my turn to officiate at the ceremony after the high priest, and I alone was aware that the serpent had crawled even into the temple and was coiled up behind the shrine. I determined to seize him and, calling upon our ancient master, strangle him there and spill his blood upon the ground.

Even as I thought this, I saw my friend from other lands enter the temple disguised as a wandering monk, and knew that my half-uttered aspiration even then was answered. Yet death stared me in the face. There, near the altar, was the sacred axe always ready to fell the man who in any way erred at the ceremony. This was one of the vile degenerations of the ancient law, and while it had been used before upon those who had only erred in the forms, I knew that the Priest himself would kill me as soon as the diamond's great flame had died away. The evening darkness would be upon us by the time that the moment in the performance permitted me to destroy the enemy of our race. So I cared not for death, for had I not faced it a thousand times as a blessed release and another chance?

At last the instant came. I stooped down, broke through the rule, and placing my hand behind the shrine caught the reptile by the neck. The High Priest saw me stoop and rushed to the axe. Another moment's delay and all hope was gone. With superhuman power, I grasped and squeezed. Through my skull shot a line of fire, and I could see my wandering monk wave his hand, and instantly the Priest stumbled and fell on his way to the axe. Another pressure, and the serpent was dead. My knife! It was in my girdle, and with it I slit his neck. His red and lively blood poured out upon the ground and—the axe fell upon my head, and the junior priest of the temple fell dead to the floor.

But only my body died. I rose upon the air and saw myself lying there. The people neither stirred nor spoke. The Priest bent over me. I saw my wandering monk smile. The serpent's blood spread slowly out beside my body, and then collected into little globes, each red and lively. The diamond on the mountain behind the temple slowly grew bright, then flashed and blazed. Its radiance penetrated the temple, while priests and people, except my wandering monk, prostrated themselves. Then sweet sounds and soft rustling filled the air, and voices in strange language spoke stranger words from the mountain. Yet still the people did not move. The light of the diamond seemed to gather around the serpent's blood. Slowly each globe of blood was eaten up by the light, except one more malevolent than the others, and then that fateful sphere of life rose up into the air, suddenly transformed itself into a small and spiteful snake that with undulating motion flew across the air and off into the night to the distant Isles. Priest and people arose in fear, the voices from the mountain ceased, the sounds died out, the light retreated, and darkness covered all. A wild cry of despair rose up into the night, and the priest rushed outside to look up at the mountain.

The serpent's blood still stained the ground, and the diamond had disappeared.

BRYAN KINNAVAN

January, 1889

THE MAGIC SCREEN OF TIME

AN OLD Hindu saying thus runs: "He who knows that into which Time is resolved, knows all."

Time, in the Sanscrit, is called Kala. He is a destroyer and also a renovator. Yama, the lord of death, although powerful, is not so much so as Kala, for "until the time has come Yama can do nothing." The moments as they fly past before us, carrying all things with them in long procession, are the atoms of Time, the sons of Kala. Years roll into centuries, centuries into cycles, and cycles become ages; but Time reigns over them all, for they are only his divisions.

Ah, for how many centuries have I seen Time, himself invisible, drawing pictures on his magic screen! When I saw the slimy trail of the serpent in the sacred Island of Destiny I knew not Time, for I thought the coming moment was different from the one I lived in, and both from that gone by. Nor then, either, did I know that that serpent instead of drawing his breath from the eternal ether, lived on the grossest form of matter; I saw not then how the flashing of the diamond set in the mountain was the eternal radiance of truth itself, but childishly fancied it had a beginning.

The tragedy in the temple, in which I was the victim—struck down by the high priest's axe—was followed by another, as I found out soon when, freed from my body, I conversed in spirit with my friend the strange monk. He told me that the next day the high priest, upon recovering from the terrible event, went into the temple where my blood still stained the ground. The object of his visit was to gain time to meditate upon new plans for regaining his hold upon the people, which had been weakened by the blackening and disappearance of the mountain diamond. His thoughts dwelt upon the idea of manufacturing a substitute for the beautiful gem, but after remaining for a while plunged in such reveries his eye was attracted by a curious scene. Upon the stand from which he had snatched the axe that let out my life-blood he saw a cloud which seemed to be the end of a stream of vapor, rising up from the floor. Approaching, he perceived that my blood had in some curious way mixed with that which remained of the stains left by the reptile whose death I had accomplished, and from this the vapor arose, depositing itself, or collecting, upon the stand. And there to his amazement, in the center of the cloud, he saw, slowly forming, a brilliant gem whose radiance filled the place.

"Ah, here," he cried, "is the diamond again. I will wait and see it fully restored, and then my triumph is complete. What seemed a murder will become a miracle."

As he finished the sentence the cloud disappeared, my blood was all taken up, and the flashing of the jewel filled him with joy.

Reaching forth his hand, he took it from the stand, and then black horror overspread his face. In vain he strove to move or to drop the gem; it seemed fastened to his hand; it grew smaller, and fiery pains shot through his frame. The other priests coming in just then to clear the place, stood fixed upon their steps at the door. The High Priest's face was toward them, and from his body came a flow of red and glittering light that shed fear over their hearts; nor could they move or speak. This lasted not long—only until the diamond had wholly disappeared from his hand—and then his frame split into a thousand pieces, while his accursed soul sped wailing through space accompanied by demoniacal shapes. The diamond was an illusion; it was my blood "crying from the ground," which took its shape from his thoughts and ambitions.

"Come, then," said my monk, "come with me to the mountain."

We ascended the mountain in silence, and once at the top, he turned about, fixing upon me a piercing gaze, under which I soon felt a sensation as if I was looking at a screen that hid something from my sight. The mountain and the monk disappeared and in their place I saw a city below me, for I was now upon the inner high tower of a very high building. It was an ancient temple dominating a city of magicians. Not far off was a tall and beautiful man: I knew it was my monk, but oh, how changed; and near him stood a younger man from whom there seemed to reach out to me a stream of light, soft yet clear, thin yet plainly defined. I knew it was myself. Addressing my monk, I said:

"What is this and why?"

"This is the past and the present," he replied; "and thou art the future."

"And he?" pointing to the young man.

"That is thyself."

"How is it that I see this, and what holds it there?"

" 'Tis the Magic Screen of Time, that holds it for thee and hides it ever. Look around and above thy head."

Obeying his command, I cast my eyes around the city spread below, and then, looking upward, I saw at first naught but the sky and the stars. But soon a surface appeared as if in the ether, through it shining still the stars, and then, as my gaze grew steadfast, the surface grew palpable and the stars went out; yet I knew instinctively that if my thoughts wandered for a moment the sky would once more fill the view. So I remained steady. Then slowly pictures formed upon the surface in the air. The city, its people, with all the color of life; and a subdued hum appeared to float down from above as if the people were living up there. The scene wavered and floated away, and was succeeded by the thoughts and desires of those who lived below. No acts were there, but only lovely pictures formed by thoughts; living rainbows; flashing gems; pellucid crystals—until soon a dark and sinuous line crept through the dazzling view, with here and there black spots and lines. Then I heard the pleasing, penetrating voice of my monk:

"Time's screen rolls on; ambition, desire, jealousy, vanity, are defacing it. It will all soon fade. Watch."

And as I watched, centuries rolled past above me on the screen. Its beauty disappeared. Only a dark background with unpleasing and darker outlines of circumstances that surround contention and greed were offered to my eye. Here and there faint spots and lines of light were visible—the good deeds and thoughts of those still of spiritual mind. Then a question fell into my mind: "What is this screen?"

"It will be called the astral light when next you are born on earth," said the voice of my monk.

Just then a mighty sound of marching filled the space. The airy screen seemed to palpitate, its substance, if any it had, was pressed together, as if some oncoming force impinged upon it; its motion grew tumultuous; and then the stars once more shone down from the sky, and I hovered in spirit on the dark mountain where the gem had been. No beings were near, but from the distant spaces came a voice that said—"Listen to the march of the Future."

BRYAN KINNAVAN

April, 1889

THE WANDERING EYE

THIS is not a tale in which I fable a mythical and impossible monster such as the Head of Rahu, which the common people of India believe swallows the moon at every eclipse. Rahu is but a tale that for the vulgar embodies the fact that the shadow of the earth eats up the white disk, but I tell you of a veritable human eye; a wanderer, a seeker, a pleader; an eye that searched you out and held you, like the bird fascinated by the serpent, while it sought within your nature for what it never found. Such an eye as this is sometimes spoken of now by various people, but they see it on the psychic plane, in the astral light, and it is not to be seen or felt in the light of day moving about like other objects.

This wandering eye I write of was always on the strange and sacred Island where so many things took place long ages ago. Ah! yes, it is still the sacred Island, now obscured and its power overthrown—some think forever. But its real power will be spiritual, and though the minds of men today know not the spirit, caring only for temporal glory, the old virtue of the Island will once again return. What weird and ghostly shapes still flit around her shores; what strange, low, level whisperings sweep across her mountains; how at the evening's edge just parted from the day, her fairies suddenly remembering their human rulers—now sunk to men who partly fear them—gather for a moment about the spots where mystery is buried, and then sighing speed away. It was here the wandering eye was first seen. By day it had simply a grey color, piercing, steady, and always bent on finding out some certain thing from which it could not be diverted; at night it glowed with a light of its own, and could be seen moving over the Island, now quickly, now slowly, as it settled to look for that which it did not find.

The people had a fear of this eye, although they were then accustomed to all sorts of magical occurrences now unknown to most Western men. At first those who felt themselves annoyed by it tried to destroy or catch it, but never succeeded, because the moment they made the attempt the eye would disappear. It never manifested resentment, but seemed filled with a definite purpose and bent toward a well-settled end. Even those who had essayed to do away with it were surprised to find no threatening in its depths when, in the darkness of the night, it floated up by their bedsides and looked them over again.

If any one else save myself knew of the occasion when this marvellous wanderer first started, to whom it had belonged, I never heard. I was bound to secrecy and could not reveal it.

In the same old temple and tower to which I have previously referred, there was an old man who had always been on terms of great intimacy with me. He was a disputer and a doubter, yet terribly in earnest and anxious to know the truths of nature, but he continually raised the question: "If I could only know the truth; that is all I wish to know."

Then, whenever I suggested solutions received from my teachers, he would wander away to the eternal doubts. The story was whispered about the temple that he had entered life in that state of mind, and was known to the superior as one who, in a preceding life, had raised doubts and impossibilities merely for the sake of hearing solutions without desire to prove anything, and had vowed, after many years of such profitless discussion, to seek for truth alone. But the Karma accumulated by the lifelong habit had not been exhausted, and in the incarnation when I met him, although sincere and earnest, he was hampered by the pernicious habit of the previous life. Hence the solutions he sought were always near but ever missed.

But toward the close of the life of which I am speaking he obtained a certainty that by peculiar practices he could concentrate in his eye not only the sight but also all the other forces, and wilfully set about the task against my strong protest. Gradually his eyes assumed a most extraordinary and piercing expression which was heightened whenever he indulged in discussion. He was hugging the one certainty to his breast and still suffering from the old Karma of doubt. So he fell sick, and being old came near to death. One night I visited him at his request, and on reaching his side I found him approaching dissolution. We were alone. He spoke freely but very sadly, for, as death drew near, he saw more clearly, and as the hours fled by his eyes grew more extraordinarily piercing than ever, with a pleading, questioning expression.

"Ah," he said, "I have erred again; but it is just Karma. I have succeeded in but one thing, and that ever will delay me."

"What is that?" I asked.

The expression of his eyes seemed to embrace futurity as he told me that his peculiar practice would compel him for a long period to remain chained to his strongest eye—the right one—until the force of the energy expended in learning that one feat was fully exhausted. I saw death slowly creeping over his features, and when I had thought him dead he suddenly gained strength to make me promise not to reveal the secret—and expired.

As he passed away, it was growing dark. After his body had become cold, there in the darkness I saw a human eye glowing and gazing at me. It was his, for I recognized the expression. All his peculiarities and modes of thought seemed fastened into it, sweeping out over you from it. Then it turned from me, soon disappearing. His body was buried; none save myself and our superiors knew of these things. But for many years afterwards the wandering eye was seen in every part of the Island, ever seeking, ever asking, and never waiting for the answer.

BRYAN KINNAVAN

May, 1889

THE TELL-TALE PICTURE GALLERY

ALTHOUGH the gallery of pictures about which I now write has long ago been abandoned, and never since its keepers left the spot where it was has it been seen there, similar galleries are still to be found in places that one cannot get into until guided to them. They are now secreted in distant and inaccessible spots—in the Himalaya mountains; beyond them, in Tibet; in underground India; and such mysterious localities. The need for reports by spies or for confessions by transgressors is not felt by secret fraternities which possess such strange recorders of the doings, thoughts, and condition of those whom they portray. In the brotherhoods of the Roman Catholic Church or in Free-masonry, no failure to abide by rules could ever be dealt with unless some one reported the delinquent or he himself made a confession. Every day mason after mason breaks both letter and spirit of the vows he made, but, no one knowing or making charges, he remains a mason in good standing. The soldier in camp or field oversteps the strictest rules of discipline, yet if done out of sight of those who could divulge or punish he remains untouched. And in the various religious bodies, the members continually break, either in act or in thought, all the commandments, unknown to their fellows and the heads of the Church, with no loss of standing. But neither the great Roman Church, the Free-masons, nor any religious sect possesses such a gallery as that of which I will try to tell you, one in which is registered every smallest deed and thought.

I do not mean the great Astral Light that retains faithful pictures of all we do, whether we be Theosophists or Scoffers, Catholics or Free-masons, but a veritable collection of simulacrae deliberately constructed so as to specialize one of the many functions of the Astral Light.

It was during one of my talks with the old man who turned into a wandering eye that I first heard of this wonderful gallery, and after his death I was shown the place itself. It was kept on the Sacred Island where of old many weird and magical things existed and events occurred. You may ask why these are not now found there, but you might as well request that I explain why Atlantis sank beneath the wave or why the great Assyrian Empire has disappeared. They have had their day, just as our present boasted civilization will come to its end and be extinguished. Cyclic law cannot be held from its operation, and just as sure as tides change on the globe and blood flows in the body, so sure is it that great doings reach their conclusion and powerful nations disappear.

It was only a few months previous to the old man's death, when approaching dissolution or superior orders, I know not which, caused him to reveal many things and let slip hints as to others. He had been regretting his numerous errors one day, and turning to me said,

"And have you never seen the gallery where your actual spiritual state records itself?"

Not knowing what he meant I replied, "I did not know they had one here."

"Oh, yes; it is in the old temple over by the mountain, and the diamond gives more light there than anywhere else."

Fearing to reveal my dense ignorance, not only of what he meant but also of the nature of this gallery, I continued the conversation in a way to elicit more information, and he, supposing I had known of others, began to describe this one. But in the very important part of the description he turned the subject as quickly as he had introduced it, so that I remained a prey to curiosity. And until the day of his death he did not again refer to it. The extraordinary manner of his decease, followed by the weird wandering eye, drove the thought of the pictures out of my head.

But it would seem that the effect of this floating, lonely, intelligent eye upon my character was a shadow or foretoken of my introduction to the gallery. His casual question, in connection with his own short-comings and the lesson impressed on me by the intensification and concentration of all his nature into one eye that ever wandered about the Island, made me turn my thoughts inward so as to discover and destroy the seeds of evil in myself. Meanwhile all duties in the temple where I lived were assiduously performed. One night after attaining to some humility of spirit, I fell quietly asleep with the white moonlight falling over the floor, and dreamed that I met the old man again as when alive, and that he asked me if I had yet seen the picture gallery. "No," said I in the dream, "I had forgotten it," awakening then at sound of my own voice.

Looking up, I saw standing in the moonlight a figure of one I had not seen in any of the temples. This being gazed at me with clear, cold eyes, and afar off sounded what I supposed its voice,

"Come with me."

Rising from the bed I went out into the night, following this laconic guide. The moon was full, high in her course, and all the place was full of her radiance. In the distance the walls of the temple nearest the diamond mountain appeared self-luminous. To that the guide walked, and we reached the door now standing wide open. As I came to the threshold, suddenly the lonely, grey, wandering eye of my old dead friend and co-disciple floated past looking deep into my own, and I read its expression as if it would say,

"The picture gallery is here."

We entered, and, although some priests were there, no one seemed to notice me. Through a court, across a hall, down a long corridor we went, and then into a wide and high roofless place with but one door. Only the stars in heaven adorned the space above, while streams of more than moonlight poured into it from the diamond, so that there were no shadows nor any need for lights. As the noiseless door swung softly to behind us, sad music floated down the place and ceased; just then a sudden shadow seemed to grow in one spot, but was quickly swallowed in the light.

"Examine with care, but touch not and fear nothing," said my taciturn cicerone. With these words he turned and left me alone.

But how could I say I was alone? The place was full of faces. They were ranged up and down the long hall; near the floor, above it; higher, on the walls; in the air; everywhere except in one aisle; but not a single one moved from its place, yet each was seemingly alive. And at intervals strange watchful creatures of the elemental world moved about from place to place. Were they watching me or the faces? Now I felt they had me in view, for sudden glances out of the corners of their eyes shot my way; but in a moment something happened showing they guarded or watched the faces.

I was standing looking at the face of an old friend about my own age who had been sent to another part of the island, and it filled me with sadness unaccountably. One of the curious elemental creatures moved silently up near it. In amazement I strained my eyes, for the picture of my friend was apparently discoloring. Its expression altered every moment. It turned from white to grey and yellow, and back to grey, and then suddenly it grew all black as if with rapid decomposition.* Then again that same sad music I had heard on entering floated past me, while the blackness of the face seemed to cast a shadow, but not long. The elemental pounced upon the blackened face, now soulless; tore it in pieces, and by some process known to itself dissipated the atoms and restored the brightness of the spot. But alas! my old friend's picture was gone, and I felt within me a heavy, almost unendurable gloom as of despair.

As I grew accustomed to the surroundings, my senses perceived every now and then sweet but low musical sounds that appeared to emanate from or around these faces. So, selecting one, I stood in front of it and watched. It was bright and pure. Its eyes looked into mine with the half-intelligence of a dream. Yes, it grew now and then a little brighter, and as that happened I heard the gentle music. This convinced me that the changes in expression were connected with the music.

But fearing I would be called away, I began to carefully scan the collection, and found that all my co-disciples were represented there, as well as hundreds whom I had never seen, and every priest high or low whom I had observed about the island. Yet the same saddening music every now and then reminded me of the scene of the blackening of my friend's picture. I knew it meant others blackened and being destroyed by the watchful elementals who I could vaguely perceive were pouncing upon something whenever those notes sounded. They were like the wails of angels when they see another mortal going to moral suicide.

Dimly after a while there grew upon me an explanation of this gallery. Here were the living pictures of every student or priest of the order founded by the Adepts of the Diamond Mountain. These vitalized pictures were connected by invisible cords with the character of those they represented, and like a telegraph instrument they instantly recorded the exact state of the disciple's mind; when he made a complete failure, they grew black and were destroyed; when he progressed in spiritual life, their degrees of brightness or beauty showed his exact standing. As these conclusions were reached, louder and stronger musical tones filled the hall. Directly before me was a beautiful, peaceful face; its brilliance outshone the

* Compare Mr. Judge's "Culture of Concentration," where the effects of several vices are described (*Theosophy*, XIV, 439-40).—Eds.

light around, and I knew that some unseen brother—how far or near was unknown to me—had reached some height of advancement that corresponded to such tones. Just then my guide re-entered; I found I was near the door; it was open; and together we passed out, retracing the same course by which we had entered. Outside again the setting of the moon showed how long I had been in the gallery. The silence of my guide prevented speech, and he returned with me to the room I had left. There he stood looking at me, and once more I heard as it were from afar his voice in inquiry, as if he said but

"Well?"

Into my mind came the question, "How are those faces made?" From all about him, but not from his lips, came the answer,

"You cannot understand. They are not the persons, and yet they are made from their minds and bodies."

"Was I right in the idea that they were connected with those they pictured by invisible cords along which the person's condition was carried?"

"Yes, perfectly. And they never err. From day to day they change for better or for worse. Once the disciple has entered this path his picture forms there; and we need no spies, no officious fellow disciples to prefer charges, no reports, no machinery. Everything registers itself. We have but to inspect the images to know just how the disciple gets on or goes back."

"And those curious elementals," thought I, "do they feed on the blackened images?"

"They are our scavengers. They gather up and dissipate the decomposed and deleterious atoms that formed the image before it grew black—no longer fit for such good company."

"And the music—did it come from the images?"

"Ah, boy, you have much to learn. It came from them, but it belongs also to every other soul. It is the vibration of the disciple's thoughts and spiritual life; it is the music of his good deeds and his brotherly love."

Then there came to me a dreadful thought, "How can one—if at all—restore his image once it has blackened in the gallery?"

But my guide was no longer there. A faint rustling sound was all—and three deep far notes as if upon a large bronze bell!

BRYAN KINNAVAN

June, 1889

THE SKIN OF THE EARTH

THE cold materialism of the 19th century paralyzes sentiment and kills mysticism. Thus it commits a double crime, in robbing man and preventing many classes of sentient beings from progressing up the ladder that leads from earth to heaven. So in telling these tales I feel sheltered behind the shield of the editor of the magazine for which I write, for, were I to be known as believing that any beings whatever other than man are affected by the mental negations of the century, my life would soon become a burden. This age is so full of ignorance that it sees not and cares nothing for the groans that are rolling among the caverns of mother earth fathoms deep below its surface. Nor will it care until its contempt for what it calls superstition shall have caused its ruin, and then—another age will have risen and other men have come.

It was not so in our Sacred Island cycles ago. Then what we call superstition was knowledge that has now been replaced by impudent scorn for aught save the empiric classification of a few facts; a heritage of glory given up for a mere statement of the limits of our ignorance. But I will plunge into the past and forget the present hour.

Seven months had rolled away since the time when, standing in the picture gallery, I had seen the simulacrum of a dear friend blacken and disappear, and now on the morning of the day when I was to pass by the mountain of the diamond, the news was brought to me how he had fallen faithless to his trust, overcome by vanity with its dark companion, doubt.

So, at the appointed hour, I waited for the messenger. Once again the white moonbeams shone into the room and, revealing the monthly dial curiously wrought into the floor and walls by a chemical art that allowed nothing to be revealed save by moonlight after the 14th day of her course, told me in a language pale and cold that this was the 17th day. I stood and watched the dial, fascinated by the symbols that crept out with the silvery light, although for years I had seen the same thing every month. But now as I looked some new combination of our ancient magic was revealed. Every now and then clouds seemed to roll across the floor, while on them rested the earth itself. This I had never seen before. Seven times it rolled by, and then I felt that near me stood the silent messenger. Turning I saw him just as he stood when he called me to the gallery.

"Do you not know this picture?" said he.

"No. All is dark to me."

"It is the sign that you are to come to the earth's hall beyond the gallery. Look again closely at that rolling ball upon the clouds, and tell me what you see."

These words seemed to come not from the man's lips, but from all about him, as if the air was full of sound. But obeying the direction I gazed at the picture and saw that the surface of the mystic globe was moving, and then that myriads of small creatures were coming through it.

"It is time," said the sounds from all about the impassive being. "That is the signal. We will go." And he turned away.

I followed while he led me up to the building and through the gallery of tell-tale pictures where still in the silence the faces changed and the soft music sounded. I would have lingered there to see those magic pictures, but a cord seemed to draw me after my guide. As we approached the other end of the gallery nothing was visible to the eye save a blank wall, but the messenger passed through it and disappeared. Afraid to stop, unable to resist the drawing of the invisible cord, I walked against the wall. One short moment of suspense and with my breath held I had passed through: it was but a cloud, or a vapor—and I was on the other side. Turning, expecting to still see through that immaterial wall, I found that it was impervious to the sight, and then the cord that drew me slackened, for my guide had stopped. Stepping up to the wall, my outstretched fingers went through it, or rather disappeared within it, for they felt no sensation. Then the messenger's voice said,

"Such is the skin of the Earth to those who live below it." With these words he walked on again through a door of a large room into which I followed. Here a faint but oppressive smell of earth filled all the space, and, standing just inside the door-way now closed by a noiselessly moving door, I saw that the whole place save where we stood was moving, as if the great globe were here seen revolving upon its axis and all its motions felt.

As I gazed, the surface of the revolving mass was seen to be covered with circling hosts of small creatures whose movements caused the revolutions, and all at once it seemed as if the moving body became transparent, and within was filled with the same creatures. They were constantly coming from the surface and moving to the centre along well-defined paths. Here was the whole globe represented in forcible miniature, and these creatures within and upon it of their own nature moved it, guided by some mysterious Being whose presence was only revealed by beams of light. Nor could the others see him, but his silent directions were carried out.

These little beings were of every color and form; some wore an appearance similar to that of man himself, others appeared like star blossoms of the sea, their pure tints waxing and waning as they throbbed with an interior pulse of light. Whatever their shapes, these seemed evanescent, translucent, and easily dissipated; in their real essence the creatures were centers of energy, a nucleolus around which light condensed, now in this form, now in that, with constant progression of type and form. Some were more swift and harmonious in their movements than others, and these I understood were the more progressed in the scale of Being. Such had a larger orbit, and satellites circled about them. Of such systems the place was full, and all owned obedience to the subtle and interior Power which I could not discern. Each system existed for the service of all the rest; each complemented and sustained the others as they swept onward in a harmony that was labor and love. Their object seemed twofold; they assisted in maintaining the revolutions of the earth upon its axis and in guiding it in its orbit. They also grew through the ever-increasing swiftness of their own motions into greater splendor and brightness, approaching greater intelligence, coming ever nearer to self-conscious reason and love, and, as they grew, stimulated the latent spark in the metals and all the underworld growth as the lambent touch of flame awakens flame.

Guided by the Unseen Power and in their automatic obedience (for to obey was their nature), there were some who, by the greatness of their own momentum and the ferment of new forces attracted and gathering about them, seemed upon the point of bursting into some fuller expansion, some higher state of intelligence and life, but they were withheld by something that was not the Power guiding them. Looking closer I saw that an antagonistic influence was at work in the place.

The orbit of many of these docile and beautiful creatures included a passage to and fro through the mystic wall. Their duties were upon the earth as well as beneath its surface; faithful fulfilment of these functions comprised an evolution into higher service and a higher form. The malign influence often prevented this. It seemed like a dark mist full of noxious vapor that deadened while it chilled. As the clouds rolled into the hall their wreaths assumed now this shape and now that, changeful and lurid suggestions of hatred, lust, and pride. Many of the creatures coming in contact with these had that influence stamped upon their sensitive spheres, giving them the horrid likeness which they were powerless to shake off, thus becoming servants of the baleful mist itself with altered and discordant motions. Others were paralyzed with the chill contact. Others were so taxed to make up for the partial suspension of their fellows' activity that their work was unsteady and their orbital revolutions checked. But still the whole throng swung on like some splendid creation, paling, glowing, throbbing, pausing, a huge iridescent heart scintillating, singing through the gloom. Here the mist was beaten back by greater efforts that jarred the harmony; there it gathered, condensed, and in its vile embrace swept in bright systems, stifling their motions, then leaving them paralyzed where they fell, while it crawled on to fresh victims. And all through this strange picture and wonderful battle I could see the dim cloud-like shapes of cities inhabited by the men of earth, my fellows, and also the rivers, mountains, and trees of the globe.

In my mind the query rose, "Why do the earth's cities look like dreams?"

And there upon the wall flashed out this sentence, while its meaning sounded in every letter:

"When you are being shown the elemental beings, the men of your earth and their cities appear as clouds because it is not to them that your mind is directed. Look yet again!"

I saw that the evil mist had gathered strength in one part of the place, and had destroyed the harmony and swiftness of so many of the little beings that the great circling globe was moving off its axis, circling more and more. So I knew that upon whatever earth this happened great changes would occur, and that in the path of the mist there would sweep over man epidemics of disease and crime. Horrified at such impending calamities I sought for an answer and looked towards my guide. As I did so he disappeared, and upon the wall his voice seemed to paint itself in living letters that themselves gave out a sound.

"It is the thoughts of men." I hid my face, appalled at owning such a heritage, and when I looked again great jets spurted through the Skin of the Earth, thoughts spouting and pouring out in miasmatic streams.

I would have asked much more, but again from some vast distance came the tones of the deep bronze bell; a shower of earth's blossoms fell about me; I had passed the wall; my guide was gone; and I was alone in my own room reflecting on what I had seen.

BRYAN KINNAVAN

October, 1889

THE TURN OF THE WHEEL

A Little Tale of Karma

I

HE WAS the son of a small ruler in Rajpootana. His father, of the warrior caste, governed a district including several villages, as well as his own small town, with justice and wisdom, so that all were prosperous and happy. The ruler was called a Rajah; he lived in a building made of stone, built on a hill that commanded the town. The son, of whom this tale tells, was born after the Rajah had been many years childless, and was the only child to whom the father's honors and power could descend. He was named Rama after the great Avatar. From the time he was born and until he could speak, a strange look was always to be seen in his baby eyes; a look that gazed at you without flinching, bold, calculating, as if he had some design on you; and yet at times it seemed to show that he was laughing at himself, sorry, too, melancholy at times.

Rama grew up and delighted his father with his goodness and strength of mind. The strange glance of his eye as a baby remained with him, so that while everyone loved him, they all felt also a singular respect that was sometimes awe. His studies were completed, a first short pilgrimage to a celebrated shrine had been made very early by his own request, and he began to take part in the administration of the affairs of the old and now feeble rajah. Each day he retired to his room alone; no one was permitted to come within three rooms of his; and on the fourteenth of the month he spent the entire day in retirement. Let us go with him in fancy to one of these monthly retreats and listen with his consent.

II

The room is an ordinary Hindu room. Hard chunam floor, the bed rolled up in the corner, on the walls one or two flat metal plaques inlaid with enamel and representing different gods and heroes. He enters and goes up to the wall in front of one of these plaques—Krishna. The strange look in his eyes grows deeper, stronger, and a stream of light seems to rush from them to the object on the wall. His lips move.

"Atmanam, atmana—" he seems to say; the rest is murmured so low we cannot hear it. The words are in his own dialect, but in the mind of the hearer they translate themselves. He says:

"This weight upon my heart is not from this life. I have known no sorrow, have lost no object that I loved. My ambitions are fulfilled; the present is bright, the future shows no shadow. When, O Krishna, shall I know that which I now know not, nor what it is that I long to learn? Yet even now a ray of hope steals into my soul."

Just as he uttered the last words a ringing sound came from the metal plaque and Rama gazed steadily at it. The plaque vibrated, and a subtle scent spread from it over the whole room. The air seemed to vibrate slowly, undulatingly, and then a dazzling shape of a young man seemed to form itself upon the floor, while the vibration centered in the form and the scent turned into light. Rama looked steadily at this being who stood there erect and terrifying, yet calm and strong with peace all about it. It was the calmness and power of it that terrified. As Rama looked, it spoke:

"Do you forget the Upanishad, 'Two birds sit in one tree; the one eats the fruit and the other looks on'?"

"No," said Rama, "I forget not. They are the personal and universal. The one who looks on is my higher self—Atman."

"I am thy higher self. I come to tell thee of three words. Forget them not, forget not me. They are: Action, Law, The Fruit of Action."

"These," said Rama, "I have heard. Action and Law I know, but the Fruit of Action, is it that which eats within?"

The form of beauty replied: "It is the ignorance of it that hurts thee. Thou art bound in thy future. This present birth of thine is to allow thee to make the Karma for thy next birth better in the end, but which will be ever dark and painful if not now ameliorated. In this present is thy future. Potential now lies the effect in what cause you make."

Then with one straight arrow-like glance into the face of Rama, the form faded, and the plaque rang a note of farewell. Across the wall there seemed to pass a picture of poverty and riches, of huts and buildings of stone. Rama left the room the next day, and never after seemed to sorrow or to be annoyed. His old father died, and he carried on the government for many years, scattering blessings in every direction, until a rival rajah came and demanded all his possessions, showing a claim to them through a forgotten branch of the family. Instead of rejecting the claim, which was just, instead of slaying the rival as he could have done, Rama resigned all, retired to the forest, and died after a few years of austerity.

III

The wheel of time rolled on and Rama was reborn in a town governed by the Rajah who had once in a former life demanded Rama's possessions. But now Rama was poor, unknown, an outcaste, a chandalah who swept up garbage and hoped that Karma might help him. He knew not that he was Rama; he only swept the garbage near the Rajah's palace.

A solemn audience was held by the Rajah with all the priests and the soothsayers present. Troubled by a dream of the night before, the superstitious ruler called them in to interpret, to state causes learnedly, to prescribe scriptural palliative measures. He had dreamed that while walking in his garden, hearing from his treasurer an account of his increasing wealth, a huge stone building seemed suddenly to grow up before him. As he stopped amazed, it toppled over and seemed to bury him and his wealth. Three times repeated, this filled him with fear.

The astrologers retired and consulted their books. The remedy was plain, one suggested. "Let the King give a vast sum of money tomorrow to the first person he sees after waking up." This decision was accepted, and the proposer of it intended to be on hand early so as to claim the money. The Rajah agreed to the direction of the stars, and retired for the night, full of his resolution to give immense gifts next day. No horrid dreams disturbed his sleep. The winking stars moved over the vault of heaven, and of all the hosts the moon seemed to smile upon the city as if, being near, she heard and knew all. The cold early morning, dark with promise of the dawn, saw the chandalah—once Rama—sweeping up the garbage near the palace where inside the Rajah was just awaking. The last star in heaven seemed to halt as if anxious that Rama should come in his sweeping to the side of the palace from which the Rajah's window opened. Slowly the chandalah crept around in his task, slowly, surely. Slowly the Rajah's waking senses returned, and as they came a hideous memory of his dream flashed on him. Starting up from the mat on which he lay, he rose and seemed to think.

"What was I to do? Yes, give gifts. But it is not yet day. Still the oracle said 'immediately on awakening'."

As he hesitated the poor garbage sweeper outside came more nearly in front of his window. The setting star almost seemed to throw a beam through the wall that struck and pushed him to the window. Flinging open the shutter to get breath, he looked down, and there before him was a poor chandalah with waistcloth and no turban, sweating with exertion, hastening on with the task that when finished would leave the great Rajah's grounds clean and ready for their lord.

"Thank the gods," said the Rajah, "it is fate; a just decision; to the poor and the pious should gifts be given."

At an early hour he gathered his ministers and priests together and said—

"I give gifts to the devas through the poor; I redeem my vow. Call the chandalah who early this morn swept the ground."

Rama was called and thought it was for prison or death. But the Rajah amazed him with a gift of many thousands of rupees, and as the chandalah, now rich, passed out, he thought he smelt a strange familiar odor and saw a dazzling form flash by. "This," thought he, "is a deva."

The money made Rama rich. He established himself and invited learned Brahmins to teach others; he distributed alms, and one day he caused a huge building of stone to be built with broken stone chains on its sides to represent how fate ruptured his chains. And later on a wise seer, a Brahmin of many austerities, looking into his life, told him briefly,

"Next life thou art free. Thy name is Rama."

BRYAN KINNAVAN

October, 1889

WHERE THE RISHIS WERE

The Rishis were the sacred Bards, the Saints, the great Adepts known to the Hindus, who gave great spiritual impulses in the past and are said to sometimes reincarnate, and who at one time lived on the earth among men.

THE world is made of seas and islands. For continents are only great lands water-encircled. Men must ever live upon sea or land, then, unless they abide in air, and if they live in the air they are not men as we know them." Thus I thought as the great ship steamed slowly into the port of a small island, and before the anchor fell the whole scene seemed to change and the dazzling light of the past blotted out the dark pictures of modern civilization. Instead of an English ship I was standing on an ancient vehicle propelled by force unknown today, until the loud noises of disembarkation roused me once again.

But, landed now, I was standing on the hill overlooking the town and bay. The strange light and the curious vehicle again obtained mastery over sense and eye, while the whole majesty of forgotten years rolled in from the Ocean. Vainly did modern education struggle and soar: I let the curtain drop upon the miserable present.

Now softly sings the water as it rolls against the shore, with the sun but one hour old shining upon its surface. But, far off, what is that spot against the sky coming nearer from the West, followed by another and another until over the horizon rise hundreds, and now some are so near that they are plainly seen? The same strange vehicles as that I saw at first. Like birds they fly through the air. They come slowly now, and some have been brought still on the land. They light on the earth with a softness that seems nearly human, with a skill that is marvellous, without any shock or rebound. From them alight men of noble mien who address me as friends, and one more noble than the others seems to say, "Wouldst thou know of all this? Then come," as he turns again to his vehicle that stands there like a bird in wait to be off.

"Yes, I will go"; and I felt that the past and present were but one, and knew what I should see, yet could not remember it but with a vagueness that blotted out all the details.

We entered the swift intelligently-moving vehicle, and then it rose up on the air's wide-spreading arms and flew again fast to the West whence it had come. It passed many more flying east to the Island, where the water was still softly singing to the beams of the sun. The horizon slowly rose and the Island behind us was hidden by sea from our sight. And still as onward we flew to the Occident, many more birds made by man like that we were in flew by us as if in haste for the soft-singing water lapping the shore of that peak of the sea mountain we had left in the Orient. Flying too high at first we heard no sound from the sea, but soon a damp vapor that blew in my face from the salt deep showed that we were descending, and then spoke my friend.

"Look below and around and before you!"

Down there were the roar and the rush of mad billows that reached toward the sky, vast hollows that sucked in a world. Black clouds shut out the great sun, and I saw that the crust of the earth was drawn in to her own subterranean depths. Turning now to the master, I saw that he heard my unuttered question. He said,

"A cycle has ended. The great bars that kept back the sea have been broken down by their weight. From these we have come and are coming."

Then faster sailed our bird, and I saw that a great Island was perishing. What was left of the shore still crumbled, still entered the mouth of the sea. And there were cars of the air just the same as that I was in, only dark and unshining, vainly trying to rise with their captains; rising slowly, then falling, and then swallowed up.

But here we have rushed further in where the water has not overflowed, and now we see that few are the bright cars of air that are waiting about while their captains are entering and spoiling the mighty dark cars of the men whose clothing is red and whose bodies, so huge and amazing, are sleeping as if from the fumes of a drug.

As these great red men are slumbering, the light-stepping captains with sun-colored cloaks are finishing the work of destruction. And now, swiftly though we came, the waters have rushed on behind us, the salt breath of the all-devouring deep sweeps over us. The sun-colored captains enter their light air-cars and rise with a sweep that soon leaves the sleepers, now waking, behind them. The huge red-coated giants hear the roar of the waters and feel the cold waves roll about them. They enter their cars, but only to find all their efforts are wasted. Soon the crumbling earth no longer supports them, and all by an inrushing wave are engulfed, drawn into the mouth of the sea, and the treacherous ocean with roars as of pleasure in conquest has claimed the last race of the Island.

But one escaped of all the red giants, and slowly but surely his car sailed up, up, as if to elude the sun-colored men who were spoilers.

Then loud, clear, and thrilling swelled out a note of marvellous power from my captain, and back came a hundred of those brilliant, fast cars that were speeding off eastward. Now they pursue the heavy, vast, slow-moving car of the giant, surround it, and seem to avoid its attacks. Then again swells that note from my master as our car hung still on its wings. It was a signal, obeyed in an instant.

One brilliant, small, sharp-pointed car is directed full at the red giant's vehicle. Propelled by a force that exceeds the swift bullet, it pierces the other, itself, too, is broken and falls on the waves with its victim. Trembling I gazed down below, but my captain said kindly,

"He is safe, for he entered another bright car at the signal. All those red-coated men are now gone, and that last was the worst and the greatest."

Back eastward once more through the salt spray and the mist until soon the bright light shone again and the Island rose over the sea with the soft-singing water murmuring back to the sun. We alighted, and then, as I turned, the whole fleet of swift sailing cars disappeared, and out in the sky there flashed a bright streak of sun-colored light that formed into letters which read:

"This is where the Rishis were before the chalk cliffs of Albion rose out of the wave. They were but are not."

And loud, clear, and thrilling rose that note I had heard in the car of swift pinions. It thrilled me with sadness, for past was the glory and naught for the future was left but a destiny.

BRYAN KINNAVAN.

January, 1891

THE COMING OF THE SERPENT

THE white rays shed over all the Island when the Diamond on the mountain shot forth its last light and continued shining until the malignant snake formed from the serpent's blood had fled all across the sea and reached the great Isle beyond. Then all became black as night to the people. Deprived of my body that lay cold and dead beside the altar, I could see the high priest bending over the corpse until the growing darkness filled him with alarm which changed to terror. As he rose up from his bending attitude I heard a solemn voice that filled all the space around utter these words:

"The cycle is ended. Thou hast completed a part of thy work, leaving a little in the new malignant snake to be done. Thou must follow it to the other Islands until fate shall lead thee elsewhere. Fear not but proceed with a calm courage, for we are ever beside thee, the same in the dark as in the light."

A sudden faintness filled my ethereal body, shadowy forms flitted about me, and I knew I was flying eastward with the vast heaving sea below me. On and on I fled and soon perceived the smell of earth. Over the other Island to the west I was floating in an atmosphere loaded with heavy emanations. I lost consciousness—and then I was born in another land, in the Island to the East, and even as a child I knew that the serpent's blood had come before me, knew full well I should meet it one day. In time I entered in company with the Druids, and one of them told of the coming of the serpent.

My teacher and narrator was a tall old man, over a century in age. A long white beard fell over his breast. Large blue eyes that seemed alive with a light of their own showed his soul gazing at you, but they were strong and fearless in expression. They pierced your being, but carried calmness and hope with them. A calmness born from many lives of struggle and triumph, a hope arising from a vast and comprehensive view of the future; for he was a seer and knew the coming and going of the great tides of time. He said:

"Boy, your questions grow out of experience in the past. The serpent is in this land. Here we came long, long ago, after many centuries of watching, from the shore of the Island of the Diamond, while this land slowly rose up from the deep to touch the surface of the water and then emerge. For your own island is far older than this. We planted huge stones of magic potency in the slime as it came near the surface, and held them in place by the same power, hoping to prepare in advance for the Serpent which we knew was to come. But human hearts and wills alone can conquer; magic stones and amulets and charms subserve but a temporary end. Many centuries passed thus, and after the land had arisen, became clothed with vegetation and inhabited by people, we sorrowfully saw the emanations from colonists were thickening day by day.

"Across the sea the Diamond Mountain threw up over the horizon a faint and beautiful light by night, a bluish haze by day. Then one night as with my brothers I sat looking westward, the light on the sky blazed up with sudden force. We knew the hour had come. The darkness fell greater as that holy light faded away, and through the air a hissing sound came across the sea. It was the serpent's blood, one drop changed into a smaller snake that flew from the West. That was the day you violated rules, throttled the ancient serpent behind the altar, and lost your life at the hands of the high priest of a false, a counterfeit religion.

"In vain our chants arose around the mighty stones that stood majestically in the plain. On and on, louder and louder, came that malignant hiss; down on the ground, even close to the stones of the Sun, fell the serpent and disappeared from our sight.

"Since then its baleful influence has been felt over all the land, and until thy coming we knew not when any Deliverer should arise. In thee is locked up the power to destroy the last remnants of the power of the serpent's blood. Perhaps thy ancient friends will help, for although thou art younger here, yet thou art older than we all. Be wise and true. Forget no duty, omit no effort, and one day the last drop of that ophidian blood will be altered by thy power and art, will be transmuted into elixir."

BRYAN KINNAVAN

March, 1893

AN OCCULT NOVEL

A TIRELESS worker, Mr. Judge was always proposing new modes of activity. One never knew what fresh idea would emanate from his indefatigable mind. One idea with which he occupied some of his lighter moments, was that of an occult novel. It was his idea that a friend of his should write this, from incidents and material to be furnished by himself, and to this idea he adhered, even having the title copyrighted, with the name of his author, despite the laughing protests of this friend, to whose outcries and statements that she never could, and never should, write a novel, Mr. Judge would smilingly reply: "Oh, yes! You will do it when the time comes." From time to time he sent to this friend suggestions, incidents and other material for this novel, the same being on odds and ends of paper, often rough wrapping paper, and being jotted down under a lamp-post at night while he waited for his tram, or in court while he waited for the case in which he was engaged to come up. On these scraps are also marginal notes, as he accepted or rejected the ideas of his own prolific mind. These notes are given here as such. It has been suggested that the recipient of these materials should still write the novel as proposed, but setting aside the fact that she could not be sure of properly rendering the real ideas of Mr. Judge, it is also thought that readers will much prefer to have the notes precisely as Mr. Judge set them down.

The printed title-page runs as follows:

IN A BORROWED BODY

The Journey of a Soul

BY

J. CAMPBELL VER-PLANCK, F.T.S.

1891

The name is filled in in the writing of Mr. Judge, and there is this marginal note. "Copyright gone to Washngn."

(All "Notes" are to be understood as being marginal ones made by Mr. Judge unless otherwise stated.) [J. N.]

MEMO. ABOUT *Borrowed Body*

The point on which it should all turn is not so much reincarnation as the use of a borrowed body, which is a different kind of reincarnation from that of Arnold's *Phra the Phœnician.*

This will also give chance to show the other two sorts of reincarnation, *e.g.*:—

(*a*) Ordinary reincarnation in which there is no memory of the old personality, as the astral body is new; and:

(*b*) Exception as to astral body; but similarity of conception to that of ordinary cases, where the child retains the old astral body and hence memory of old personality and acquaintance with old knowledge and dexterity.

A CHAPTER

The Assembling of the Skandhas

On the death of body, the Kama principle collects the Skandhas in space, or at the rebirth of the Ego the Skandhas rush together and assemble about it to go with it in the new life.

ANOTHER

The Unveiling of the Sun

There is the real and unreal Sun. The real one is hidden by a golden vase, and the devotee prays:

"Unveil, O Pushan, the true Sun's face," etc. A voice (or other) says "thou art that vase" and then he knows that he alone hides the true Sun from himself.

Pushan is the guide and watches on the path to the Sun.

The eulogy of the Sun and the Soul are enshrined in a golden rose or lotus in the heart which is impregnable.

The theme of the book is not always teacher and pupil.

He first strives for some lives ordinarily and then in one he grows old and wise, and sitting before a temple one day in Madura he dies slowly, and like a dissolving view he sees the adepts round him aiding him; also a small child which seems to be himself, and then thick darkness. He is born then in the usual way.

Twice this is repeated, each time going through the womb but with the same astral body.

Then he lives the third life to forty-nine,* and comes again to die and with the same aid he selects a foreign child who is dying.

Child dying. Skandhas collecting, child's Ego going—left, spark of life low: relatives about bed.

He enters by the way the mind went out and revivifies the body. Recovery, youth, etc., etc.

This is his borrowed body.

MEMO. NO. 2

A couple of Incidents for the Book

I. A round tower used by the fire worshippers in Ireland and other isles in early ages. A temple is attached to it; quaint structure—one priest and one neophyte.

People below the tower coming into the temple grounds as the religion is in its decadence.

On the top of the tower is the neophyte, who in the face of the prevailing scepticism clings to the dead faith and to the great priest. His duty is to keep a fire on the tower burning with aromatic woods. He leans over the fire; it burns badly; the wood seems green; he blows it up; it burns slightly; he hears the voices of the disputers and sellers below; goes to the tower and gazes over while the fire goes slowly out. He is a young man of singular expression, not beautiful but powerful face; intense eyes, long dark hair, and far-gazing eyes of a greyish colour unusual for such hair. Skin clear with a shifting light flowing from it. Sensitive face; blushes easily, but now and then stern. As he still gazes, the fire goes out. Just then a tall old man comes up the stairs and stands upon the tower top at opposite side, looking at the fire and then at the young man and withdraws not his gaze for an instant. It is a sternly powerful drawing look. He is very tall, dark brown eyes, grey hair, long beard. The young man feels his look and turns about and sees the fire out completely, while its last small cloud of smoke is floating off beyond the tower. They look at each other. In the young man's face you see the desperate first impulse to excuse, and then the sudden thought that excuses are useless bcause childish,

* Compare Judge's statement in a letter to Olcott, March 4, 1880: "I have lived at one time in India 19 years, and twice before about 2 or 3 years each time, so, you see, I am not so much younger than you, as I thought." (*The Theosophist*, March, 1931.) Olcott was born in 1832, W.Q.J. in 1851.—Eds.

for he knew his duty—to keep the small spiral of smoke ever connecting heaven with earth, in the hope, however vain, that thus the old age might be charmed to return. The old man raises his hand, points away from the tower and says "Go." Young man descends.

II. *A battle.*—In the hottest a young soldier armed to the teeth, fighting as if it made no matter whether he win or lose, die or live. Strange weapons, sounds and clouds.

Wounded, blood flowing. It is the young man of the tower. He sinks down, taken prisoner. In a cell, condemned, for they fear his spiritual power. Conflict between the last remnant of the old religion and the new, selfish faith.

Taken to his execution. Two executioners. They bind him standing and stand behind and at side; each holds a long straight weapon with a curved blunt blade, curved to (fit?) about the neck. They stand at opposite sides, place those curved blunt blades holding his neck like two crooks. They pull—a sickening sound: his head violently pulled out close to the shoulder leaves a jagged edge. The body sways and falls. It was the way they made such a violent exit for a noble soul as they thought would keep it bound in the astral earth sphere for ages.

III. That young man again. He approaches an old man (of the tower). Young one holds parchments and flowers in his hand, points to parchments and asks explanation. Old one says, "Not now; when I come again I will tell you."

Note.—Keep this, Julius.

W. Q. J.
Z. L. Z.

The next batch of notes is headed by the single word: *"Book."* Then follow four lines of shorthand. After these the words:

"Incidents showing by picture his life in other ages; the towers; the battle; the death; the search for knowledge and the sentiment expressed in the flowers."

Eusebio Rodriguez de Undiano* was a notary in Spain who found among the effects of his father many old parchments written in a language which was unknown to him. He discovered it was Arabic, and in order to decipher them learned that tongue. They contained the story.

* Compare Mr. Judge's pen names, "Eusebio Urban" and "Rodriguez Undiano."—Eds.

Note.—No initiates; Lytton only.

Eusebio de Undiano is only one of the old comrades reborn in Spain who searches likes Nicodemus for the light.

Note.—Yes.

Eusebio de Undiano finds in his father's parchments confirmation of what the possession of the body has often told him.

Note.—Yes.

This person in the body never gave his name to anyone and has no name.

An autobiographical story? No? *Yes!* Related by one who was struck; by an admirer who suspected something? No; because that is hearsay evidence; the proof is incomplete, whereas he relating it himself is either true, or a mere insane fancy. It is better to be insane than be another's tool.

Stick to the tower and the head-chopping business. Let him be that young man and after the head loss he wanders in Kama Loca and there he sees the old man who was killed on the tower soon after the fire went out. The old man tells him that he will tell all when they return to earth.

He wanders about the tower vicinity seeking a birth, until one day he sees vague shapes suddenly appearing and disappearing. They are not dressed like his countrymen down below on the earth. This goes on. They seem friendly and familiar, the one requesting him to go with them, he refuses. They are more powerful than he is, yet they do not compel him but show him their power. One day one was talking to him; he again refuses unless something might show him that he ought to go. Just then he hears a bell sound, such as he never heard before. It vibrates through him and seems to open up vistas of a strange past and in a moment he consents to go.

They reach Southern India and there he sees the old man of the tower, whom he addresses, and again asks the burning question about the parchment. The old man says again the same as before and adds that he had better come again into the world in that place.

The darkness and silence. The clear, hot day. The absence of rain. After listening to the old man he consents inwardly to assume life there and soon a heavy storm arises, the rain beats, he feels himself carried to the earth and in deep darkness. A resounding noise about him. It is the noise of the growing plants. This is a rice field with some sesamum in it. The moisture descends and causes the expanding; sees around, all is motion and life. Inclosed in the sphere of some rice, he bemoans his fate. He is born in a Brahmin's house.

Note.—Shall the question of reincarnation—through cloud and rain and seed, and thus from the seed of the man—be gone into?

He is the young man. He knows much. He dies at nineteen. Strange forms around his bed who hold him. They carry him back to the land of the towers. He recognizes it again and sees that ages have passed since the fire went out, and in the air he perceives strange shapes and sees incessantly a hand as of Fate, pointing to that Island. The towers are gone, the temples and the monuments. All is altered. They take him to a populous city and as he approaches he sees over one house a great commotion in the air. Shapes moving. Bright flashes, and puffs as of smoke. They enter the room, and on the bed is the form of a young boy given up to die, with relatives weeping. His guides ask him if he will borrow that body about to be deserted and use it for the good of their Lodge. He consents. They warn him of the risks and dangers.

The boy's breathing ceases and his eyes close, and a bright flash is seen to go off from it (the body). He sees the blood slowing down. THEY push him, and he feels dark again. Boy revives. Physician takes hope. "Yes; he will recover, with care." He recovers easily. Change in his character. Feels strange in his surroundings, etc.

The place in India where he went after death which was again sudden (how?). A large white building. Gleaming marble. Steps. Pillars. A hole that has yellowish glow that looks like water. Instruction as to the work to be done, and the journey to the land of the tower, in search of a body to borrow. As to bodies being deserted by the tenant that might live if well understood and well connected with a new soul. The difference between such a birth and an ordinary birth where the soul really owns the body, and between those bodies of insane people which are not deserted, but where the owner really lives outside. Bodies of insane are not used because the machine itself is out of order, and would be useless to the soul of a sane person.

Note.—Julius; keep these. I will send them now and then. But before you go away, return to me so I can keep the run of it. May change the scheme. The motive is in the title I gave you.

Note.—No one who has not consciously lived the double life of a man who is in the use and possession of a body not his own can know the agony that so often falls to one in such a case. I am not the original owner of this body that I now use. It was made for another, and for some little time used by him, but in the storm of sickness he left it here to be buried, and it would have been laid away in the earth if I had not taken it up, vivified its failing energies and carried it through some years of trial by sickness and accident. But the first owner had not been in it long enough to sow any troublesome seeds of disease; he left a heritage of good family blood and wonderful endurance. That he should have left this form so well adapted for living, at least seems inconceivable, unless it was that he could not use it, sick or well, for any of his own purposes. At any rate it is mine now, but while at first I thought it quite an acquisition there are often times when I wish I had not thus taken another man's frame, but had come into life in the ordinary way.

A Couple of Incidents for The Book

Incident of the letter and picture.

There was a very curious old man (sufficient description to add).

Sent a small cardboard in which was a picture, a head, and over it appeared to be placed a thin sheet of paper, gummed over the sides to the back. He asked if I could tell him anything of the picture which was visible through the thin paper. Having great curiosity, I lifted up the thin paper, and at once there seemed to be printed off from its underside a red circle surrounding the head on the board. In one instance this circle turned black and so did the entire inside space including the head which was then obliterated. In the other the red circle seemed to get on fire inward, and then the whole included portion burned up. On examining the thin paper on underside there were traces of a circle, as if with paste.

He laughed and said that curiosity was not always rewarded.

Took it to several chemists in Paris, who said that they knew of no substance that would do this. The old chemist in Ireland said a very destructive thing called Fluorine might be liberated thus and do it, but that it was only a thing with chemists and analysts.

(*Note by the compiler.*—In his travels Mr. Judge met many strange people and saw some extraordinary sights. Now and again he would tell one of these to be included in the novel, but just in this unfinished and vague way. When asked to tell more, he would smile and shake his head, saying: "No. No—little brothers must finish it.")

Another Incident

The temple on the site of the present city of Conjeveram was about to be consecrated, and the regular priests were all ready for the ceremony. Minor ceremonies had taken place at the laying of the cornerstone, but this was to exceed that occasion in importance. A large body of worshippers were gathered not for the gratification of curiosity, but in order to receive the spiritual benefits of the occasion, and they filled the edifice so that I could not get inside. I was thus compelled to stand just at the edge of the door, and that was, as I afterwards found out, the best place I could have selected if I had known in advance what was to take place. A few days before, a large number of wandering ascetics had arrived and camped on a spot near the temple, but no one thought much of it because used to seeing such people. There was nothing unnatural about these men, and all that could be said was that a sort of mysterious air hung about them, and one or two children declared that, on one evening, none of the visitors could be found at their camp, nor any evidence that men had been there. But they were not believed, because the ascetics were there as usual the next morning. Two old men in the city said that the visitors were Devas in their "illusionary form," but there was too much excitement about the dedication to allow of much thought on the subject. The event, however, proved the old men right.

At the moment when the people in the temple were expecting the priests to arrive, the entire body of ascetics appeared at the door with a wonderful looking sage-like man at their head; they entered the edifice in the usual formal way of the priests and the latter, on arriving, made no disturbance, but took what places they could, simply saying: "They are the Devas." The strangers went on with the ceremonies, and, all the while, a light filled the building and music from the air floated over the awestruck worshippers.

When the time came for them to go, they all followed the leader in silence to the door. I could see inside, and as I was at the door could also see outside. All the ascetics came to the entrance, but not one was seen to go beyond it, and none were ever perceived by any man in the city again. They melted away at the threshold. It was their last appearance, for the shadow of the dark age was upon the people, preventing such sights for the future. The occurrence was the topic of conversation for years, and it was all recorded in the archives of the city.

In a Borrowed Body

I must tell you first what happened to me in this present life, since it is in this one that I am relating to you about many other lives of mine.

I was a simple student of our high Philosophy for many lives on earth, in various countries, and then at last developed in myself a desire for action. So I died once more, as so often before, and was again reborn in the family of a Rajah, and in time came to sit on his throne after his death.

Two years after that sad event, one day an old wandering Brahmin came to me and asked if I was ready to follow my vows of long lives before, and go to do some work for my old master in a foreign land. Thinking this meant a journey, only, I said I was.

"Yes," said he, "but it is not only a journey. It will cause you to be here and there all days and years. Today here, to-night there."

"Well," I replied, "I will do even that, for my vows had no conditions and master orders."

I knew of the order, for the old Brahmin gave me the sign marked on my forehead. He had taken my hand, and covering it with his waist-cloth, traced the sign in my palm under the cloth so that it stood out in lines of light before my eyes.

He went away with no other word, as you know they so often do, leaving me in my palace. I fell asleep in the heat, with only faithful Gopal beside me. I dreamed and thought I was at the bedside of a mere child, a boy, in a foreign land unfamiliar to me, only that the people looked like what I knew of the Europeans. The boy was lying as if dying, and relatives were all about the bed.

A strange and irresistible feeling drew me nearer to the child, and for a moment I felt in this dream as if I were about to lose consciousness. With a start I awoke in my own palace—on the mat where I had fallen asleep, with no one but Gopal near and no noise but the howling of jackals near the edge of the compound.

"Gopal," I said, "how long have I slept?"

"Five hours, master, since an Old Brahmin went away, and the night is nearly gone, master."

I was about to ask him something else, when again sleepiness fell upon my senses, and once more I dreamed of the small dying foreign child.

The scene had changed a little, other people had come in, there was a doctor there, and the boy looked to me, dreaming so vividly, as if dead. The people were weeping, and his mother knelt by the bedside. The doctor laid his head on the child's breast a moment. As for myself, I was drawn again nearer to the body and thought surely the people were strange not to notice me at all. They acted as if no stranger were there, and I looked at my clothes and saw they were eastern and bizarre to them. A magnetic line seemed to pull me to the form of the child.

And now beside me I saw the old Brahmin standing. He smiled.

"This is the child," he said, "and here must you fulfil a part of your vows. Quick now! There is no time to lose, the child is almost dead. These people think him already a corpse. You see the doctor has told them the fatal words, 'he is dead!' "

Yes, they were weeping. But the old Brahmin put his hands on my head, and submitting to his touch, I felt myself in my dream falling asleep. A dream in a dream. But I woke in my dream, though not on my mat, with Gopal near me. I was that boy, I thought. I looked out through his eyes, and near me I heard as if his soul had slipped off to the ether with a sigh of relief. The doctor turned once more and I opened my eyes—his eyes—on him.

The physician started and turned pale. To another I heard him whisper "automatic nerve action." He drew near, and the intelligence in that eye startled him to paleness. He did not see the old Brahmin making passes over this body I was in and from which I felt great waves of heat and life rolling over me—or the boy.

And yet this all now seemed real as if my identity was merged in the boy.

I was that boy and still confused, vague dreams seemed to flit through my brain of some other plane where I thought I was again, and had a faithful servant named Gopal; but that must be dream, this the reality. For did I not see my mother and father, the old doctor and the nurse so long in our house with the children. Yes; of course this is the reality.

And then I feebly smiled, whereon the doctor said:

"Most marvellous. He has revived. He may live."

He was feeling the slow-moving pulse and noting that breathing began and that vitality seemed once more to return to the child, but he did not see the old Brahmin in his illusionary body sending air currents of life over the body of this boy, who dreamed he had been a Rajah with a faithful servant named Gopal. Then, in the dream, sleep seemed to fall upon me. A sensation of falling, falling, came to my brain, and with a start I awoke in my palace on my own mat. Turning to see if my servant was there, I saw him standing as if full of sorrow or fear for me.

"Gopal, how long have I slept again?"

"It is just morning, master, and I feared you had gone to Yamâ's dominions and left your own Gopal behind."

No, I was not sleeping. This was reality, these my own dominions. So this day passed as all days had, except that the dream of the small boy in a foreign land came to my mind all day until the night when I felt more drowsy than usual. Once more I slept and dreamed.

The same place and the same house, only now it was morning there. What a strange dream I thought I had had; as the doctor came in with my mother and bent over me, I heard him say softly:

"Yes, he will recover. The night sleep has done good. Take him, when he can go, to the country, where he may see and walk on the grass."

As he spoke I saw behind him the form of a foreign-looking man with a turban on. He looked like the pictures of Brahmins I saw in the books before I fell sick. Then I grew very vague and told my mother: "I had two dreams for two nights, the same in each. I dreamed I was a king and had one faithful servant for whom I was sorry, as I liked him very much, and it was only a dream, and both were gone."

My mother soothed me, and said: "Yes, yes, my dear."

And so that day went as days go with sick boys, and early in the evening I fell fast asleep as a boy in a foreign land, in my dream, but did no more dream of being a king, and as before I seemed to fall until I woke again on my mat in my own palace with Gopal sitting near. Before I could rise the old Brahmin, who had gone away, came in and I sent Gopal off.

"Rama," said he, "as boy, you will not dream of being Rajah, but now you must know that every night, as sleeping king, you are waking boy in foreign land. Do well your duty and fail not. It will be some years, but Time's never-stopping car rolls on. Remember my words," and then he passed through the open door.

So I knew those dreams about a sick foreign boy were not mere dreams, but that they were recollections, and I condemned each night to animate that small child just risen from the grave, as his relations thought. But I knew that his mind for many years would not know itself, and would ever feel strange in its surroundings, for, indeed, that boy would be myself—inside—and he—without—his friends not seeing that he had fled away and another taken his place. Each night I, as sleeping Rajah, who had listened to the words of sages, would be an ignorant foreign boy, until, through lapse of years and effort unremittingly continued, I learned how to live two lives at once. Yet horrible at first seemed the thought that, although my life in that foreign land as a growing youth would be undisturbed by vague dreams of independent power as Rajah, I would always, when I woke on my mat, have a clear remembrance of what at first seemed only dreams of being a king, with vivid knowledge that, while my faithful servant watched my sleeping form I would be masquerading in a borrowed body, unruly as the wind. Thus, as a boy, I might be happy, but as a king miserable, maybe. And then, after I should become accustomed to this double life, perhaps my foreign mind and habits would so dominate the body of the boy, that existence there would grow full of pain from the struggle with an environment wholly at war with the thinker within.

But a vow once made is to be fulfilled, and Father Time eats up all things and ever the centuries.

BIOGRAPHICAL NOTES

JASPER NIEMAND'S sketch of Mr. Judge's life has been considerably enlarged in this edition of the LETTERS, by the addition of material taken from her four-part story of W. Q. J., published in AE's (George Russell's) *Irish Theosophist,* beginning in February, 1896. This account she herself evidently summarized when preparing the second book of letters.

Almost all the quotations have been lengthened, also, by reference to the complete texts in the *Path* Magazine (then beginning its first year under the name *Theosophy*), where articles on Mr. Judge by his students and friends continued to appear for three months. A few of these have been added here, as well as letters and articles of especial relevance.

Nor would this section be complete without some of W. Q. J.'s own words—the description of his first meeting with Mme. Blavatsky. The relationship thus renewed between H. P. B. and her "friend, brother and son—W. Q. J.," speaks for itself.

> It was her eye that attracted me, the eye of one whom I must have known in lives long passed away. She looked at me in recognition at that first hour, and never since has that look changed. Not as a questioner of philosophies did I come before her, not as one groping in the dark for lights that schools and fanciful theories had obscured, but as one who, wandering many periods through the corridors of life, was seeking the friends who could show where the designs for the work had been hidden. And true to the call she responded, revealing the plans once again, and speaking no words to explain, simply pointed them out and went on with the task. It was as if the evening before we had parted, leaving yet to be done some detail of a task taken up with one common end; it was teacher and pupil, elder brother and younger, both bent on the one single end, but she with the power and the knowledge that belong but to lions and sages. So, friends from the first, I felt safe.

WILLIAM Q. JUDGE

WILLIAM QUAN JUDGE, son of Alice Mary Quan and Frederick H. Judge, was born at Dublin, Ireland, on April 13th, 1851. His father was a Mason and a student of mysticism. His mother died in early life at the birth of her seventh child. The lad was brought up in Dublin until his thirteenth year, when the father removed to the United States with his motherless children, taking passage on the Inman Liner, "City of Limerick," which arrived in New York harbour on July 14th, 1864. Of the years of William's childhood there is little to be said, though we hear of a memorable illness of his seventh year—an illness supposed to be mortal. The physician declared the small sufferer to be dying, then dead; but, in the outburst of grief which followed the announcement, it was discovered that the child had revived, and that all was well with him. During convalescence, the boy showed aptitudes and knowledge never before displayed, exciting wonderment and questioning among his elders as to when and how he had learned all these new things. He seemed the same, and yet not the same; he had to be studied anew by his family, and while no one knew that he had ever learned to read,* from his recovery in his eighth year, we find him devouring the contents of all the books he could obtain, relating to Mesmerism, Phrenology, Character-Reading, Religion, Magic, Rosicrucianism, and deeply absorbed in the Book of Revelation, trying to discover its real meaning.

Perhaps the magnetic link so abruptly renewed in his illness was never fully vitalized in the physical sense, for the lad never acquired a strong physique. Without being sickly, he was frail, but indomitable and persevering beyond his years. An anecdote of his boyhood illustrates these traits. He was with other boys upon the bank of a stream. His companions swam to an island a little way off from the bank, from which vantage-ground they jeered and mocked their younger comrade, who could not swim. The small William's heart rose hot within him; he plunged into the water, resolved to get to that island or perish. When out of his depth he let himself sink, touched bottom, ran a few steps on the river's

* Compare the account in the "Tea Table Talk," p. 152.—Eds.

bed, rose, of course, kicked, sank, took a step and another, repeated the process, and thus struggling, rising, sinking, scrambling, and, above all, holding his breath, he actually reached the margin of the island, to be drawn out, half unconscious, by his astonished playfellows. Nothing could be more characteristic of Mr. Judge.

The elder Judge, with his children, lived for a brief period at the old Merchants' Hotel, in Cortland Street, New York; next in Tenth Street, and then settled in Brooklyn. William began work in New York as a clerk, and afterwards entered the Law Office of George P. Andrews, who later became Judge of the Supreme Court of New York. There the lad studied law, while living with his father, who, however, died soon after. On coming of age, William Q. Judge was naturalized a citizen of the United States, in April, 1872. In May of that year he was admitted to the Bar of New York. His conspicuous traits as a lawyer, in the practice of Commercial Law, which became his specialty, were his thoroughness, his inflexible persistence, and his industry, which won the respect of employers and clients alike. As was said of him, then and later: "Judge would walk over red-hot ploughshares from here to India to do his duty."

In 1874 he married Ella M. Smith, of Brooklyn, by whom he had one child, a little girl of great charm and promise, whose death in early childhood was long a source of deep, though quiet, sorrow to both. Mr. Judge in especial was a great lover of children, and had the gift of attracting them around him. If he sketched on the deck of a steamer the children would sidle up, coming nearer and nearer, until they were leaning against him or perching wherever a resting-place could be had—often before he had seemed to notice their presence. The children of his friends always gave him joyous welcome, and not infrequently he was dragged to the floor, the common playground, amid their toys. A child, in the company where he was, was sure to find the haven of his arms at last, and nestle there while the metaphysical discussion went on above its curls. But, however animated the argument, you would not find that small form, so gently cradled, to be ever so little disturbed.

Soon after his marriage, Mr. Judge heard of Madame Blavatsky, in this wise. He came across a book which greatly interested him: *People from the Other World*, by H. S. Olcott. Mr. Judge wrote to Colonel Olcott, asking for the address of a good medium, for at this time the tide of occult inquiry and speculation had just set in, and the experiences of numbers of people, including those of Madame Blavatsky, at the "Eddy Homestead," were the talk of all the world. While no medium was forthcoming, Mr. Judge was invited to call upon H. P. B.

The call was paid at 40, Irving Place, New York, and H. P. Blavatsky then for the first time in this life met her most devoted pupil and friend face to face,* in a relationship which continued unbroken, and justified that which H. P. Blavatsky herself wrote of it—*"till death and after."* Storms there were, no doubt, as well as fullest sunshine, for the pupil was a powerful mind and the teacher was the sphinx of her era, so that intellectual tussles followed as a natural sequence; but whatever the pupil thought of the teacher was said *to her,* boldly—not a doubt nor a fear concealed when these arose, as arise they must when the hour of occult teaching and trial dawns. That H. P. B. honored this openness is evidenced by her long letters—there are some of forty-eight pages—in which many a puzzle is explained with profound affection.

There has been a recent attempt to make capital out of some passing episode, turning it into a prolonged enmity on the part of Mr. Judge toward H. P. B. New, perhaps, to their odious trade, the slanderers were more silly than expert; they were unaware of the existence of these letters of H. P. B., which not only show how complete was the final understanding, but which also show through what arts, and of what individual, the temporary want of comprehension arose. Never was karmic line more plainly marked out nor karmic tool more mercifully—yet plainly—exposed by H. P. B. This effort was as vain as will be every other attempt to separate that teacher and that pupil. The final verdict of H. P. B. upon the relationship is an ample one. It extends over the ten years previous to her departure from our midst and is replete with a noble gratitude constantly poured forth. The splendid friendship went on its rejoicing way, a thing of life immortal, destined to pass beyond the confines of the tomb, as beyond many a mortal life.

Mr. Judge spent much of his time with H. P. B. at Irving Place, New York, in study, under her direction and instruction, and helped her with *Isis Unveiled* [as indicated in his Paris letter, p. 199]. He was one of the number present at her rooms on

* For Mr. Judge's account of that first meeting, see p. 261, the quotation from his article, "Yours Till Death and After" (reprinted in *Theosophy,* V, 289).—Eds.

September 7, 1875, when the first proposal for the Theosophical Society was made, and its organization begun. *Isis* was published in 1877, and a little over a year later, Madame Blavatsky and Col. Olcott went to India, while Mr. Judge was left to carry on the T. S. in New York as best he could—these *three* being, as H. P. B. subsequently wrote, the only founders who remained true to the Cause and to the Society. It was a position in which the young lawyer seemed quite over-weighted, but he did all that he could. Much or little it might have been on the external plane, and at that time. We cannot say. He was a disciple under trial, soon to be accepted and recognized, but already, so far as this life goes, a neophyte, one of a band who have taken the vow of interior poverty, and whose unseen and unrecorded work is regarded as being of far more importance than exterior, visible work. The main current of such lives runs underground. Already H. P. Blavatsky had written and said that he had been a part of herself and of the Great Lodge "for aeons past" (her exact words), and that he was one of those tried Egos who have reincarnated several times immediately after death; assisted to do so, and without devachanic rest, in order to continue his Lodge work. It is a matter of record that, when the seven years' probation of this life were over, the Master best known in connection with the T. S. sent to Mr. Judge, through H. P. B., his photograph, inscribed upon the back "to my colleague," with a cryptogram and signature; and, a little later, a letter of thanks and advice was delivered to Mr. Judge in Paris by H. P. B. A message sent to him through H. P. B. in writing from the Lodge at about this time ends by saying: "Those who do all that they can, and the best they know how, do enough for us."

Mr. Judge's was a difficult task, indeed, when she, who was then the one great exponent, had left the field, and the curiosity and interest excited by her original and striking mission had died down. The T. S. was henceforth to subsist on its philosophical basis, and this, after long years of toil and unyielding persistence, was the point attained by Mr. Judge. From his twenty-third year until his death, his best efforts and all the fiery energies of his undaunted soul were given to this Work. We have a word picture of him, opening meetings, reading a chapter of the *Bhagavad Gita*, entering the Minutes, and carrying on all the details of the same, as if he were not the only person present; and this he did, time after time, determined to have a society. Will, such as this, makes its way through every obstacle. Through his unremitting labour, he built up the T. S. in America, aiding the Movement as well in all parts of the world, and winning from The Master the name of "Resuscitator of Theosophy in America." His motto in those days was, "Promulgation, not Speculation." "Theosophy," said he, "is a cry of the Soul."

The work went slowly at first. There was no very great activity, but the link was kept unbroken, and correspondence with H. P. Blavatsky was brisk. Amid such external work as he could find to do, the young disciple still kept up the inner search. It was a period of darkness and silence, the period of probation. Through such a period had passed H. P. Blavatsky, and of it she said and wrote: "For long years I thought Master had quite deserted me." She had seen the Master in London, in the physical body, following, as if an official, in the suite of some Indian prince, and, in an interview which was given to her in Hyde Park, the Master told her she might come to Thibet, but left her to find her way thither unaided, and also to discover where she should go when she reached that country, all of which she accomplished after several failures and some years of search and apparent desertion. Of such a period the author of *Light on the Path* wrote in some explanatory notes in *Lucifer,* that though the Master might really be near the neophyte and might extend to him the utmost comfort which one soul could give to another, yet the neophyte would feel himself utterly alone, and that not one has passed through this period of suffering without bitter complaint. Complaint was wrung from this strong soul, whose portrait is feebly attempted here, in letters of sacred privacy to his teacher, H. P. Blavatsky, and to Damodar, his fellow-disciple.*

The shadow portrayed in those letters lifted, the disciple came to know even as he was known, and in 1888 we find H. P. B. writing in certain official documents of him as being then "a chela of thirteen years' standing, with trust reposed in him," and as "the chief and sole agent of the Dzyan (Lodge) in America." (This, it will be remembered, is the name by which what is called "The Lodge" is known in Thibet.)

Mr. Judge had been in South America, where H. P. B. said there was a branch of the Great Lodge, and where he saw many

* See also Mr. Judge's letter from London and Paris, in 1884.—Eds.

strange things.* In that country he contracted the dreaded Chagres fever, which racks the system of its victims as by fire, often carrying them off in the twentieth year. Mr. Judge was always a great sufferer from this torturing disease—though he never stayed his work for it—and 1896 was the twentieth year.

To Europe he went, too, in 1884, meeting H. P. B. in Paris and spending some little time with her there, and thence to India, where he arrived just after the outbreak of the Coulomb scandal.† After a brief stay there, Mr. Judge returned to America and the duties of his professional and theosophical life. The moment was critical, a turning-point. As so often happens, the scandal attracted public attention to the Theosophical Society, and letters of inquiry began to pour in. Mr. Judge seized the tide at the flood and carried the bark of the Society on to wider fortunes. The press took the matter up, reporters called, inquirers became members, the community became aware of the quiet, forceful worker in its midst. His method and his manner won the respect of those who heard him; the press began to accept his articles on Theosophy, and later on those of others; from scoffing and jeering and being unable to admit a theosophical item without insulting comment, it passed to giving these like other items of news. Later still, the personal influence of Mr. Judge induced the editors of the New York *Sun* to retract a libel which they had published against the T. S. and Madame Blavatsky, and a libel suit instituted against that journal by Mr. Judge was withdrawn.‡

Mr. Judge instituted *The Path* magazine in 1886, meeting all its deficits and carrying on its various activities, as well as those of the T. S. He wrote unceasingly, books, articles, letters. He lectured all over the States, and did the work of several men. Every spare moment was given to Theosophy, and taken from his meals and his rest. Finally, when the New York Headquarters were bought, and when the work had increased to large proportions, Mr. Judge relinquished his profession and gave his entire life and time to the Society. His health, always frail, continued to give way. A day free from pain was rare with him. Often he was in very real

* See "A Weird Tale," p. 207.—Eds.

† For a full account of this incident, see *The Theosophical Movement* (E.P. Dutton & Co., New York: 1925), Chapters V and VI.—Eds.

‡ The retraction (see the above text, p. 223) was accompanied by a long article of Mr. Judge's on H.P.B., "The Esoteric She," published on September 26, 1892 (reprinted in *Theosophy* IX, 142).—Eds.

danger. But always he was scornful of every suffering, working when another man would have been prone, when his friends and doctors were shocked at his being about at all. As the T. S. grew, his working staff grew also, but he out-worked and out-tired them all. Dauntless, indomitable, he was ever inaugurating fresh plans of work.

He had his sorrows, too, but the cheerfulness of his aspect, his undaunted energy, never failed him. To those who would ask his advice in the crises which were wont to shake the tree of the T. S., he would make answer: "Work! Work! Work for Theosophy!" And when at last the Great Betrayal came to him, and some of those whom he had lifted and served and taught *how* to work, strove to cast him down and out of the Society, in their ignorance of their own limitations, he kept the due silence of the Initiate. He bowed his defenceless head to The Will and The Law, and, passing with sweet and serene heart through the waters of bitterness—consoled by the respect and trust of the community in which his life had been spent, and by the thousands of students who knew and loved him—he exhorted all to forgiveness and renewed effort. He reminded them that there were many [mistakes] committed by the unbrotherliness of his opponents, but they themselves would in time come to see and comprehend the wrong done to the Work by action taken which at the time they did not understand in all its bearings.* He begged the students to be ready to meet that day, and to take the hands which would then be extended by those who had ignorantly shared the wrong done to him, and through him, to all. In this trust he passed behind the veil. On the 21st of March, 1896, he encountered "Eloquent, Just and Mighty Death."

* * * * *

So much for the open and material facts of his life. There is much more that must be left unsaid. His claim upon us was that of The Work. The Work was his Ideal. He valued men and women only by their theosophical Work, and the spirit in which that work was done. He held Right Thought to be of the best Work. He worked with anyone who was willing to do Work in the real sense, careless whether such were personal friends, strangers,

---

* The history of the period to which this passage refers may be found in the *Theosophical Movement*, beginning at Chapter XIX.—Eds.

or active or secret foes. Many a time he was known to be energetically working with those who were attacking him, or planning attack in supposed concealment, and his smile, as this was commented upon, was a thing to be always remembered—that whimsical and quaint smile, followed by some Irish drollery.

[The following section is part of the last installment of Jasper Niemand's memoir of Mr. Judge, which, though not published until June, 1896, was written before his death, and we have retained the present tense throughout. At the end was appended a note about Mr. Judge's passing, dated on what would have been his 45th birthday, and giving the message which concludes the biographical sketch. —Eds.]

The mind of Mr. Judge has a very pronounced duality. It is immensely practical and also profoundly mystical. As a man of business he is successful; it was once said of him by a wealthy merchant that he was a man who could have sold anything he undertook to sell. His practical gift has its most brilliant exposition in his power of organization. He is indeed a master-builder, and to this faculty the T.S. in America owes its strength and its growth. He is far-seeing, prompt, and resourceful in emergency, never deterred by expediency, mere public opinion, nor by any consideration of a personal nature, from carrying out that which he has resolved to do. He fears nothing, except his own conscience. When plans of work are under consideration, he consults all the principal workers and members living in the districts for which the plan is proposed. He collates the opinions of all and is guided by those which are of worth, and thus, like an able general, he never moves far from his base of supplies, but carries his support with him.

As a mystic, Mr. Judge has another office, simple yet profound, rarely visible on the surface, yet luminous: In the years 1887-88, he wrote, by the order of the Master and to two friends who are now husband and wife, a series of letters since published under the title, *Letters that have Helped Me*. It would be difficult to trace the lives in which these letters have been as a light to the soul. In them is found that gift which the occultist who has in any degree *become* must possess in rare perfection—the art of evolving souls.

For thus act the Bearers of the Flame, the Brethren of the burning Heart, from one generation to another. Such are the servants of Krishna. Such are the evolvers of soul. And those who have come into closer contact with the man of whom the Master wrote in 1887 through H. P. B., that "he of all chelas suffers most and ask or even expects the least,"—those who have worked with true devotion and in the true spirit with William Q. Judge, whether near or far in the body—know well the uplifting, widening force which flows through him, ripening the character, developing the higher nature and letting patience have her perfect work.

Working thus on varied planes, the life of William Q. Judge goes on its quiet way. Its depths lie hidden, but from them wells an irresistible force that stimulates to devotion, to self-denial, to unsparing, unceasing activity for the world. A friend to all men and women, he is yet impersonal always; personal flattery or personal following he meets with impatience, and soon sets the offender upon his own feet. To him, the ideal friend is one who teaches us to stand on our own base, to rely upon the inner self, and this is the part of friendship as he himself plays it.

A lady, being recently asked if she had not received psychic teachings from Mr. Judge, replied: "I will tell you the kind of psychic teaching he gave me. It was this: *'Cast no one out of your heart'.*" So we find him ever accepting all, as in the One Self, closing no door to anyone; leaving the way always open to all who may wish to return to him or to the work; excluding none who are in that work, whether friend or foe; offering a hand to his adversaries, and ready to offer it again when it is rejected; conquering personal animosity by the sheer force of his character, as he goes steadily on with that work from which it sought to remove him. Seeing in him our most constructive and most indefatigable worker, we can well understand that he is the towering mark against which every force subversive to evolution is being hurled. To obliterate our trust in the "Resuscitator," to dim his reputation and impede his building hand, is to enfeeble the work.

April 13th, 1896

A message in 1893 foreshadowed the storm and lightnings of the judicial charges against W.Q.Judge, the crisis of November 3rd, 1894, and the death of William Q. Judge:

"Take yet more courage. We have not left you comfortless. The Lodge watches ever. A new day will dawn. But there is much darkness yet to traverse and Judge is in danger. You must watch, and stand, and *stand* and STAND."

On Page 50 of the first book of LETTERS is a letter from an Adept, from which a certain portion ("private instruction") is omitted. That omitted portion runs as follows:

"*Is the choice made? Then Y. will do well to see W.Q.J. and to acquaint him with this letter. For the first year or two no better guide can be had.* For when the 'PRESENCE' *is upon him, he knows well that which others only suspect and 'divine.'* ——— *is useful to 'Path,' but greater services may be rendered to him, who, of all chelas, suffers most and demands, or even expects, the least.*"

If this extract be fitted into the original letter its immense importance in respect to Mr. Judge may be realized by the intuitive student. J. N.

ABOUT THE "LETTERS"

To the Editor of THE IRISH THEOSOPHIST:

Dear Sir and Brother,—A report having arisen that William Q. Judge did not himself write *Letters that have Helped Me,* we ask your fraternal assistance in correcting this rumour. It is false. It attributes the letters to the dictation or the teaching of the Master "Hilarion," who is known to have been in daily (physical) intercourse with Mr. Judge in 1888 in New York. The letters began in 1886, and had ended in 1888, so far as those already published are concerned. The letters do, in fact, continue to the present day, and we are not the only persons to receive such, as extracts now appearing in your columns—none of them being from letters to ourselves—amply testify.

NOTE.—This letter was originally published in the *Irish Theosophist,* February, 1895.—Eds.

Those of us to whom the Master Hilarion is objectively, as well as psychically known, have the best of reasons for asserting that these letters were not from him, and we do so state now and here. Matter from him, whether "inspired" or objectively dictated, is in quite another style. [The Master spoken of is the author of *Light on the Path*.—Eds.]

Moreover, on page 50 of the little volume referred to, is a letter printed in italics, beginning, "Says Master." That letter is one written *through* H. P. B. by her Master, and is in the modification of her handwriting to which Colonel Olcott refers as being the form in which her Master first wrote through her. The "private directions" omitted from that letter assign to Mr. Judge the office of "*guide*," therein assigned to him by the Master, and specify the interior source of his inspiration:

". . . He knows well that which others only suspect or 'divine'." We shall be happy to show the original to any Esotericist whom you may indicate.

Your readers may be interested to hear that a second volume of such *Letters* will probably appear.

With thanks for the courtesy of your columns, we are,

Fraternally yours,

Julia C. Keightley
Archibald Keightley

London, Jan. 13th, 1895

LAST DAYS OF WM. Q. JUDGE

MR. JUDGE came to the conclusion that climates were of no avail and determined to return to New York, where he would be in the midst of friends and close to the Headquarters of his work. He intended to devote his evenings to writing a book on "Occultism," and we spent many hours talking over its contents and the general outline of the work. Students will never see that book, and those who knew something of the vast fund of information on occult matters possessed by W.Q.Judge will appreciate their loss and the loss to the cause of Theosophical education. * * *

On February 22d, at about 2:30 P.M., he drove in a closed carriage to the apartment on the third floor of 325 West 56th Street, the last time but one that he was out of doors. Ill as he was, his contempt for the precautions that all orthodox invalids take—in the shape of shawls, rugs and so forth—was characteristic of the man, though alarming to his friends.

From that day he grew weaker and weaker, with rare spurts of renewed strength, though down to the very last he retained his power of energizing and inspiring others. Some two weeks before his death he was warned by Dr. Rounds, who was attending him daily, that his only chance of living would be destroyed unless he would consent to absolutely give up all work. This he reluctantly agreed to do, but the first effect of such a change in his whole life's practice was to bring about a reaction that threatened an immediate collapse. After this he read but little, and then only the lightest sort of literature. He would doze whenever he could, as his nights were broken by his cough, and for weeks before he finally passed away he had not been able to get more than three hours continuous sleep at any one time. Hardly able to whisper, so weak that he had to be supported from chair to chair, torn to pieces by his racking cough—that made it impossible for him to lie down—he still held fast to life and did so until the time had come for him to relax his effort and die. And throughout it all he preserved his magnificent power of endurance and self-control.

On the morning of March 19th, he asked me to make full enquiries in regard to health resorts in the South and to report to him at once. At the same time I was to telegraph Mr. E. A. Neresheimer to call on him. He said that if he could "only get to some place where he could sit in the midst of sunshine and flowers," he might yet perhaps recover. Mr. Neresheimer called that afternoon, and it was after he had said good-bye, and when I was sitting by the side of Mr. Judge's sofa, that the "Rajah" suddenly roused the body out of the half-sleep in which it had been lying, and with his unmistakable force said: "There should be calmness. Hold fast. Go slow." I took this at first to apply particularly to the contemplated journey to a warmer climate, and it was not until several days later when his papers had been examined that the full significence of this message appeared. It had meanwhile been applied to all the matters that came up for decision, and it was well that this was done, for hasty action taken during the day or two following his death might, as I now see, have brought lasting disaster on the Society. * * *

Dr. Rounds afterwards said that the condition of his lungs could not have caused his death; that death had been due to "failure of the heart's action." But all the doctors who had examined him had agreed that his heart was as sound as a bell, and from this it is safe to conclude that he died as H.P.B. died, from no immediate physical cause, but because the right time had come.

—E. T. HARGROVE

The Path, May, 1896

[From E. T. Hargrove's address on March 23, 1896:]

His last message to us was this: "There should be calmness. Hold fast. Go slow." And if you take down those words and remember them, you will find that they contain an epitome of his whole life-struggle. He believed in Theosophy and lived it. He believed because he knew that the great Self of which he so often spoke was the eternal Self, was *himself*. Therefore he was always calm.

He held fast with unwavering tenacity to his purpose and to his ideal.

He went slow, and never allowed himself to act hastily. He made time his own, and he was justice itself on that account. And he had the power to act with the rapidity of lightning when the time for action came.

We can now afford to console ourselves because of the life he lived, and should also remember that this man, William Quan Judge, had more devoted friends, I believe, than any other living man—more friends who would literally have died for him at a moment's notice, would have gone to any part of the world on the strength of a hint from him. And never once did he use that power and influence for his own personal ends—never once did he use that power, great as it was, not only in America, but in Europe, Australasia and elsewhere as well, for anything but the good of the Theosophical movement.

Poor Judge. It was not the charges that stung him, they were too untrue to hurt. It was the fact that those who had once most loudly proclaimed themselves his debtors and his friends were among the first to turn against him. He had the heart of a little child and his tenderness was only equalled by his strength . . . . He never cared what people thought of him or his work so long as they would work for brotherhood. . . . His wife has said that she never knew him to tell a lie, and those most closely connected with him theosophically agree that he was the most truthful man they ever knew.

W.Q.Judge, in a letter dated August 5th, 1895, wrote: "What I want to work at is a Napoleonic propaganda which I hoped to, but cannot, assist. . . . We have to fill the air with Theosophy and the T.S. in A. . . . We have to pour in force at those points."

—E. T. HARGROVE

"MY ONLY FRIEND"

H. P. BLAVATSKY ON WILLIAM Q. JUDGE

[There is no one—not even H.P.B. herself—concerning whom so great a range of contradictory opinion exists among Theosophists as in regard to William Q. Judge. She was the great Personage who was the target for all the *outside* enemies of Theosophy, the Theosophical Movement, and the Parent Theosophical Society. "I ask no one to help or defend me. But Judge's case is different, and more difficult of proof or disproof," as she herself said, on a momentous occasion—that of the Coues-Collins conspiracy—"and I now call upon all those who will remain true to their pledges to do their duty *when the time comes,* and especially by their American brother." How was Judge's case "different" from her own? His enemies were all *within* the Movement, within the Society.

It will, therefore, be of interest and value to all students to place together here some of the statements, public and private, formal and informal, which H.P.Blavatsky made in reference to Mr. Judge. They are all *unique*—all such as she made in regard to no others—and the circumstances under which and in which they were made but adds to their importance. Readers of *The Theosophical Movement* may refer to it for the setting of events in which her various utterances were made.—EDS.]

To WILLIAM Q. JUDGE, *General Secretary of the American Section of the Theosophical Society:*

MY DEAREST BROTHER AND CO-FOUNDER OF THE THEOSOPHICAL SOCIETY:

In addressing to you this letter, which I request you to read to the convention summoned for April 22d, I must first present my hearty congratulations and most cordial good wishes to the assembled Delegates and good Fellows of our Society, and to yourself—the heart and soul of that body in America. We were several to call it to life in 1875. Since then *you have remained alone* to preserve that life through good and evil report. It is to you chiefly, if not entirely, that the Theosophical Society owes its existence in 1888. Let me then thank you for it, for the first, and perhaps for the last time publicly, and from the bottom of my heart, which beats only for the cause you represent so well and serve so faithfully. I ask you also to remember that, on this important occasion, my voice is but the feeble echo of other more sacred voices, and the transmitter of the approval of Those whose presence is alive in more than one true Theosophical heart, and lives, as I know, pre-eminently in yours.

(From H.P.B.'s first message to the American Theosophists, April, 1888.)

In answer to your letter I can only say as follows: If W. Q. Judge, the man who has done most for Theosophy in America, who has worked most unselfishly in your country, and has ever done the biddings of Master, the best he knew how, is left alone . . . then I say—let them go! They are *no* Theosophists; and if such a thing should happen, and Judge be left to fight his battles alone, then I shall bid all of them an eternal good-bye. I swear on MASTER'S holy name to shake off the dust of my feet from every one of them. . . . I am unable to realize that at the hour of trouble and supreme fight. . . any *true* Theosophist should hesitate for one moment to back W.Q.J. *publicly* and lodge in his or her protest. Let them read Masters' letter in the preliminary. . . . All that I said about W.Q.J. was from HIS words in HIS letter to me. . . . Do with this letter what you like. Show it to anyone you please as my firm determination. . . .

H. P. B.

He or she, who believes that under any circumstances whatever, provocations, gossips, slander or anything devised by the enemy, H.P.B. will ever dream even of going against W.Q.J.—does not know H.P.B.—even if he or she *does* know H.P.Blavatsky, or *thinks* he knows her.

The idea is absurd & preposterous.

If W.Q.J. gets *riled* under any provocation—for more than five minutes by the city clock, then he is flap-doodle. H.P.B. would give 7 dozens of Bridges, 77 dozens of Noyses, the whole esoteric brood in the U.S.A. for one W.Q.J. *who is part of herself for several eons.* Those having ears will hear, those who are deaf & blind, let them provide themselves with *false* ears & glass eyes, or —vanish away.

The Esoteric Section and its life in the U.S.A. depends on W.Q.J. remaining its agent & what he is now. The day W.Q.J. resigns, H.P.B. will be virtually dead for the Americans. W.Q.J. is the *Antaskarana* between the two *Manas*(es), the American thought & the Indian—or rather the trans-Himalayan Esoteric Knowledge. DIXI. H.P.B.

P.S. W.Q.J. had better show, & impress *this* on the minds *of all those whom it may concern.* H.P.B.

(From a letter of H.P.B.'s in 1889.)

KEEP THE LINK (the *Antaskarana*) UNBROKEN! DO NOT LET MY LAST INCARNATION BE A FAILURE.

(The last words of H.P.B.)

FROM H. P. B.'S LETTERS

[The following extracts from the letters of H. P. Blavatsky are in several instances prophetic. Addressed to more than one person, the originals are all in the possession of the sender. Some are written as late as 1890, as will be seen by the allusion to Mrs. Besant's trip to America. Two are evidently to Mr. Judge (so stated), who was prevailed upon to give them to friends on account of their prophetic nature.—Ed., *Irish Theosophist.*]

"If knowing that W. Q. J. is the only man in the E. S. in whom I have confidence enough not to have extracted from him a pledge, he misunderstands me or doubts my affection for him or gratitude, then in addition to other things he must be a flapdoodle.* . . . There is nothing I would not do for him and I will stick to him till death through thick and thin. . . . He says and writes and prints he is my agent (of the Master rather, not mine). Therefore it is easy for him to say that any alterations are as by myself. . . . And look here, if he does protest . . . against what I say about him in my forthcoming Instructions, then I will curse him on my death-bed. He does not know *what I do.* He has to be defended whether he will or not. He has much to endure and he is overworked. But so have I, and if he threatens me with such a thing [as resignation] then I had better shut up shop. . . . May our Savior, the mild Jesus, have him in his keeping."

"He *who does all and the best that he can* and knows how does ENOUGH for Them. This is a *message* for Judge. His *Path* begins to beat *The Theosophist* out of sight. It is most excellent. . . . *The Path* alone *is his certificate* for him in Theosophy."

". . . Oh, my poor crushed chum, what would I give to help him. I try to be with him as much as I can. I am often watching him. . . . He should gather strength from one who is oftener with him than he knows of."

"Judge . . . whom I trusted more perhaps than I did Olcott—or myself."

NOTE.—Published in *The Irish Theosophist,* June, 1895.—Eds.

* Of "flap-doodle" it has been said: "a convenient term which she (H.P.B.) often used, with many shades of meaning, but all of them derogatory."—Eds.

"My Co-Founder, W. Q. Judge, General Secretary in America."

"Master *wants* Judge to be elected for life, for reasons of His own—that's God's truth. . . . Less than you would I want to see X ——— or anyone (save Judge) elected for life. . . . But if I do not like the idea it is because I trust *no one* any longer, save Judge, and Olcott perhaps. I have lost my last faith in mankind and see and smell (rightly, if you please) Judases everywhere. But with Judge it is different. . . ."

"My dear W. Q. J. . . . my *only* friend. . . . Judge has done for me so much lately, I owe him such gratitude, there is nothing I would not do for him. . . . 'Pon my word, I never knew I cared so much for him personally. . . . I will never forget Judge's loyalty and devotion, his unswerving friendship. . . ."

"Thanks for all, my dear old chum [W. Q. J.]; may the Masters protect him. His ever and till and AFTER death."

[To W. Q. Judge.] "Well, sir and my *only* friend, the crisis *is* nearing. I am ending my *S. D.* and you *are* going to replace me, or take my place in America. I know you will have success if you do not lose heart, but do, *do* remain true to the Masters and *their* Theosophy and THE NAMES. . . . May They help you and allow *us* to give you our best blessings. I am offered any amount of money, an income, board, lodging, all free to come to America and work without you, i.e., *against*. . . . I rather lose the whole American lot to the last man, X ——— included, than YOU. Perhaps soon now, you will know why. . . . Now be so kind as to write to me plainly (so that I could read) what you expect me to do and what I must *not* do. And I *give you my word* that I shall follow your instructions. Let us understand each other, mutually. But till now no one ever said to me a word about you asking to do this or that. Write to me direct and I will do it. Goodbye, my Irish crocodile, and may Masters protect you."

". . . Affairs and events may be turned off by unseen hands into such a groove that you will be unanimously elected for life—just as Olcott and I were—to go on with the work after our deaths. Do you understand what it means? It means that, unless you consent, you force me *to a miserable* life and a MISERABLE DEATH, with the idea preying upon my mind that there is an end of Theosophy. That for several years I will not be able to help it on, and steer its course, because I will have to act in a body which will have to be assimilated to the *Nirmanakaya,* because even in occultism there are such things as a failure and a retardment and a misfit. . . . Nothing that you will do will ever be discountenanced by me, my beloved W. Q. J."

"If I thought *for one moment* that *Lucifer* will 'rub out' *Path* I would never consent to be the editor. But listen, then, my good old friend. Once that the Masters have proclaimed your *Path* the *best,* the most *theosophical* of all theosophical publications, surely it is not to allow it to be rubbed out. . . . One is the fighting, combative Manas; the other (*Path*) is pure Buddhi. . . . *Lucifer* will be Theosophy militant and *Path* the shining light, the Star of Peace. If your intuition does not whisper to you 'IT IS SO', then that intuition must be wool-gathering. No, sir, the *Path* is too well, too *theosophically* edited for me to interfere."

"I trust Judge more than anyone in the world. . . . He has numerous enemies who work against him underhand and openly too, as ______ does. Now I have to hold in check and counterwork their machinations when they write or say to Olcott that Judge is a liar, etc. Now this is a ______ lie. . . . I am thinking of going to U. S. with Annie Besant when the spirit moveth me."

[To William Q. Judge in 1888.] "Well, my *only* friend, you ought to know better. Look into my life and try to realize it—in its outer course at least, as the rest is hidden. I am under the curse of ever writing, as the wandering Jew was under that of being ever on the move, never stopping one moment to rest. Three ordinary healthy persons could hardly do what *I have* to do. I live an artificial life; I am an automaton running full steam until the power of generating steam stops, and then—good-bye! . . .

"The night before last, however, I was shown a bird's eye view of the present state of Theosophy and its Societies. I saw a few earnest, reliable Theosophists in a death-struggle with the world in general and with other—nominal but ambitious—Theosophists. The former are greater in number than you may think, and *they prevailed,* as *you in America will prevail* if you only remain staunch to the Master's programme and true to yourselves.

And last night I saw ∴ and now I feel strong—such as I am in my body—and ready to fight for Theosophy and the few true ones to my last breath. The defending forces have to be judiciously—so scanty they are—distributed over the globe, wherever Theosophy is struggling against the powers of darkness.

"Is Judge ready to help me to carry on the sacrifice—that of accepting and carrying on the burden of life, which *is* heavy? My choice is made and I will not go back on it. I *remain* in England in the midst of the howling wolves. Here I am needed and nearer to America; there in Adyar there are dark plots going on against me and poor Olcott."

[To W. Q. Judge.] "Take my place in America now and, after I am gone, at Adyar. If you have no more personal ambition than I have—and I know *you have not*, only combativeness—then this will be no more sacrifice for you than it was for me to have Olcott as my President. . . . I am yours truly in the work forever. Dispose of me. I will . . . help you with all my powers. . . .

"Well, I have raised a 'Frankenstein' [the T. S.], and he seeks to devour me. You alone can save the fiend and make of him a *man*. Breathe into him a soul if not the spirit. Be his Savior in the U. S. and may the blessings of my SUPERIORS and yours descend on you. Yours—the 'old woman', but one ready to offer you her *inner* life if you begin and proceed with the work. . . . But as the ranks thin around us, and one by one our best intellectual forces depart, to turn *bitter* enemies, I say—Blessed are the pure-hearted who have only intuition, for intuition is better than intellect. . . .

Yours ever, H. P. B."

HISTORY REPEATED

(The following letter of H. P. Blavatsky [evidently a letter to "Julius"—see *Path* IX, 255], dated Ostende, March 19th, 1887, seems so applicable to the present hour that we have permission to repeat it thus in print.—Ed., *Irish Theosophist*, February, 1895.)

Dear ———,

Having heard from my dear old W. Q. Judge how kindly disposed you are toward me, and having received from him several messages on your behalf, let me tell you how grateful I feel for your kind expressions of sympathy.

Yes, the work has brought upon me contumely, ignominy of all kinds, hatred, malice and slander. Were it only from the outsiders I would mind very little. But, sad to say, it is the "Theosophists" chiefly who tear me to pieces. Our mystic *birds* are so wise as to soil their own nest instead of leaving it and choosing another. True, "there are many *mansions*" in our Father's house, but for the world we are one. And it does seem hard that I should have created a "Frankenstein" only to turn round and try to rend me in pieces!

Well, so be it, for it is my Karma. "Barkis is willing" even to become the manure for the theosophical fields, provided it does bring crops some day. Unfortunately, the "birds" peck out even the manure, and thus we had but *weeds* so far.

* * * * *

Dear and far distant friend, that is private and strictly confidential. I open my poor old aching heart before you. If Judge has such a great esteem for you, *you must be* worth all that *he* thinks.

Have patience; *The Secret Doctrine* will teach you more definite things than *Isis* now ever could. The latter was only an "essay balloon." I hope you will be satisfied with the last and final work of my life.

Yours sincerely and truly gratefully,
H. P. BLAVATSKY

NOTE.—The expression "Barkis is willing," H. P. B. said once was a mantram unconsciously made by Dickens. She used it upon occasion to certain persons on meeting (or writing) them for the first time. Spoken, it had such peculiar force as to alarm one who thus heard it from her lips and as she used it.—ED., *Irish Theosophist*.

ON W. Q. J.

Words of Students and Friends

I FIRST met William Q. Judge in the winter of 1885. He was at that time a devoted student of the *Bhagavad Gita*. It was his constant companion, and his favorite book ever after. His life and work were shaped by its precepts. That "equal-mindedness" and "skill in the performance of actions" inculcated in this "Book of Devotion," and declared to constitute "Yoga," or union with the Supreme Spirit, Mr. Judge possessed in greater measure than any-one I have ever known. His devotion never wavered; his anchorage seemed ever sure and steadfast, and herein lay his strength. His skill in the performance of actions was marvellous, his executive ability of the highest order. He was never disturbed by passion or blinded by resentment, and when openly and strongly assailed, he held steadily on his course, working for the one object of his life, the success of the T. S.

And so he worked on to the end, friends rallying around him and aiding him in his work. People on the other side of the ocean never understood Mr. Judge's position in America, where he was well known in connection with his work, nor how impossible it would be to shake confidence in him. It is true the issues raised were seemingly altogether personal, and it took some time to make clear to the whole Society their real nature. When, however, these issues became clear and people had time to consider them, the verdict was overwhelming, and those who were present at Boston last April [1895] will never forget the scene there enacted [when the T. S. in A. was formed]. It has been my lot to preside over many conventions, both medical and Theosophical, but I never witnessed such a scene before and never expect to again. There was no noisy demonstration, but the very air throbbed with sympathy and appreciation.

He was never narrow, never selfish, never conceited. He would drop his own plan in a moment if a better were suggested, and was delighted if some one would carry on the work he had devised, and immediately inaugurate other lines of work. To get on with the work and forward the movement seemed to be his only aim in life. . . . For myself, knowing Mr. Judge as I did, and associating with him day after day—at home, in the rush of work, in long days of travel over desert-wastes or over the trackless ocean, having travelled with him a distance equal to twice around the globe—there is not the slightest doubt of his connection with and service of the Great Lodge. He did the Master's work to the best of his ability, and thus carried out the injunction of H. P. B. to "keep the link unbroken."

J. D. BUCK

For the last four years, nearly, most of our communication has been personal, much of this period having been spent under the same roof. I have had good opportunity to study the character of the man and I do not hesitate to place my estimate of him on record.

There is not one act in the life of William Q. Judge that has come under my observation, that savors of selfishness or of a desire to further any personal end.

Perhaps I am not qualified to pass on the merits as an occultist of the man whose memory I hold in such grateful esteem; but I can, at least, speak of what has passed before my eyes in the ordinary affairs of life, and in these affairs I have invariably found him to be the soul of unselfishness, honor, generosity, and all the other virtues that men hold so dear in other men. The severity which some saw in him was on the outside, only. He was not always patient with folly and faintheartedness, yet even these drew from him pity rather than condemnation, and nothing except deliberate cowardice persisted in, and treachery to the Cause itself, seemed to place the offender outside the pale of his present sympathy and attention.

He was singularly free from the vice of constantly seeking to explain and justify his actions. He believed in doing the present good act, in carrying out the present good intention, leaving the result where it belonged. Even when something occurred which, apparently, called for particular explanation and justification, he usually neither explained nor justified. The most striking example of this, of which I have any knowledge, grew out of a letter that I received from him in 1887, in which letter was folded another on different paper and written, in blue, in the hand made so familiar by reason of the frequent "exposures" of "so-called Mahatmic messages." The enclosure was directly in explanation of a matter that was no more than hinted at in Judge's own letter, and when I wrote, making a jocular allusion to his effort at precipitating a letter for my benefit, he answered, in a direct, straightforward way, that he had done nothing of the kind and would not; but, contrary to his usual custom, he gave a theory of how such things might be accomplished. Some years afterwards we met in St. Louis and I showed him the letter and the enclosure. After turning the papers over for a moment, he looked me straight in the face and said, in the simplest manner, "I can't explain it. It's a dead give-away." And there the matter rested. But for my certain belief in his integrity I might have doubted him then, might have given some heed to the cry of "fraud" later. Years after the occurrence I found out, independently of Judge, the truth about the matter, and my faith in his sincerity was abundantly justified.

Among all my friends and acquaintances, William Q. Judge was least wasteful of time. He seemed never to rest, for work was his rest. And yet he was not, in any sense, an unsociable man. . . . During the last few years, he seemed to become more and more absorbed in his work, and yet, much as he was struggling through, and it was enough to appall the ordinary hardworking man, he never hesitated to take on some other burden if it appeared to promise well for the movement in which he was so thoroughly wrapped up. Notwithstanding the busy life that he led, he was one of the most accessible men that I ever knew, and one of the few who was always ready to accept a suggestion. He did not know everything, and was aware of the fact, but he did know how to utilize the material that he found ready to his hand.

Though he was always the same kindly friend to me, never in all these years writing or speaking a harsh word to me, I am aware that in his intercourse with the many people whom he met "the Irish boy" sometimes came between himself and others. To those who were aware of the real inner life of the man this is enough explanation for the apparent contradictions and failings on the everyday plane of life that he shared in common with the rest of mankind. That he ever deliberately wounded or deceived anyone is unthinkable to me.

ELLIOTT B. PAGE

In the summer of 1894 we were privileged to have him stay at our house for several weeks, and since then he spent at least one evening a week with us until his illness forced him to leave New York. . . . Day after day he would come back from the office utterly exhausted in mind and body, and night after night he would lie awake fighting the arrows of suspicion and doubt that would come at him from all over the world. He said they were like shafts of fire piercing him; and in the morning he would come downstairs wan and pale and unrested, and one step nearer the limit of his strength; but still with the same gentle and forgiving spirit. Truly they knew not what they did.

Perhaps the most striking evidence of his greatness was the wisdom with which he treated different people and the infinite knowledge of character shown by him in his guidance of his pupils. I do not believe he was the same to any two people. . . . His most lovable trait was his exquisite sympathy and gentleness. It has been said of him that no one ever touched a sore spot with such infinite tenderness, and I know many that would rather have been scolded and corrected by Mr. Judge than praised by anyone else.

It was the good fortune of a few of us to know something of the real Ego who used the body known as Wm. Q. Judge. He once spent some hours describing to my wife and me the experience the Ego had in assuming control of the instrument it was to use for so many years. The process was not a quick nor an easy one and, indeed, was never absolutely perfected, for to Mr. Judge's dying day, the physical tendencies and heredity of the body he used would crop up and interfere with the full expression of the inner man's thoughts and feelings. An occasional abruptness and coldness of manner was attributable to this lack of co-ordination. Of course Mr. Judge was perfectly aware of this and it would trouble him for fear his friends would be deceived as to his real feelings. He was always in absolute control of his thoughts and actions, but his body would sometimes slightly modify their expression. * * *

Mr. Judge told me in December, 1894, that the Judge body was due by its Karma to die in the next year and that it would have to be tided over this period by extraordinary means. He then expected this process to be entirely successful, and that he would be able to use that body for many years, but he did not count upon the assaults from without, nor the strain and exhaustion due to the

"Row." This, and the body's heredity, proved too much for even his will and power. Two months before his death he knew he was to die, but even then the indomitable will was hard to conquer and the poor exhausted, pain-racked body was dragged through a miserable two months in one final and supreme effort to stay with his friends. And when he did decide to go, those who loved him most were the most willing for the parting. I thank the Gods that I was privileged to know him. It was a benediction to call him friend.

G. HIJO

My acquaintance with William Q. Judge antedated considerably my interest in Theosophy. We were introduced by a newspaper man who spoke of him to me as a thoroughly honest good fellow but a crank about some incomprehensible Oriental philosophy, a knowledge of which would not be, to any practical mind, compensative for the difficulty of understanding it. If my memory serves me rightly, we met first upon an occasion when H. P. Blavatsky was induced to try, in presence of some reporters, if she could open up communication with the diaphanous remainder of a night watchman who had been drowned in an East River dock. Olcott was present, in command, prominent and authoritative; and Judge, in attendance, reserved and quiet. The spook was shy and the reporters were sarcastic. The only one apparently annoyed by their humor was the Colonel. Mr. Judge's placidity and good nature commended him to the liking of the reporters and made a particularly favorable impression upon me, which was deepened by the experiences of an acquaintance that continued while he lived.

In all that time, though I have seen him upon a good many occasions when he would have had excellent excuse for wrath, his demeanor was uniformly the same—kindly, considerate and self-restrained, not merely in such measure of polite self-control as might be expected of a gentleman, but as if inspired by much higher regards than mere respect for the covenances of good society. He always seemed to look for mitigating circumstances in even the pure cussedness of others, seeking to credit them with, at least, honesty of purpose and good intentions, however treacherous and malicious their acts toward him might have been. He did not appear willing to believe that people did evil through preference for it, but only because they were ignorant of the good, and its superior advantages; consequently he was very tolerant.

But that meekness of spirit—a strange thing, by the way, in a brainy and rather nervous Irishman—by no means made of him a weak, or yielding character who could be bluffed into doing what his judgment did not approve, or turned aside by influence from any course of action upon which he had deliberately resolved. And careful deliberation upon things was one of his strongest characteristics. His mind was very active, quick and resourceful in suggestion, but I do not recall having ever known of his trusting its impulses until he had thoroughly weighed and considered them. Not infrequently, matters that seemed to me of trivial importance, things that might as well be settled right off, and about which there did not appear to be room for two opinions, he would take under advisement over night, or even longer. And candor compels me to admit that such things, as a rule, turned out to be much more important, and with chains of effects more serious, than had at first seemed possible, fully justifying his caution.

Now, and for a good while past, I have had no doubt of his receiving aid in his deliberations, and guidance toward correct conclusions, from intelligences with prescience beyond that of ordinary men, but when I first noted his habit of deliberation I regarded it simply as a proneness to "chew over" things—prudent but rather un-Irish.

Many journalists work very hard, but I have never known anyone, even in that toilsome field of labor, so indefatigable and persistent as William Q. Judge. No matter how much those about him might endeavor, by their assistance, to lighten his burden, the effort was hopeless, for a moment's leisure, when he should have been resting, only gave him opportunity to think of something else to do.

J. H. CONNELLY

His life was an example of the possibility of presenting new ideas with emphasis, persistence, and effect; without becoming eccentric or one-sided, without losing touch with our fellows; in short, without becoming a "crank."

Those who have heard him speak, know the singular directness with which his mind went to the marrow of a subject, the simplicity of his words, the unaffected selflessness that radiated from the man. The quality of "common sense" was Mr. Judge's preeminent characteristic. He had the gift of words, but also the far greater gift of a sense of proportion, of a co-ordinating faculty which reduced those words to their proper place, as mere tools or agents, attracting no attention to themselves. His sentences were short and plain; his manner cool and quiet; but what he said was remembered, for his words appealed to the sense of truth; they seemed to "soak in," like the showers which the farmers prize, while a "torrent of eloquence" would have run off, leaving dry ground.

Whether true or not, it might well be that Wm. Q. Judge was, as has been said, one of the signers of the Declaration of Independence. His qualities were those which characterized the leaders of that period. There was energy on the one hand, and intellect on the other; but there was also a dominating and tenacious common sense, which was not a dull conservatism, but a balancing quality which converted intellect into clear judgment, and blind expansive energy into cool steady work.

For the lack of this, we find that the intellectual element of the French Revolution furnished only a chaos of visionary schemes, while its emotional and animal energies were expended in destructive heat, fury, and froth.

W. Main

Mr. Judge joined another office to that of evolver. He was a conserver. When one came to work under him, one was at first surprised, perhaps annoyed even, at his insistence in small things. It was, keep your desk thus; or, dip your pen thus; or, make your entries and copy your letters in this fashion, and not in your own way. Presently one found that the sum total of attention in these details was greater celerity with less waste of energy, or greater mental freedom often obtained by greater ease of bodily action. All he did had a meaning when you came to put it together.

In thinking of this helper and teacher of ours, I find myself thinking almost wholly of the future. He was one who never looked back; he looked forward always. While the activities of the body and the mind were engaged each moment in the duty of that moment, yet his heart was set upon the promise of the future, and the song of his soul echoed the music of cycles yet to come. We think of him not as of a man departed from our midst, but as a soul set free to work its mighty mission, rejoicing in that freedom and resplendent with compassion and power. His was a nature that knew no trammels, but acknowledged the divine laws in all things. He was, as he himself said, "rich in hope." He wrote recently that we should now turn our attention to work in the United States in order to have there "a world compelling and sky defying place for Theosophy."

That future as he saw and sees it is majestic in its harmonious proportions. It presaged the liberation of the race. It struck the shackles from the self-imprisoned and bade the souls of men be free. It evokes now, to-day, the powers of the inner man. . . . Death, the magician, opened a door to show us these things. If we are faithful, that door will never close. If we are faithful—only that proviso. Close up the ranks, and let Fidelity be the agent of heavenly powers. To see America, the cradle of the new race, fit herself to help and uplift that race and to prepare here a haven and a home for Egos yet to appear . . . for this he worked; for this will work those who come after him. And he works with them.

JULIA W. L. KEIGHTLEY

A friend of old time and of the future—as such does William Q. Judge appear to me, as doubtless he does to many others in this and other lands.

The first Theosophical treatise that I read was his *Epitome of Theosophy;* my first meeting with him changed the whole current of my life. I trusted him then, as I trust him now, and all those whom he trusted; to me it seems that "trust" is the bond that binds, that makes the strength of the Movement, for it is of the heart. And this trust he called forth was not allowed to remain a blind trust, for as time went on, as the energy, steadfastness and devotion of the student became more marked, the "real W. Q. J." was more and more revealed, until the power that radiated through him became in each an ever-present help in the work. As such it remains to-day, a living centre in each heart that trusted him, a focus for the Rays of the coming "great messenger."

Having been engaged in active T. S. work in Boston for over seven years, it has been my Karma to be brought in touch with him under many different circumstances, the various crises, local and general, through which the Society has safely passed. In all these, his was the voice that encouraged or admonished, his the hand that guided matters to a harmonious issue. Of his extraordinary power of organization, his marvellous insight into the character and capacity of individuals, his ability of turning seeming evils into powers for good, I have had many proofs.

That he was a "great occultist" many know by individual experience, but none have fathomed the depths of his power and knowledge. The future will reveal much in regard to him that is now hidden, will show the real scope of his life-work. We know that to us that life-work has been an inestimable boon, and that through us it must be bestowed on others. The lines have been laid down for us by H. P. B., W. Q. J., and Masters, and we can take again our watchword, that which he gave us at the passing of H. P. B., "Work, watch and wait." We will not have long to wait.

Speaking of Mr. Judge as anybody might have known him—as a human being like ourselves—he was humble, unassuming, modest, strong, patient, meek, courageous, an organizer beyond comparison, with powers similar to those possessed by H. P. B., and never using them in any way but to smooth the path for those who desired to follow the road to knowledge. He was kind and patient, as we do not often find with tremendous forcefulness; he had extraordinary powers of organization, with a perception that could look into the very motives and minds of others, could see traitors around him, could read the hearts of those desirous of injuring him, and yet in all his intercourse with them, paving the way for them, remaining ever kind. For the one who most injured him, he had only this to say when friends about him spoke their denunciations: "Never mind what others do. Put no one out of your heart. Go on with the work you see. Work will tell in time, and all these follies of others—follies of ignorance—will fall to nothing. Then, when the time comes, we will all have gained strength; when those who have fallen away for a while come back, there we will be with open arms, as strong brothers, to help them find the path and smooth out the effects of errors that they have created through ignorance."

ROBERT CROSBIE

Wm. Q. Judge was an Adept—a great one, however much the true man was hidden behind the one of clay. Is it reasonable to suppose that at a time when the Great Lodge had for foes the intellectual giants—the Spencers, Mills, Huxleys, and Darwins—of an era the very apotheosis of materialistic agnosticism, they sent tyros or babes to do battle for the world? Nay; they sent their best and bravest; were there no other proof of this, the work accomplished would be sufficient. Right royally did H. P. B. march down to Armageddon; confounding the learned by her wisdom, mocking materialism by her wonderful exhibition of abnormal and at first sight supernatural powers. But she was the Knight errant, who fought amid the beating of drums, and the clash and clamor, the excitement and glory, of a princely tournament. None the less royally did Wm. Q. Judge do his knightly duty on his silent, unnoticed field of battle. His place, his task, it was to teach ethics; to turn aside the craze for phenomena and wonder-working into the more healthy, lasting channels of love for our fellow men. H. P. B. laid the foundations well; but it was left for Wm. Q. Judge to build strongly and safely thereon.

Yet while we reverence the Adept, let us not therefore lose sight of the man, for even in his simplest life he was great. Those who have seen him lay aside every care, and for the moment become the mirth-loving gleeful companion, will not need to be reminded of this beautiful side of his character. To the children and the humble and lowly in the Society, he was a revelation. They heard of him with awe, they approached him with fear and trembling, they instantly recognized their own, and became his sworn friends forever. This was wonderful—how wholly the very humblest in our ranks, who came into his presence personally, loved and trusted him.

JEROME A. ANDERSON

My acquaintance with him dates from 1888; he was the only man I ever met with whom I felt safe in all directions. The depth of his nature as it appeared to me was fathomless. His character was balanced, for he had an all-absorbing ideal; his thoughts and doings emanated from the soul and not from superficial motives. He was careless of the impressions that he might produce by anything he said or did, the personal element being mostly absent, and he was sincere always, unless it was at times when he would permit the surface man to prevail, and submitted to the frolics and idiosyncrasies of his more human nature; but even then there was mastery supreme.

He had the faculty of observing and synthesizing circumstances, persons and events; in fact here I often detected what people sometimes call occult knowledge. He was an occultist; he had the power of self-control, and could subdue the turbulent wanderings of the mind, sit still in the midst of his own nature, supported by his ideal, and view any and every situation dispassionately. What wonder that he saw clearly! In matters Theosophical all his mind and soul was aglow and alive with deepest interest; whatever question or problem arose he would view it starting with his basic ideal of the spiritual unity of all things, *the Self;* sublime harmony was contained in its comprehension, and a mode of adjustment for everything found in its source.

This philosophy he claimed is brought to view in the book of books, the *Bhagavad Gita,* and he used to say that the *Gita* and *Secret Doctrine* were quite enough for him to attempt to understand and to follow in this life.

He never tired of making things plain and simple. . . . He was called by some *"The Rajah."* I wrote him once at the end of a period of prolonged anxiety, worry and trouble in my affairs, asking what was the lesson to be learned from it, as I could not make the application myself. His reply was: "The lesson is not different from anything in life. It is just Karma, and being applied to large circumstances seems larger, but is in reality no more than the small ones of others. Calmness is the best lesson to learn, with an indifference to results. If all comes right it is well, and if you have been calm and detached then it is better, for you shall have made no new Karma of attachment by it. Calmness also preserves health in all affairs more than anything else, and leaves the mind free to act well."

From him I learned to disentangle principle from condition. He viewed all questions from the standpoint of the principle or essence that each contained in itself, without reference to personality, and his quick perception of every situation, together with the application of his ideal principles, enabled him to judge correctly at all times.

Whenever his advice was followed on the lines of his own example in any matter in or outside of the Society's work, it would invariably simplify the most complicated situation; in other words, the standpoint of truth and the establishment of harmony was ever the attitude which he held towards everything he touched. He was non-argumentative, because he thought by argument no one could be finally convinced—"each has to hew out his own conviction"—nevertheless he was easily approachable, gentle, sympathetic, but above all strong and powerful, whenever and wherever it was necessary to put in a word at the right time, or to act on the spot.

E. August Neresheimer

To the mystical element in the personality of Mr. Judge, was united the shrewdness of the practised lawyer, the organizing faculty of a great leader, and that admirable common sense, which is so *un*common a thing with enthusiasts. . . . In his teaching was embodied most emphatically that received by the prophet Ezekiel when the Voice said to him: "Stand upon thy feet, and I will speak to thee."

It was the upright and self-dependent attitude that the Chief insisted upon, and he emphatically discouraged anything that savored of weakness, of want of self-reliance, or of what H. P. B. was so fond of calling "flap-doodle and gush," and he turned a face of stern resistance to those who expected to reach the heights he had climbed by clinging to his garments. But when one came to him who really needed aid, no one could be more ready to stretch out a helping hand, to respond with a bright smile of encouragement, to say just the word that was necessary, and no more.

He was the best of friends, for he held you firmly, yet apart. He realized the beautiful description Emerson gives of the ideal friend, in whom meet the two most essential elements of friendship, tenderness and truth. "I am arrived at last," says Emerson, "in the presence of a man so real and equal . . . that I may deal with him with the simplicity and wholeness with which one chemical atom meets another. . . . To a great heart he will still be a stranger in a thousand particulars, that he may come near in the holiest ground."

Upon that "holiest ground" of devotion to the highest aim, of desire alone for the welfare of others, the Chief was always to be approached. And blended with the undaunted courage, the keen insight, the swift judgment, the endless patience, that made his personality so powerful, were the warm affections, the ready wit, the almost boyish gaity that made it so lovable. . . .

One of the Chief's last messages to us said: "They must aim to develop themselves in daily life in small duties." . . . There was a beautiful story of Rhoecus, who could not recognize in the bee that buzzed about his head the messenger of the Dryad, and so lost her love.

KATHERINE HILLARD

It is necessary that just those souls in whom we have felt most of reality should disappear from us into the darkness, in order that we may learn that not seeing, but inwardly touching, is the true proof that our friend is there; in order that we may learn that the vanishing and dissipation of the outward, visible part, is no impairing or detriment to the real part which is invisible. This knowledge, and the realizing of it in our wills, are gained with the utmost difficulty, at a cost not less than the loss of the best of our friends; yet if the cost be great, the gain is great and beyond estimating, for it is nothing less than a first victory over the whole universe, wherein we come to know that there is that in us which can face and conquer and outlast anything in the universe, and come forth radiant and triumphant from the contest. Yet neither the universe nor death are real antagonists, for they are but only Life everywhere, and we are Life.

CHARLES JOHNSTON

To a greater extent than I have ever realized I know he entered into my life and I am equally sure into the lives of thousands, and this fact I see we are to acknowledge as time passes more and more. . . . He swore no one to allegiance, he asked for no one's love or loyalty; but his disciples came to him of their own free will and accord, and then he never deserted them, but gave more freely than they asked, and often in greater measure than they could or would use. He was always a little ahead of the occasion, and so was truly a leader.

E. B. RAMBO

Judge was the best and truest friend a man ever had. H. P. B. told me I should find this to be so, and so it was of him whom she, too, trusted and loved as she did no other. And as I think of what those missed who persecuted him, of the loss in their lives, of the great jewel so near to them which they passed by, I turn sick with a sense of their loss: the immense mystery that Life is, presses home to me. In him his foes lost their truest friend out of this life of ours in the body, and though it was their limitations which hid him from them, as our limitations do hide from us so much Spiritual Good, yet we must remember, too, that these limitations have afforded to us and to the world this wonderful example of unselfishness and forgiveness. Judge made the life portrayed by Jesus realizable to me.

ARCHIBALD KEIGHTLEY

William Q. Judge was the nearest approach to my ideal of a MAN that I have known. He was what I want to be. H. P. B. was something more than human. She was a cosmic power. W. Q. J. was splendidly human: and he manifested in a way delightfully refreshing, and all his own, that most rare of human characteristics—genuineness. His influence is continuingly present and powerful, an influence tending steadily, as ever, in one direction—work for the Masters' Cause.

THOMAS GREEN

I knew him with some degree of intimacy for the past eight years, meeting him often and under varied conditions, and never for one moment on any occasion did he fail to command my respect and affection, and that I should have had the privilege of his acquaintance I hold a debt to Karma. A good homely face and unpretentious manner, a loving disposition, full of kindliness and honest friendship, went with such strong common sense and knowledge of affairs that his coming was always a pleasure and his stay a delight. The children hung about him fondly as he would sit after dinner and draw them pictures.

A. H. SPENCER

What he was to one of his pupils, I believe he was to all—so wide-reaching was his sympathy, so deep his understanding of each heart—and I but voice the feeling of hundreds all over the world when I say that we mourn the tenderest of friends, the wisest of counsellors, the bravest and noblest of leaders. What a man was this, to have been such to people of so widely varying nationalities, opinions and beliefs—to have drawn them all to him by the power of his love—and, in so doing, to have brought them closer to each other. There was no difficulty he would not take infinite pains to unravel, no sore spot in the heart he did not sense and strive to heal.

G. L. G.

Mr. Judge has lived hundreds of lives. So have all men, but very few have any recollection of them. Mr. Judge's existence has been a conscious one for ages, whether alive or "dead," sleeping or waking, embodied or disembodied. In the early part of his last life I do not think he was completely conscious twenty-four hours a day, but several years ago he arrived at the stage where he never afterwards lost his consciousness for a moment. Sleep with him merely meant to float out of his body in full possession of all his faculties, and that was also the manner in which he "died"—left his body for good. In other bodies, and known under other names, he has played an important part in the world's history, sometimes as a conspicuous visible figure. At other times, he worked quietly behind the scenes, or, as in his last life, as a leader in a philanthropical and philosophical movement.

CLAUDE FALLS WRIGHT

W. Q. J.

A Sculptor's Appreciation

[The following appeared in the *New York Journal,* May 7th, 1896, and is an appraisement of our late Chief's character from a standpoint whose merits are recognized by few in the T.S. on this the sceptical side of the Atlantic. In America, phrenology, as a scientific method of estimating disposition and ability, is a generally accepted fact, and Mr. Lindstrom, whose remarks, as recorded, appear to be chiefly founded upon phrenological observation, has evidently strong enough belief in this science, to induce him to join the T.S. on its evidence as to a noble character.

Some little acquaintance with phrenology on the part of the writer,* and a careful study of such photographs of Mr. Judge as he has been able to obtain, enables him to say that Mr. Lindstrom's deductions, as reported, appear perfectly accurate, and that if any journalistic embellishments have been introduced, they are so well within the truth as to be indistinguishable from it. T.]

William Quan Judge, the head of both esoteric and exoteric branches of the Theosophical Society in America, died on March 21st. August Lindstrom, a sculptor, who had never seen Mr. Judge in life, made a cast of the dead man's head, from which he modelled the bust unveiled at Madison Square Garden during the recent convention of Theosophists. Yesterday Mr. Lindstrom said:—

"While making the death mask I was struck by the shape of Mr. Judge's head, which was utterly unlike anything I had ever seen. Most of the heads of remarkable men show the development of one faculty in particular, or, perhaps, of several, and to the neglect of other faculties. I saw at once that Mr. Judge's head evidenced a high and uniform development of all the faculties, well-balanced throughout. This is the remarkable combination I found: —A tremendous will power, with an equal development of gentleness; thorough practicability and adaptability conjoined to a highly

---

NOTE.—From *The Theosophic Isis,* June, 1896.—Eds.

* "T." or "P.T." (Philip Tovey?), whose articles appeared regularly in *The Theosophic Isis.* His "Mind and Brain" appeared in the May, 1896, issue. —Eds.

idealistic nature, and a gigantic intellect hand in hand with selflessness and modesty.

"There are only two heads that I know of in history that compare with his—Michael Angelo's and Savonarola's. The back of Angelo's head is almost identical with the back of Mr. Judge's. There is a difference however, in the forehead.

"In addition to the death mask, I had six photographs to assist me in modelling the bust. A comparison of these photographs is a study. One taken at the age of twenty placed by the side of one taken a year ago, when he was about forty-four years old, makes such a contrast that no one would believe they pictured the same person. It shows that by his great will power this man overcame all his youthful tendencies, with the result of completely changing the form of his skull. I make bold to say that another such highly developed head is not to be found between Maine and California. He had only time to plan his work when carried off in his prime by death. Had he lived to the age of seventy his influence would have been felt by the whole nation.

"I consider the nose as giving the best index to character of any feature. His nose was his most distinguishing feature, and shows great power and at the same time complete control over every thought and act, and although strong, it is of the delicate and sensitive type. His mouth showed tenderness and firmness present in equal proportion. His cheek bones also gave evidence of will strength. His hair was soft and showed refinement and gentleness. Taken altogether there was harmonious development, with no defects present, and careful examination of his head from every aspect proves that he was a great and noble man. If such a man as he would devote his life to the Theosophical Society, I think it must have a great mission and I shall ask to be admitted as a member."